In this important historical stu... ...Glen
Barclay examines the people...
island groups of the Pacific: M...
Melanesia, and Polynesia. He...
the knotty problems of the or...
these peoples and he descrit...
various social and political organizations
– ancient cultures that were to be
transformed by the arrival of European
explorers.

The first r   tween
Pacif   ˙k
n˙

A HISTORY OF THE PACIFIC

Other books by Glen Barclay, published by Sidgwick and Jackson

STRUGGLE FOR A CONTINENT

THE RISE AND FALL OF THE NEW ROMAN EMPIRE

A HISTORY OF THE
PACIFIC

from the Stone Age to the present day

Glen Barclay

TAPLINGER PUBLISHING COMPANY
NEW YORK

First published in the United States in 1978 by
TAPLINGER PUBLISHING CO., INC.
New York, NY

Copyright © 1978 by Glen Barclay

Library of Congress Catalog Card Number: 78-51996

ISBN 0-8008-3902-1

Printed in Great Britain

Contents

List of Illustrations

List of Maps

Introduction

To write a history of all the peoples who have been vitally concerned in Pacific Ocean affairs would be almost equivalent to writing a history of the world. There are, however, some fairly obviously defensible ways of limiting the scope of such a study. It is thus reasonable to concentrate on the peoples who have lived longest in those territories furthest removed from any continental land mass. One does not have to try to define too rigidly where Oceania ends and Asia begins, to agree that the inhabitants of the Polynesian Spearhead, for example, have shared a historical experience which can be separated from that of their homeland, Asia, at least until the intervention of Japan. By the same token, Australia, which did not experience a Polynesian migration, has little more than a commercial relationship with the region until the problems of imperial defence encourage interest in the strategic significance of the various island groups. Oceanic concerns are accordingly far less important throughout most of Australian history than European or Asiatic. By contrast, New Zealand, although geographically more remote, is intensely concerned from the outset with the Polynesian presence, both in the home islands and in the groups to the north.

There are also limitations of material. There is no doubt that the Melanesians have chronologically a prior claim to attention over the Polynesians. The fact is, however, that their history as distinct from their anthropology is nothing like as fully documented as that of the Polynesians. Nor with the exception of the Fijians do they seem to have been involved in exchanges with other island peoples in the manner characteristic of Polynesian history. It is perhaps easier to say simply that the experience of the peoples of New Guinea and the Solomon Islands really requires a quite separate and distinct study from that of the other Pacific island peoples.

I

The Adventurers

Man has lived in the Pacific for as long as he is known to have lived anywhere. The most recent skeletal finds in Australia indicate a humanoid presence on that continent dating back to around 500,000 BC, while Java Man, *Pithecanthropus Erectus*, flourished further north about 350,000 BC. *Homo Sapiens* himself admittedly appeared much later, and may have originated elsewhere. Human remains found in Australia have been dated at around 40,000 BC and others, in the highlands of Papua-New Guinea, at 10,000 BC.[1] However, the artefacts found in South Australia and Tasmania are similar to those also found in Indonesia, as well as in Thailand, on the Asian mainland, indicating that progressive settlement of the South and South-west Pacific basin from Asia was well under way before the end of the last Ice Age. There is indeed a remote possibility that the first settlers might have come from even further afield. Geneticists have discovered that one of the variants of the iron-binding serum protein, transferrin, is present in small quantities in Melanesians and Australian aborigines, as well as in Africans and American Negroes. On the other hand, the blood serum Gmc, which is common in Africa, is totally absent in New Guinea natives, whose closest genetic links have been found to be with South-east Asia.[2]

What seems beyond question is that, wherever the Pacific peoples might have come from in the first place, they reached the Pacific by way of Asia. The process of settlement seems to have begun with a movement of short-statured, dark-featured and frizzy-haired people south and east from southern China and northern Indo-China, towards the end of the Ice Age. Their migrations were inspired by the shortage of food, by the desire for warmer climates as the glaciers came nearer, and by pressure from more northern or western peoples, themselves retreating before the glaciers. These first adventurers reached Tasmania about 9000 BC, by way of the Malay Peninsula, Indonesia, New Guinea and Cape York. They were accompanied or possibly even preceded by a physically similar but ethnically distinct Negroid people who settled in New Guinea and Cape York. These groups were in their turn followed by migrations of Veddoid people, also dark-featured but with straighter hair, and usually taller, who settled on the north and south coasts of New Guinea, and around the shores of the Gulf of Carpentaria in Australia. A fourth racial type may also have been on the move at this time : some researchers identify an Anoid strain, tall, fair-skinned and with abundant straight hair, akin to the Ainu of Japan, who may have settled in the larger land masses of the region, eventually becoming predominant in South Australia.[3]

These assorted groups obviously provided the ingredients for the most various of racial mixes. People tall and short, dark and fair, with hair sparse and abundant, wavy, frizzy and straight, had all established themselves in the South and South-west Pacific before 1000 BC. Any variety of human size, appearance or pigmentation can be found somewhere among the inhabitants of the Ocean. To add to the confusion, there is no need to assume that this first process of settlement involved any element of planned migration. The time-span is quite long enough to allow for the most gradual and unorganized of dispersions. Two hundred generations is sufficient for human life to spread itself from China to Tasmania, especially as these first adventurers would not actually have needed any unusual skills or technology to accomplish their voyages. Even today, it would be physically possible to make one's way from the Malay Peninsula to Indonesia, and thence to New Guinea, without ever losing sight of land. Cape York would be barely more than a day and a night's sail from the southernmost point of New Guinea, under favourable conditions. In fact, these early movements would have been mainly undertaken at a time when glacial movements had forced the land masses considerably closer together than they are now. Under these conditions, primitive rafts, without any navigational aids whatever, would have been fully adequate to carry their occupants as far south as Australia, as far east as New Guinea and as far north as the Bismarck Archipelago. The area of their settlement in fact extended over the area south of a line drawn from the Philippines to the Ellice Islands, and west of one drawn from the Ellice Islands to Fiji. This area, subsequently known as Melanesia, incorporated all the larger land masses in the Pacific, except for New Zealand and Hawaii and of course Australia, as well as the bulk of its population. New Guinea, for example, covers an area of about 280,000 square miles, with a population in pre-European times of probably a million and a half; the Solomon Islands are 11,500 square miles in area, with an estimated population of 160,000; the New Hebrides, 3,585 square miles, with 70,000 people; and New Caledonia, 11,500 square miles, with 27,000. Unfortunately, almost nothing is actually known of the pre-European history of these territories, and what is known comes within the sphere of Asian history rather than Pacific. The pirate-trader princes of the Moluccas, for example, certainly claimed New Guinea as part of their dominions, and the presence of Malay elements in the local languages suggests that traders and explorers from the Moluccas might have ventured as far east as 140° 90' beyond the frontier of present day West Irian. They also pushed inland and coined the word *papuwa* – frizzy-haired = Papuan, to describe the people they met there.

Even less is known of the history of the next wave of settlers. Wilhelm G. Solheim deduces from archaeological and linguistic evidence that Asian wanderers entered the Pacific Ocean proper about 2500 BC. Radio-carbon dating has certainly established the first appearance of human life on Saipan, in the Marianas, at around 1500 BC.[4] The rest of Micronesia was presumably reached and partially settled over the next few hundred years. But the fact is that pre-Japanese history of the region is still quite unknown, and the size of its population cannot even be guessed at. All that one is justified in saying is that it cannot have been very large: the total land area of the region is only 1,042 square miles, divided among at least as many islands, most of them tiny coral atolls, quite incapable of supporting any human life.

The effect of the settlement of Melanesia was substantially to extend the frontiers of Asia, in the sense that it could no way be regarded as a feat of maritime adventure, as distinct from simple human endurance. Even Micronesia can be not unfairly categorized as a group of offshore islands. The task of populating the Pacific Ocean itself, which is the real subject of this account, and which involved an epic of seafaring unmatched in human experience, was not undertaken until near the beginning of the Christian Era.

This is where the story becomes unavoidably complicated. The people who swept over the Pacific Ocean between AD 100 and 1000, the 'heroes of the sea', in the words of Andrew Sharp, 'whose like may never be seen again', were descendants of the same East Asian peoples who had earlier settled in the Marianas.[5] Linguistic studies of the various tongues of what became known as Polynesia confirmed that these languages together formed one element in a linguistic super-family of Malay–Polynesian speech. Archaeological studies of pottery and adzes in the Pacific Islands indicated a link between Malay–Polynesian speakers and the Lungshan cultures of South China, themselves linked with the cultures of North China. Biological evidence is consistent with the findings of linguistics and archaeology: the prevalence of so-called 'shovel-shaped' incisors among Polynesians is a distinctive Mongolian trait, and reinforces the proposition that the Polynesians originated as a mixed Caucasoid–Mongolian racial group, who launched out into the Pacific Ocean from much the same parts of Eastern Asia as the first adventurers, with whom they intermarried extensively.[6]

The Polynesians themselves are not mysterious, and the heroic nature of their voyages is attested by their simple presence on the most widely dispersed islands of the Pacific Ocean. However, there seems little doubt that even more remarkable but quite unrecorded voyages were made across the Pacific from west to east by other peoples, before the first Polynesian thrusts took place; and there are certainly grounds for supposing that at least one mysterious voyage from east to west must have happened shortly after the last of the Polynesian epics of settlement had been completed. Evidence for the first of these suppositions is provided by the massive and accumulating indications of direct Asian impact on the peoples of Central and South America over a period of some 2,000 years. For example, motifs characteristic of the Chavin de Huantar culture of Northern Peru, dated around 800 BC, closely parallel motifs found only in China 100 years earlier. Temples built in the form of pyramids constructed in receding stages appear both in Cambodia in Asia and in Yucatan in Central America at about the same period. Angkor Wat in Cambodia and Chichen Itza in Mexico, both built in the twelfth century AD, have in common the lotus motif, the gradual development of vaulted galleries and the use of half-columns to flank doorways. The resemblances are far too minute and recondite to be merely coincidental. As Heine-Geldern and Ekhom summarize the situation: 'There is no psychological law which could have caused the peoples on both sides of the Pacific to stylize the lotus plant in the same manner and to make it surge from the mouth of a jawless demon's head, to invent the parasol and use it as a sign of rank and to invent the same complicated game. There is no explanation other than the assumption of cultural relationship.' Even more convincing evidence is provided by the comparatively new research technique of ethnobotany, which has confirmed that cotton plants in Asia possess thirteen large chromosomes, and wild plants in the Americas thirteen small ones. However, woven cotton materials discovered in Peru and dated back to 2500 BC were found to have twenty-six chromosomes, made up of two sets, one of large chromosomes and one of small. The individuals in each set were so distinctive that they could be traced back to a wild American parent, and a cultivated Asian one. The Asian cottons had been cultivated by the Harappans, the founders of the Indus Valley civilization, sometime before 2500 BC.[7]

There seems no possible doubt that the seeds could have been carried from Asia to America only by human agency. They could not have been blown by the winds, because the winds blow the opposite way. They could not have been carried by birds, because birds do not eat cotton seeds. They could not have floated on the waves, because salt water would have destroyed their powers of germination. They could hardly have been carried by land across the Bering Straits and through the Arctic Circle, because the cold would have killed them. Therefore it seems that they must have been carried by men, in ships, across the temperate or tropic zones of the Pacific. The Harappans, in fact, had the technology to accomplish this at the time in question. Their civilization, more remarkable in many of its scientific achievements than those of Egypt or Mesopotamia, probably matured as early as 3500 BC. One of the most striking areas of its pre-eminence was in shipbuilding. An artificial dock built at Lothal, at the mouth of the Gulf of Cambay, was capable of taking ships of up to 70 tons deadweight and more than 80 feet in length. The Harappans had devised a unique method of making ships water-tight by stitching the planks of the hull together with palm fibres. They also mastered the technique of constructing vessels with three or even four masts to make the greatest possible use of the winds, 3,000 years before the Europeans did. By 2000 BC, their ships were carrying goods to Egypt, some 2,600 miles away, as well as to Sumer, which would have involved voyages of nearly 1,500 miles across open sea between Lothal and the Persian Gulf. The Harappan civilization itself ended about 1700 BC but its contributions to navigation lingered on among other Asian peoples: 3,000 years later, the kings of Sumatra and Ceylon were waging war across 1,200 miles of ocean for the control of the Malay Archipelago.[8]

In other words, navigators from the mainland of Asia must have been traversing the Pacific from west to east certainly after, probably before, and very likely during the period of Polynesian discoveries. We have no proof at all that they ever completed the return journey. On the other hand, it would seem that somebody somehow must have reached the outskirts of Polynesia from the American mainland in east-to-west voyages in historic times, and possibly earlier. For example, the sweet potato or *Cumar* has been dated back in Peru to about AD 100. However, it was widely cultivated in Hawaii by AD 1250, 200 years after the island was reputedly settled by the Polynesians, whose name for the vegetable, *Kumara,* clearly echoes the Quicha Indian word. Winds could not possibly have blown the tubers from Peru to Hawaii. Birds are unlikely to have carried them, and in any case birds could not have told the Hawaiians the Indian name. One can only suppose that men in ships must have brought the sweet potato from America to Polynesia, just as men must have brought cotton seeds from Asia to America.[9] How or when this happened is anybody's guess, but one must admit the possibility that some Polynesians, having covered the 2,400 miles from the Marquesas to Easter Island, sailed on another 2,000 miles into the unknown, until they fetched up in South America; and that they or their descendants attempted to make the return trip, and by sheer luck happened across Hawaii, some 200 years after other Polynesians had settled there. It is not a likely story, but it fits the known facts, and it only had to happen once.

The same process might also explain what appears to be a definite, although not necessarily a direct, link between the Harappans and Polynesia. The only form of genuine writing found in the Pacific Islands is incised on wooden blocks in Easter Island. It is still undeciphered, but appears to be essentially a mirror-image of Harappan script, itself almost wholly unintelligible as yet. Wooden tables inscribed during the period of the Harappan civilization are not likely to have survived into modern times. The most plausible explanation is that the script was taken to Easter Island by the Harappans before the arrival of the Polynesians. The Polynesians, naturally, were unable to read the script, but adapted it to their own purposes. It might also, of course, have been brought to Easter Island in historic times from South America, having been taken there by the Harappans, probably along with the cotton seeds.

The important thing about these supposed east-west contacts is that they can only have been extremely rare and wholly accidental. Recent attempts to demonstrate that the thrust of Polynesian settlement might actually have come from this quarter, rather than from west-to-east, can only be termed inconclusive. Eric de Bisschop, even with the aids of modern navigational instruments and the immense advantage of knowing where he was going, failed totally either to reach Tahiti from Peru, or Peru from Tahiti, and died on the second leg of his unsuccessful journey. Thor Heyerdahl and his colleagues went further than any Polynesians are known to have gone, drifting 4,300 miles in a raft of balsa logs tied together with rope from Callao in Peru to an uninhabited reef off the Taumotu Archipelago. It was a human achievement of truly Polynesian greatness, but it did nothing to prove that the Polynesians had ever done it themselves.

What the Polynesians are known to have done is impressive enough by any human standards. In simple terms, between AD 100 and 300 they swept across the sea from Asia to Samoa and the Marquesas, and thence to Tahiti; in about AD 800, they moved further south, to the Australs and east, to Easter Island; and around the year 1000, they reached even further north, to Hawaii. Wanderers from Tahiti had meanwhile settled in the Cook Islands, and reached New Zealand, the last and by far the largest of the Polynesian island groups, about the same time as their fellows were making landfall at Hawaii. It is impossible to exaggerate the quality of seamanship which these voyages demanded: Samoa, for example, is about 3,500 miles from the Marianas; Hawaii, 2,600 miles from Tahiti; Easter Island, 2,400 miles from the Marquesas; and New Zealand, 1,400 miles from Tonga. For comparison, the longest voyage out of sight of land known to have been undertaken regularly by the Vikings, with whom the Polynesians are frequently compared, was the 300-mile run between Norway and Iceland. What must be appreciated, however, is that the sailors who accomplished these terrific journeys did so entirely by accident, in the sense that they literally did not know where they were going. The Polynesian canoe was admittedly a superb achievement of Stone Age technology. In 1842, for example, the Fijians built a double canoe 118 feet long, 24 feet wide and 6 feet deep from keel to deck. It could carry up to 250 warriors, with food and provisions for a moderately long voyage. Sharp calculates its effective carrying capacity for peaceful purposes as 'thirty persons, two boars, three sows, twelve piglets, thirty fowls, ten dogs, twenty rats, a hundred balled or potted breadfruit and banana plants, and twelve tons of water-gourds, seeds, yams, tubers, coconuts, adzes and weapons'.[10] It is of course true that this monster was built with the aid of metal tools introduced by the Europeans, and that the genuine Stone Age vessel might have been somewhat smaller. However, a canoe even half the size of the Fijian boat would still have been adequate to carry a number of people and the necessities for their survival, ample for the foundation of a viable settlement. These canoes were also admirably seaworthy under favourable conditions. They were 'built of heavy planks, hewn with infinite labor from logs split by means of wedges fashioned from hard rock, and fitted with lugs and stiffening ribs. . . . The joints were cut with such precision that they scarcely needed caulking. The hulls were decked with planks shaped to provide fittings for the control of rigging. . . . The two hulls were bridged with heavy timbers on which decking was laid. A deck-house and platform were provided for the chiefs.'[11] A mast 50 feet high carried a large lateen-type sail, with yard and boom each half as long again as the mast. These ships would have managed a speed of five to seven knots under normal conditions, and up to fifteen knots with a fair wind on the quarter. They were, in other words, magnificent vessels for voyages of not more than a few days' duration, in the course of which they could cover from 200 to 300 miles with little trouble.

This, in fact, was what they were designed to do. The longest planned voyages which the Polynesians are known to have undertaken regularly were the round trips between Rotuma and the Ellice Islands, 200 miles; Tonga and Fiji, 220 miles; Tonga and Rotuma, 300 miles; and Tonga and Savaii, 360 miles direct, or two trips of 180 and 170 miles each, if broken at Tafahi. In other words, the same order of distance as the Norway–Iceland circuit. Even these voyages had become rare by the time the Europeans made their appearance. Dr A. T. Wilson of the University of the Waikato, and C. H. Hendy of Columbia University have suggested that the great Polynesian journeys were all undertaken during a period of unusual warmth, when storms were comparatively few and mild, and were abandoned with the onset of the Little Ice Age, commencing in the fifteenth century, which produced a sharp increase in the frequency of violent storms over the next 400 years. In fact the Polynesian canoe had serious disadvantages as a long-distance vessel. It was subject to racking strains when the wind was forward of the beam, and was liable to be tossed about helplessly in rough weather; it was extremely slow when sailing down wind, and constantly buried its bow in the water; and it suffered from the inherent weakness of all sailing ships, that it could make little if any headway against the wind. Its crew also lacked any navigational aids. They could not take accurate bearings from the position of the stars, because they had no means of allowing for longitudinal displacement. They could not work out their position from the operation of ocean currents, because they had no means of calculating the effects of these currents on their vessels. They could not have followed birds to a landfall, as has sometimes been suggested, because they would not have known where the birds were flying to, and they could not have seen the birds flying at night. Their great voyages were unintentional epics of seamanship and endurance, not planned voyages of discovery and exploration.

Given the natural capacity of the Polynesians for population increase, it is not surprising that even the utterly unplanned arrival of a canoe or two at a fertile island should have provided the basis for a substantial settlement by the time the Europeans arrived. It must also be remembered that we have only the most general idea as to how substantial these settlements actually were. The first European visitors were not reluctant to make estimates of the population of the islands they encountered, but these estimates were based on utterly unreliable modes of calculation. The simplest was to make a quick guess at the number of people arriving on the beaches to observe the newcomers, and adjust this according to the proportion of the total population the sightseers might be presumed to represent. The main trouble with this method was that even the islanders themselves generally had no idea of the numbers of tribes living further inland, who had made no appearance on the scene. A slightly more scientific approach was to ask the local chiefs the numbers of their warriors, and multiply this by the supposed number of non-combatants per warrior. The weakness here was that the chiefs themselves often could not be sure, and were for obvious reasons most unlikely to be telling the truth. It is thus hardly surprising that estimates wildly differ of the populations of the Polynesian islands in pre- and even post-European times.

There is, however, no doubt that the Hawaiians were the greatest of the Polynesian peoples in numbers and in terms of social evolution, if not of territorial possessions. The eight inhabited islands of their Group cover an area of some 6,435 square miles in all, nearly as large as Fiji, and larger than any other truly Polynesian Group except New Zealand. Their population at the time of the coming of the Europeans has been estimated at between 300,000 and 400,000. Aesthetically, they were perhaps not particularly distinguished, except for their *tapa*, or bark-cloth, considered to be the finest in the Pacific, and the magnificent cord-and-feather cloaks and helmets worn by their nobles. The helmets were peculiarly impressive creations, woven from the rootlets of the *'ie'ie* vine and ornamented with red and yellow feathers, usually running in a line of tufts along the centre of the woven cap or compacted into a high crest, strikingly reminiscent of the headgear of Greece or Rome. By custom, Hawaiian nobles had themselves preceded at public cere-monies by great standards or *kahili*. These were similarly woven of red and yellow feathers, in the form of cylinders 18 inches or so in diameter, and borne on the ends of poles up to 20 feet high, thus adding further to the classical European effect.

Although their pageantry was undoubtedly most impressive, the Hawaiians' public buildings or *heiau* were in general undistinguished in workmanship although adequate in size. They never achieved any written language and their technology was in some ways extraordinarily un-developed. Even by Stone Age standards, the Hawaiian digging-stick must be the most truly primitive and unproductive agricultural instru-ment ever known. Where they were truly pre-eminent, however, was in the field of social organization. This was demonstrated by the sheer scale of their public works. Their great agricultural terraces, their irrigation ditches and above all the great sea-walls with which they protected their crops from damage by salt water, were all noteworthy examples of the use of mass labour organized for utilitarian purposes. But the Hawaiian system of administration was significant for its sheer intensity, even more than for its practical achievements. By 1810, Kamehameha of Kohala had developed an effective system of centralized control over a large number of subjects – a system without precedent in the Polynesian world. He had not just brought Polynesian social evolution to its most complex stage : he had prepared the way for a completely new departure in political development. The specialization of function had gone about as far as it could go. Irving Goldman notes that the Chief's household by then included 'guardians, foster parents, wet nurses, all *kahu* (professional priests and craftsmen), a keeper of the household goods, a chief executioner, night guards, a chief steward, a treasurer, a reader of signs, an orator, a guardian of the royal genitals, a pipe lighter and massagers. The administration consisted of a chief counsellor, a chief priest, a war leader, a council of military strategists, common warriors, historians, and readers of omens.'[12]

Most important, however, was the innovation of the *kalai-moku*, or island administrator. The social significance of this office lay in the fact that it was open to commoners. It would thus have permitted the growth of a genuine managerial group, exercising power on behalf of the chiefs,

who were thus freed from the distractions of authority and allowed to
concentrate on cultivating the arts of good living. Hawaiian society
indeed was coming increasingly to resemble that of Europe in the *ancien
régime*. An embryonic capitalist system appeared, based on the use of
pigs as a reserve currency; intoxicating liquors were produced; and
adultery became fashionable and light-hearted, to the point of becoming
a popular spectator sport. European missionaries, doubtless unfamiliar
with the more high-spirited aspects of aristocratic life in their own
societies, described with horror and relish a variety of Hawaiian cricket,
in which the men 'rolled little balls towards the outspread legs of women
seated before them. If the pellet struck its target, the couple retired for
sexual intercourse'.[13] Sodomy provided another acceptable form of
relaxation; while the professionalization of boxing, wrestling and prostitution had a twofold effect : the nobility were guaranteed their enter-
tainment, and opportunities for social advancement and profit were
opened to all who possessed the requisite talents, temperament and
physical attributes, no matter how lowly their social origins.

Nothing remotely comparable with Hawaiian social and political
sophistication was ever attained by the second most populous Polynesian
people, the New Zealand Maoris. Physical considerations provide a
sufficient explanation. Hawaii was compact enough to make a centralized
form of administration possible; and it was fertile enough to permit
the accumulation of resources necessary to support a non-productive
ruling class. New Zealand, by contrast, maintained about half the
population of the Hawaiian Group on nearly sixteen times the area. Its
three main islands covered some 103,736 square miles. Population was
concentrated in the more fertile areas, such as Taranaki and the Waikato,
but the various tribes were so dispersed that nobody could have ever
thought seriously of conquering the whole country. The tribes had
indeed quarrelled fiercely over territory in the first years of settlement
but as they spread themselves over the huge areas available to them,
they settled down to the more agreeable custom of fighting for prestige,
exercise, or simply to acquire human bodies to supplement their available stock of protein. Technologically, they were little more advanced
than the Hawaiians, although they did at least add a footrest to the
basic digging-stick. Their public works were less impressive, consisting
merely of their fortified villages or *pas*, terraces, and earthwork wind-
breaks. They were, however, by no means deficient in their capacity for
design or craftsmanship. Maori clothing was the best as well as the most
beautiful in the Pacific; meeting houses were carved and painted in

enormously intricate and elaborate patterns of red, black and white; and ornaments of greenish nephrite were worked with great art and labour, by a painstaking process of abrasion.

But for the European intervention, the Tahitian Group might have become the predominant power in the Central Pacific. Their fourteen islands covered some 600 square miles, with a total population of perhaps 200,000. Density of population on the fertile plains of the volcanic islands was indeed the highest in the Pacific, at about 1,000 to the square mile. Production of the staple items of breadfruit and coconut, as well as of fowls and pigs, was nonetheless sufficient to satisfy domestic requirements, and even to allow for surpluses to be exported to neighbouring islands. The land was well-watered and its fertility enhanced by a system of irrigation ditches comparable to those in Hawaii. Fishing was safe and easy within the sheltering reefs. The Tahitians' village assembly-places or *marae*, whose main function was to serve as venues for feasting, were the most elaborate in Polynesia. One marae in the Papara district was designed to have an eleven-step pyramid 50 feet high, and an attached court that measured 367 by 267 feet. The misfortune of the Tahitians was that the sheer wealth and diversity of society which their islands could afford delayed the attainment of political unity. The Group was able to support all too many rich and powerful chiefs. Tahiti itself was split into some twenty feudal districts or fiefdoms, not counting those on unruly Raiatea. Something like genuine integration was achieved only in the eighteenth century, just in time to be crushed by European imperialism.

Samoa and the Marquesas can claim to be the real points of origin of Pacific Polynesian culture. Adventurers from these two Groups carried their arts and traditions to Tahiti, Easter Island, the Australs, Hawaii, the Cooks and New Zealand, over a period of about 1,000 years. Samoa itself could be regarded as the most benign and attractive of all the Pacific Islands. The climate was the most equable and the soil the most fertile and consistently well-watered. There was no winter, properly speaking. Population pressure was not excessive : Samoa's 1,130 square miles easily supported its 70,000 people. Life may well have been almost too easy. The acquisition of territory was not a serious concern, so the Samoan chiefs fought for prestige and honour, the demands of which were insatiable. They also developed an incredible and far from efficient specialization of handicrafts. J. B. Stair lists the following recognized guilds.

house builder, canoe maker, small canoe maker, wooden bowl maker, preparer of turmeric, preparer of lamp-black, paddle maker, fish-bait preparer, sailmaker, drum maker, maker of split bamboo fishing pots, barber, tattooer, maker of tattooing instruments, fishhook maker, maker of stone hatchets, maker of nets, weaver of garment mats, weaver of house mats, siapo maker, arrowroot maker, basket weaver, ornamental screen maker, and plaiter of sennit.

Goldman notes further that 'skill was a minor issue in such meticulous specialization'.[14] Consistent with this multiplicity of crafts was the complex system of social organization, through assemblies of family representatives, ranging from a Great Fono embracing the whole of Samoa, which may never have actually functioned in practice, to small local village assemblies. As with the Tahitians, such fragmentation hardly made for unity.

The Marquesans were too scattered as well as too disunited to achieve anything like integration before the fatal impact of the Europeans. Physically, theirs was the least rewarding of the Pacific Island groups. Their combined area of 500 square miles was inadequate to support a population estimated at between 50,000 and 100,000. Agriculture was rendered unreliable by an erratic climate, with scorching droughts. Fishing was difficult and dangerous, as the absence of any encircling reef meant that the Marquesans had to venture out into the open sea to catch what they could. The population was dispersed in fertile, isolated valleys, cut off from one another by densely wooded mountain ranges. Rivalry among the isolated tribes was guaranteed by the continuous economic uncertainty. The Marquesans did indeed attempt to safeguard themselves against their periodic droughts by retaining one-quarter of each year's breadfruit crop as a reserve store, but they dissipated the benefits of this system by a suicidal custom whereby the victors killed off the breadfruit trees of the losers in a tribal conflict. This certainly provided a strong incentive to fight to the death rather than surrender and face starvation. It also meant that the victors gained nothing economically from their triumph except the bodies of the defeated, and would have to find somebody to fight and eat next year. It is thus all the more remarkable that the Marquesas should have remained one of the undoubted centres of Polynesian civilization. Their sailors reached more distant lands than those of any other island group, while their craftsmen built great ceremonial *maraes* or *tohuas*, developed the arts of wood carving and tattooing to a high degree of refined technical perfection, and constructed monumental wooden images of deified tribal ancestors, some 8 feet high. Personal ornaments and diadems of tortoise- or sea-shell were elegant and meticulously proportioned. At the same time, the Marquesas can only be regarded as one of those centres of civilization from which it would be a positive joy to escape to a provincial periphery.

One of the striking features of pre-European Polynesia is that its most assertive and perhaps most influential race – the Tongans – developed on one of the smallest and least populous of the Groups. Moreover, their achievements did not end with the European incursion, as did those of virtually all of their fellow-islanders. The Tongans not only developed the political organizations among the Pacific peoples corresponding to the European concepts of nation and empire : they also alone among the Pacific peoples maintained at least a formal independence in the face of the flooding imperialism of the nineteenth and early twentieth centuries; and even more impressively, they refused to give the faintest indication of dying out during the period when the hope was repeatedly being expressed that the Pacific would become a Polynesian graveyard and a white man's ocean. The Tongans are survivors.

This most formidable of Polynesian civilizations arose on a Group of some 160 islands, only six of which were ever actually inhabited, and two of which, Tongatapu and Vava'u, were of any significant size. The total area of the Group was about 260 square miles, with a surprisingly constant population of between 27,000 and 30,000. The inhabited islands were tolerably fertile, although only volcanic Vava'u, with a total area of 46 square miles, could be termed notably so, its reddish clay being widely covered with a rich black mulch of decaying vegetation. Even the less obviously fertile soil of Tongatapu had the useful characteristic of swelling when wet and crumbling quickly to dust when dry, so that little water would be lost by evaporation on the surface, and plantations could be fairly easily kept free of weeds. The Tongans certainly made the maximum use of whatever natural resources were available to them. European visitors were impressed by the general scene of orderly agriculture with elaborate terraces and neatly fenced plantations, and by the massive stone walls built to trap fish brought in by the tides. The Tongans were indeed superb craftsmen, on both a large and a small scale. They constructed by far the biggest megalithic monument in Polynesia, apart from the very largest of the statues of Easter Island. In about AD 1200, the formidable chief Tui Tonga Tuitaui built a gateway in the form of a gigantic trilithon, known as *Ha' amonga 'a*

Maui ('the burden of Maui carried on a carrying stick'). The gateway, consisting of three slabs of unstratified limestone, each of about 30 tons in weight, carefully squared and morticed, was perhaps built as a memorial to honour great chiefs of the past, or to symbolize unity among Tui Tonga Tuitaui's sons. The Tongans also developed the craft of pottery, although they subsequently lost this particular skill. However, their wooden bowls and weapons were beautifully shaped and polished, and decorated with precise, elaborate but artistically restrained incised ornamentation. Their level of artistic refinement obviously makes it impossible to regard them as merely physically magnificent brawlers, the samurai of the South Pacific, despite their creation of a society dedicated to military and masculine values.

The Tongans developed the most aggressively stratified and aristocratic society in Polynesia. It carried inequality of status to the limits of human possibility : no two Tongans could occupy the same social position under any circumstances. The rewards of status were also developed to the extreme. The supreme Chief, the Tui Tonga, formally held sole right to all the land in the Group. Women of common rank were at the sexual disposal of the chiefs, who also held arbitrary powers of life and death over their inferiors. Commoners were frequently beaten up or even put to death merely on suspicion of having withheld tribute. A servant accused of overfeeding the daughter of a chief to such an extent that her figure lost its athletic symmetry was duly executed. The basic assumption of inequality of privilege was even perpetuated in Tongan concepts of the afterlife : nobles swaggered off into a paradise of feasting and gratification (*Bultotu*), not unlike what they had already enjoyed in the physical plane of existence; while commoners, having already endured what must frequently have amounted to a hell upon earth at the hands of their lords, could look forward to nothing more rewarding than total extinction. Sentimentality was not a weakness of the Tongans.

The fact is that the Tongan solution to the besetting Polynesian problems of feudal anarchy was supremely successful. This ruthless, arrogant, cultured race enjoyed unity and civic peace for periods vastly longer than those contrived by any other island people. The Tongans indeed lived in almost complete peace with themselves and their neighbours for some 600 years, between AD 1200 and 1800. Moreover, unlike other islanders who dwelt in fortified towns and villages, clustered together for mutual protection, the Tongans lived virtually weaponless, in houses dispersed among their plantations, with lanes providing easy communication. They achieved, in short, a model of rationally ordered civilized society.

Their freedom from external assaults was doubtless due, at least in part, to simple physical qualities. The Tongans are among the tallest races of mankind; in youth, among the best-proportioned; and in maturity, without any doubt the heaviest. In a Stone Age society, where survival was overwhelmingly a matter of physical prowess, the Tongans could count on being left alone. They were in fact admired as well as feared : with their olive complexions, strong features and distinctively chiselled lips, they were invariably regarded as extraordinarily handsome people by other Polynesians as well as Europeans. Pre-eminent in fighting ability, social organization and physical beauty, the Tongans easily obtained the respect of their fellow-islanders.

This was just as well, considering who their nearest neighbours were. The Fijians were from five to ten times as numerous as the Tongans, with a population estimated at from 150,000 to 250,000. Their 300 islands covered an area of 7,500 square miles, one of the largest island groups of the Pacific. They were perhaps the most talented, ingenious, disconcerting and ferocious of all the island peoples. Ethnically, they were predominantly Melanesian. Their culture was however essentially Polynesian. Characteristically, the Fijians themselves never bothered to develop traditions of their own origins, until they found that gullible Europeans expected them to provide some appropriate legend. They then made up the tale of the mighty and wholly imaginary chief Lutunasobasoba, who came to the island of Viti Levu in his great canoe Kaunitani. What is really significant is that the Fijians developed to the highest degree 'almost every art known to the Polynesians, and many others besides'.[15] Their chiefs' houses were 'large, soundly constructed and skilfully ornamented with lashings or bindings of dyed cords'.[16] Chief Tanoa's house in Bau was 125 feet long and 42 feet wide. Fijian canoes were, at their best, the fastest and most seaworthy vessels in the Pacific. Like the Samoans and Tongans, they developed the art of pottery, kneading the clay with fine sand and rubbing it with an infusion of mangrove clay after firing, to give it a dark red colour and a slight glaze. Fijian oil cups, water pots and clubs were beautifully shaped, polished and lavishly incised with undulating patterns. The supremely conceited Tongans unhesitatingly accepted the Melanesian Fijians as their superiors in both aesthetics and technology; and Tongan nobles developed the custom of making a Grand Tour of the Fijian Islands, to admire and copy the superbly constructed

and ornamented weapons of the Fijians, and to learn from them how to
master their huge double canoes. Fijian skills in surgery and the use
of herbal medicaments were noted throughout the region. Along with
the Hawaiians, they developed the use of alcoholic drinks. They terraced,
irrigated and reclaimed the land, dug canals, and built bridges and stone
canoe-docks which survive today. They were not merely cultured : they
were also, superficially at least, friendly and sociable. European visitors
regretfully noted that the Tongans, so much more physically attractive
by European standards, were customarily surly and unresponsive, while
the fearsome-looking Fijians were by contrast amiable and friendly.

This, like most such early impressions, was rather misleading. In many
ways, the Fijians had habits as alarming as their appearance. There was
no doubt about the latter, for the Fijian is one of the most physically
daunting of human beings. His features tend to be at once harsher and
more cleanly defined than the normal Polynesian cast; his towering
height is accentuated by bushy and kinky hair; and his generally thinner
and darker skin makes his enormous muscularity still more evident.
Fijians went in for social bloodshed on a scale far more wholesale than
the normal Polynesian practice. Cannibalism was indeed general throughout the islands, and partially explains the almost total lack of concern
for ethnic differences shown by the Pacific peoples : the fact that black,
brown and white people all taste the same when cooked properly helps
one to believe in the fundamental unity of the human race. However,
cannibal feasts were both more common and more substantial in places
like Bau than elsewhere in the Pacific. The Fijians were also distinguished
for the frequency of their human sacrifices : heavy canoes were launched
over the bodies of slain enemies, and prisoners were slaughtered in order
to wash the decks of canoes with blood or to keep a chief's war-club
properly lubricated. Victims were lowered into holes dug for the corner
posts of temples or important houses; they would be encouraged with
sharp stakes to grasp the butts of the poles, after which earth would be
tipped in and rammed down on top of them to ensure a firm foundation.
Widows of chiefs and princes would be strangled so that they could keep
their dead husbands company in the after-life; the women of a defeated
tribe were normally massacred as part of the victory celebrations; and
some measure of population control was achieved by simply burying alive
the sick, old and any others whose existence had become an encumbrance
to their relations. This was done in a typically jovial way : the candidate
for euthanasia would be invited to come and look at the big sea-monster;
hit on the head with a club while thus distracted; and heaved into a

grave already dug by his family, who would cheerfully suppress any last struggles. Fijians had unusually strong motivations to remain healthy and self-reliant, but they were not by any means regardless of the importance of human life. Warfare was conducted with praiseworthy moderation. The armies involved in any engagement would never number more than 1,000 men on either side; ways would usually be found to break off the encounter before anybody actually got killed; and treachery and betrayal were esteemed the highest achievements of the military art, in that they were the most economical of life. In all, probably not more than a couple of thousand Fijians on average met their deaths annually in all the wars and organized bloodletting which enlivened the island scene.

The last, the most mysterious and incontestably the most tragic of the Polynesian peoples of the Pacific were the Easter Islanders. Their small territories covered some 60 square miles. Their estimated pre-European population of 7,000 would thus have represented the highest population density in the Ocean. It was their achievement to attain two of the outstanding peaks of Polynesian culture. They were the only islanders to develop what appears to have been an authentic form of writing, not merely mnemonic but ideographic and pictographic, and derived, as has been mentioned, from the Indus Valley script of the Harappans. They were also the most extraordinary megalithic stonemasons in the Pacific. The huge stone images discovered on Easter Island have aroused as much interest as the pyramids of Egypt and Mexico. Some 600 have been found, dating from the twelfth to the seventeenth century, ranging in height from 3 to 70 feet, and averaging about 18 tons in weight. About 200 had been placed in position on the *ahus*, great ceremonial stone platforms with central altars, usually flanked by long wings of stone; about 300 were embedded in the ground; and the remainder were still in the quarries where they had been carved. The images themselves were fashioned out of volcanic *tufa* or limestone and originally coated with red ochre and white pigment. Their characteristic form was that of a torso, with the head carved as a quadrilateral, the base or chin being wider than the forehead. The lips were thin, wide and turned down at the ends; the nostrils were wide and raised; and the eyebrows emphatically ridged. Other physically details were lightly sketched: the pectoral muscles were defined, but the arms were barely indicated and were generally foreshortened, with the hands resting on the abdomen or at the sides.

Speculation of the most extraordinary kind has been aroused by these remarkable megaliths. It has even been suggested that they portray astronauts from outer space, with whose superhuman aid the Easter Islanders carved the images and moved them to their present sitings. The faces of the images are indeed most un-Polynesian in contour. However, Oceanic art seldom attempts to be strictly representational, even when there were no particular technical problems to be overcome; and anybody might be forgiven for abandoning the attempt to hew out anatomically correct Polynesian features on a 70-foot limestone block. The legends of the Easter Islanders themselves do not suggest anything remotely strange or astronomical about the origin or the purposes of the megaliths. They simply state that they were 'walked' from the quarries by the *mana* (prowess) of great chiefs, which need imply nothing more than that the images were constructed to honour conquering chiefs and were built and erected for them by the peoples they enslaved.

Conquest, tyranny and destruction are in fact the leitmotivs of the history of Easter Island, of which the megaliths remain as inexpressibly tragic and disturbing symbols. By representing the triumphs of successive warrior-chiefs, they record also the collapse of the Polynesian system and the destruction of its people. The Easter Islanders clearly responded even less satisfactorily than the Marquesans to the physical challenges of their environment. These were indeed great. The land was barren, hilly and devoid of streams or natural lakes. Springs, when present at all, were almost invariably in inaccessible spots, although volcanic craters functioned to some extent as reservoirs. Population was crowded on the narrow and comparatively fertile coastal fringe. Unlike the Tongans, who succeeded in denying themselves the destructive joys of feudal rivalry for over six centuries, the Easter Islanders seem to have become ever more fragmented into small groups, subservient initially to the *ariki* (kings) of whom there were supposed to have been fifty-seven. Their powers were subsequently taken over completely by the *matu to'a* or warriors, who assumed all political and religious authority. The kings remained sacred but totally powerless. A tradition of warfare developed, culture declined and all sense of corporate effort was lost. What this actually meant in terms of human suffering is implied by the characteristic style of the small wooden statues or figurines, which are as typical of Easter Island culture as the great stone megaliths. These are models of a human figure, depicted, unlike the megaliths, with meticulous detail. The lower ribs protrude, the sternum is clearly visible, the face is gaunt and the neck marked by a goitre and an excrescence on the back. Before the Second World War, anthropologists assumed that these figurines were intended to represent decaying corpses. Closer acquaintance with the physical appearance of malnutrition, as seen in the victims of the worst concentration camps, has suggested an explanation far more feasible : the figures simply show human beings in the extremities of starvation.[17] The picture becomes totally consistent. The megaliths celebrate the victories of the *matu to'a*; the figurines, the human consequences of these victories.

Obviously more can be affirmed of the culture of the Polynesians than of their history in pre-European times. For practical purposes, the historical record begins with Tonga where, somewhere around AD 950, one of the most interesting, pragmatic and durable of political experiments was undertaken, and the independence of the Group assured to this day. Tonga had already been settled for perhaps 600 years. Close cultural relations had been maintained with Samoa and apparently New Caledonia, with regular and frequent visits being made between all three places. Even closer relations had been developed with Fiji, from whom the Tongans had already learned the arts of pottery and probably megalithic carving. They also may have learned the techniques of making and using weapons from the formidable Fijians. Certainly until the beginning of the tenth century, Tongan chiefs were relying on imported Fijian advisers and administrators to keep their own unruly subjects in order. Some Tongan genius reversed this process of foreign dependence in the tenth century, and thereby helped to preserve the national identity of his people. The circumstances, in the absence of any written documentation, are unavoidably vague. The story is that Ahoeitu, the offspring of a union between a Tongan woman and Tangaroa, the ancestral God of the Polynesians, lived in the sky with his divine father and, presumably, at least half-divine half-brothers. He was murdered by them while still in the sky, for reasons which are not recounted; was restored to life by his father Tangaroa; and was sent down to earth to govern Tonga as a sacred chief or Tui Tonga, replacing a previous Tui Tonga who was descended from worms and whose name the legend does not deign to record. The point of the story would seem to be that one far-sighted man realized that Tonga lacked the space and resources to be able to afford unbridled feudal rivalry, and sought to unite his people by establishing a tradition of sacred and unchallengeable kingship.

This, of course, was not a peculiarly Tongan notion. The Samoan royal titles of Tui'ana and Tuiatua on the island of Upolu were also held to be of divine origin. The Tui Tonga himself was probably a Tongan version of the Tui Manu'a, the ceremonial sacred paramount chief of all Samoa. What the Tongans introduced was above all a note of practicality. Admittedly, once the Tui Tonga had entered a house, it could no longer be occupied by its owners, and nobody could eat, drink or sleep in a house where the Tui Tonga had done any of these things. On the other hand, violation of these sacred prohibitions (*tapus*) did not necessarily involve the death of the transgressor, as elsewhere in Polynesia. Similarly, the ceremonial obeisance, touching the royal feet with the backs of one's hands, was considerably more informal than the Hawaiian prostration.

The innovation of the Tui Tonga certainly seems to have initiated an impressive expansion of Tongan influence in the Pacific. Tongan nobles, no longer having a supreme position to contend for, found time to voyage out to other islands in search of excitement, visiting Easter Island, Rotuma, Futuna and Samoa itself. Rotuma and Futuna soon came under formal Tongan control. At the same time, affiliations were developed with the formidable Fijian chiefs of Verata, Bau and Lau. The Fijian Tui Matuliki actually migrated to Tonga with his whole tribe, to become subject to the Tui Tonga. Meanwhile, successive Tui Tongas established permanent residences for themselves on the Samoan islands of Upolu and Savai'i. And, at last, some time about the beginning of the thirteenth century, one of the most remarkable episodes of Pacific history occurred : the Tongans occupied Samoa.

It is unfortunate that the details of this extraordinary event are completely unknown. Legends speak only of an occupation, followed by an expulsion early in the seventeenth century. The absence of any epic stories suggests that both the arrival and departure of the Tongans might have been comparatively bloodless : they simply paid a visit to Samoa and stayed for 400 years. Meanwhile, the Tongan system itself had been undergoing some modifications. The fact that the eleventh Tui Tonga Tuitaui felt constrained to build the great trilithon in his own honour suggests that he might have felt his position to be a little precarious, as indeed does his formal title : 'the Lord who strikes at the knee'. A sacred ruler who feels constrained to keep his subjects at a safe distance by lashing out at the legs of anybody who comes within range of his club cannot be too confident about his own sacredness. His successors had real grounds for concern. The nineteenth Tui Tonga was assassinated under circumstances which have not been recorded; the twenty-second was murdered by Fijians hired by other Tongan chiefs; and when the twenty-third Tui Tonga, the tyrannical Takalaua, was killed by his own people, the validity of the title and the stability of the nation were both seriously in question. The situation was saved by Takalaua's heir,

Kau-ulu-fonua Fekai, who put the assassins to death, and then acted to preserve the symbolic value of the Tui Tonga by handing over responsibility for administration and the collection of tribute to a new hereditary line, the Tui Haa Takalaua. He retained for himself and successive Tui Tongas the condition of privilege without power enjoyed by European constitutional monarchs. Authority was further delegated to the governors of 'Eua, Ha'apai, Vava'u, Niuatoputapu and Niuafo'ou; and a Tongan clan was founded on the island of Mangaia.

This was the last great political development the Polynesians were able to achieve with the technology of their own culture. Similar attempts to achieve political unity in Tahiti and Hawaii had failed. One of the reasons was that the early success of the Tongans in overcoming feudal anarchy had made it unnecessary for them to develop the characteristic Polynesian feature of the fortified village. It was therefore difficult for local areas of resistance to develop once a central authority had been introduced. By contrast, unification in the other islands had to await a technological breakthrough which would place in the hands of a unifying tyrant weapons not available to his feudal rivals. The new weapons were on the way, even as Kau-ulu-fonua was dividing the sacred and temporal lines of authority in Tonga. The Europeans were at last breaking out of their distant homelands to sweep over the Americas and into Asia and the Pacific. Savagery was coming to the South Seas.

II

The Imperialists

European man did not reach the Pacific before the sixteenth century for the same reason that American man did not reach the moon before the twentieth: he lacked the equipment. The obstacles in the way of long-distance ocean travel out of sight of land were enormous. Chief among the practical problems was the simple one that sailors really had no reliable way of knowing where they were going, except by following a familiar coastline. Exceptionally brave men might be prepared to sail out into the unknown for a few days and might even be able to get back home, reckoning by currents, winds or the stars. The only people who seem to have embarked regularly on trips out of sight of land which must have lasted for weeks were the Harappans, who presumably had learned to make use of the monsoon winds to guide them from Lothal to the Arabian Gulf and back again. Some assistance was provided at about the beginning of the twelfth century by the invention of the compass, apparently by the Chinese, who had also discovered by 1122 that the magnetic north indicated by a compass needle did in fact vary from the true north.[1] Indian seafarers were regularly using their own form of compass, described as 'an iron fish in a bowl of oil', as a guide to navigation by 1218.[2] In the meantime, the Arabs had introduced the three-masted sailing ship to the Mediterranean. Even more important, German shipwrights had developed the stern rudder possibly as early as the mid-twelfth century, certainly by 1242, and this made it possible for a ship to take advantage of a wind on either quarter.[3] Two Genoese sailors, Doria and Vivaldi, put this new technology to the test in 1291, when they attempted to sail around Africa. They were never heard of again. However, new incentives to discover a sea route to Asia were provided by the return of the Polos to Europe in the following year with accounts of parts of the world enormously more attractive, richer, more civilized and better managed than Europe itself. They were followed by the Dominican, Odoric of Pardenone, who returned with remarkable stories of lands he had never seen and impressive ones of those which he apparently had seen, such as Coromandel, the East Indies and Canton. Indeed it would not have been difficult to make almost anywhere else on earth sound more appealing than Europe in the fourteenth century. In 1338 the English began a series of attempts to conquer France which raged sporadically over the next 115 years. In 1347 the Black Death spread from Genoa to the eastern Mediterranean and thence over all Europe, killing off one-third of the population in three years and effectively destroying the whole demographic foundation of medieval society.[4] Starvation and despair led to bloody popular uprisings like the Jacquerie in France in 1358 and the Peasants' Revolt in England in 1381. The continent itself came under pressure from both the west and the east. The easy and tolerant rule of the Moors in southern Spain was jeopardized by attempts by the African Moors to enforce their authority in Spain, at about the same time that the Ottoman Turks captured Adrianople in 1362. The Four Horsemen were riding high over Europe.

Threat of foreign invasion did not of course lead to anything remotely like a united response from the Europeans. The English and French were too busy fighting each other to be concerned with what happened in Spain or the Balkans. England in any case went to war with the kingdom of Castile in 1392 for control of the trade routes through the Bay of Biscay. A call by Pope Boniface IX for a crusade against the Infidel Turk in 1396 summoned a disorderly rabble of adventurers rendered unemployed by a temporary lull in the English–French wars, who looted their way through the countries they were supposed to defend and were shattered by the Turks at Nicopolis after succeeding in convincing most East Europeans that the West was considerably more to be feared than the Turk.

Europe was in fact contracting rapidly at the dawn of the Age of Discovery. But it would be misleading to represent the voyages west of the Portuguese and Spanish as an organized response to the Ottoman advance from the east. There could have been no voyages anywhere but for the fact that the compass had passed into general use among European seafarers by 1405. The technical advantage of knowing which

way one was going was soon put to the test by the Portuguese in a raid
against the African port of Ceuta in 1415. Nine years later, they pushed
out boldly to reach the Canaries, the approximate location of which
was known since a French ship had been blown there in 1330. But it was
of relatively little use to know which way one was going, unless one
knew where one was. European sailors were able to make a rough
approximation of latitude by using two movable pieces of wood in the
form of a cross to measure the vertical angle between the horizon and
whatever heavenly body they were taking their reckonings from. This
naturally allowed immense opportunities for error. So did the only
available means of gauging the speed at which the ship was travelling.
This was to throw a piece of wood into the water at the bow of the ship,
while a sailor recited Hail Marys or other stock sentences. One would
then decide how long the wood had taken to reach the stern by the
number of sentences the sailor had got through, assuming that one knew
roughly how long it took on average to speak each sentence, and making
due allowance for the rate at which the sailor spoke and the speed and
direction of any currents which might be flowing, if one happened to
know about them. A certain technological advance was made by the
adaptation of the astrolabe to maritime purposes in 1480. This device
consisted in its simplest form of 'a disc marked in degrees with a
swivelling pointer mounted at the centre. The pointer was fitted with
aperture sights, one at each end. The instrument was suspended vertic-
ally from a ring at the top. The observer held the ring in his left hand,
and with his right aligned the sights with his chosen star. He then read
off the angle shown by the upper end of the pointer'.[5] In fact, he
normally did not bother. In any case, one could get an accurate reckoning
with this instrument only when the deck of the ship was still, which was
likely to happen only when one was becalmed. Sailors accordingly had
in practice to lug the astrolabe ashore, to get a steady base from which
to take a sighting. It was not going to help much in crossing the Atlantic.

It was nonetheless extremely desirable that somebody should make
the attempt. The reason was not at all that the Turk was ferociously
closing the land trade routes with the East. It was rather that he was all
too tolerantly leaving them in the hands of the rapacious pirates who
had controlled them hitherto. Europe depended absolutely on trade with
the East. It was not simply a matter of luxury goods. Spices and condi-
ments of all kinds were an indispensable precaution against famine, both
as the only means available of preserving meat, and as a way of rendering
it palatable, once preserved. Trade in any vital commodity naturally

offers the greatest opportunities for human rapacity. The various levies extorted along the land route by carriers, Bedouin marauders and customs officials raised the price of spices in Alexandria to more than twenty times their original cost in India. And this was before the Venetians, the lords of the Eastern Mediterranean, took their cut.

This situation was hardly altered by the Turkish invasions. Mohammed II had confirmed the trading privileges of the Venetians and Genoese in the Levant after his capture of Constantinople in 1453. His concessions were admittedly followed by sixteen years of war between Venice and the Ottoman Empire, starting in 1463, which had adverse effects on trade. However, the victorious Turks allowed the Venetians to resume their enormously profitable and profiteering trade in the Levant in 1479. Turkish advances in many ways improved the lot of the East Europeans, but they did nothing to help the West.

There was only one way to break the Venetian stranglehold, since the Turks were not going to do it. In 1487, Bartholomeu Dias rounded the southern tip of the African continent, under royal command from Prince Henry of Portugal, and entered the Indian Ocean. The situation was temporarily confused when Christopher Columbus returned in 1493, claiming to have reached India by sailing due west, but faith in the eastern route was justified when Vasco da Gama sailed into Calicut harbour, India, in 1498. The Venetian stranglehold had been broken.

The effect on trade was immediate and spectacular. In the last five years of the fifteenth century, Venice imported on average each year £3·5 million worth of spices, and Portugal £224,000. In the first five years of the new century, the comparable figures were Venice £1 million annually and Portugal £2·3 million.[6] There was no question of the land route through the Levant being closed at this time : the Egyptians repeatedly sent fleets into the Indian Ocean in an attempt to force the Portuguese to abandon the alternative sea route they had found and go back to using the caravan route through Egyptian dominions. So did Selim I, after he had overrun the Mameluke Empire in Syria and Egypt, not over an issue of trade but because the Mamelukes had sided with the Shah of Persia against the growing Ottoman power. All such efforts failed. The land routes did remain in operation. Indeed, they continued to carry on occasion more trade than was borne by ship in certain years, but only because the Portuguese were as excessive in their charges as the Venetians had been, and also thanks to the corruptibility of Portuguese officials who were frequently prepared to send cargoes by land if adequately bribed.

These Portuguese ventures were, of course, essentially Asian affairs:
the nearest they came to the Pacific proper was when they reached the
Moluccas, the original Isles of Spice, in 1512. It was not until 1519 that
a European expedition actually traversed the Pacific. The voyage was
perhaps more illuminating for what it failed to discover than for what
it actually found: Ferdinand Magellan managed to sail around the
southern tip of South America and right across the Pacific, missing all
the Polynesian islands and finally making landfall at Guam, in
Micronesia. This first encounter between Europeans and the peoples of
the Pacific set a precedent to be all too faithfully followed in later
meetings: the islanders stole a skiff belonging to one of Magellan's ships;
the Spanish landed forty men, burned between forty and fifty houses
belonging to the islanders, as well as several small boats, and killed seven
of the inhabitants. This was only a foretaste.

It is not really surprising that the Europeans tended in these situations
to act with quite uninhibited ferocity. They were probably fierce men
to begin with, and the conditions under which they voyaged could only
have made them fiercer. The ships of the sixteenth century were durable
enough, and even large enough: the five ships of Magellan's squadron
ranged between an estimated 75 and 120 tons in either displacement or
capacity, and carried about 245 men in all. But they must have been
hellishly uncomfortable: they leaked, so that in wet weather there would
probably have been no dry space anywhere; they were soon infested
with rats and cockroaches; and the men had literally nowhere to sleep
except on the deck itself. Food and drink presented almost unimaginable
problems. The latter was probably the less serious: water supplies in the
cask quickly became unbearably foul, but the ships carried sufficient wine
to provide a normal allowance of one and a half litres per man each
day.[7] Food was quite a different story: by the time they reached the
Pacific, Magellan's men were surviving on ship's biscuit, reduced to
powder by worms and befouled by rats, sawdust and 'the hides which
kept the rigging from chafing on the yards'.[8] Scurvy was naturally
rampant, its most disagreeable effect being to cause the gums to swell
until they covered the teeth, thus making it impossible for the sufferer
to eat anything. It is indeed most probable that no men can ever have
suffered such intense physical discomfort for so long as those who sailed
from 1519 to 1522 with Ferdinand Magellan, on the greatest of all epics
of human discovery. Conditions such as these would have coarsened the
susceptibilities of even the most refined gentleman-adventurers. But the
men who sailed in the ships of Spain and Portugal in the sixteenth

century were in general bloody-minded and grasping soldiers of fortune, accustomed to careers of rapine and murder in the *reconquista* against the Moors, and looking for further employment of the same kind. European culture and religion were brought to the Pacific by a heroic band of foul-smelling, physically tortured and generally rapacious villains, in what can only be described as an advanced state of physical decay. Even apart from problems of health, they had a hard trip. Three of the ships had mutinied, two members of their crews had been killed in the fighting, two more had been marooned, another abandoned, and another executed; the *Concepcion* was wrecked, the *Santiago* was sunk, the *San Antonio* fled for home to libel Magellan and those continuing to sail with him; and only the *Vittoria* completed the round trip on 8 September 1522, leaving 170 of the original expedition lost on the way.[9]

Neither Spain nor Portugal was as yet concerned with the Pacific Ocean and its peoples as such. The target of the Portuguese was Asia. That of the Spanish was America. Cortez had already begun the loot and destruction of the Aztec Empire in 1519. In 1527, Alvaro de Saavedra sailed across the Pacific from Mexico, in search of islands alleged to have been visited years before by the Inca Tupac Yupanqui, who was supposed to have brought back gold, silver and slaves. The only islands which the Inca is likely to have encountered would have been the Galapagos, from which he could have brought back nothing but bird-droppings. De Saavedra at all events fetched up on the Marshalls in Micronesia, where he enjoyed a friendly and bloodless landfall. In 1537, six years after Pizarro had begun his assault on the Inca Empire, Hernando de Gujalva similarly crossed from Peru, this time pacifically encountering the inhabitants of the Northern Gilberts in Melanesia. In 1564 the Spanish established themselves in Asian waters, when Miguel Lopez de Legaspi crossed from Mexico to found a settlement in the Philippines. This did involve certain collisions with the Micronesians on the way, in which a few Spaniards were killed with 'spears, slings and clubs',[10] but a new incentive had arisen for serious Pacific exploration. Rumours were current of a whole new continent somewhere in the southern ocean, and the Spaniard Alvaro de Mendaña left Callao in Peru in 1567 to find it. He certainly found the Solomon Islands sometime between February and June 1568. This confrontation of cultures was not wholly amicable, however, despite de Mendaña's genuine anxiety to treat in a suitably Christian way any natives that his expedition met. Misunderstandings and total suspicion on both sides were exacerbated by the readiness of the Spanish to fire off their arquebuses at any available human target in moments of uncertainty. The result was a prolonged series of exchanges which left eleven Spanish and at least twenty-six natives dead, and, on the island of Guadalcanal, every village within reach of the shore burned to the ground. Spanish exploration in the Pacific had commenced in an unpromisingly blood-stained manner.

Spain itself was, of course, already coming under enormous pressure. The English were to enter the Pacific in 1572, also in search of the fabulous riches of the 'southern continent', but primarily to sack the Spanish American Empire. But a considerably more serious opponent was closer at hand. The Dutch provinces had risen in revolt against Spanish rule in 1555. The singularly waterlogged and beleaguered nature of their country appears to have fostered in the Dutch remarkable qualities of determination, seamanship and sheer physical strength. They were already world leaders in maritime technology. Half the trade of the Baltic was in their hands by 1578.[11] Another enormously flourishing market had been developed with Lisbon, trading in produce brought by the Portuguese from Asia. Philip II of Spain attempted to strike at the commercial wealth of his rebellious provinces by closing down the Lisbon trade when he inherited the Portuguese Empire in 1580. The Dutch response was characteristically forthright: the United Netherlands declared their independence in the following year, and in 1590 Dutch raiders began to swoop on the outposts of the Portuguese Empire in Africa, as a preliminary to an onslaught on the Asian Empire itself.

There could be little doubt how this struggle would end. The Portuguese had always faced immensely greater difficulties in Asia than the Spanish had in America. The Spanish had had the great advantage there of having to deal with the military technology of the Stone Age: Spanish swords could cut through the feather or hide armour of the Aztecs or Incas, and their own steel carapaces were invulnerable to the obsidian-edged clubs of their enemies. The Portuguese faced far more serious problems: the Asians had better swords, bigger if not necessarily better guns and often bigger ships, up to twice the displacement of the average Portuguese caravel. The Portuguese had been able to acquire and maintain an Eastern Empire because the Asian warships they actually encountered were not held together like their caravels by iron nails, which could resist the shattering impact of roundshot. The only Asian ships that were sturdy enough and heavily enough armed to have challenged them successfully, the war-junks of China, were kept by imperial decree on coastguard duty around the shores of the Middle Kingdom itself.

The Portuguese were hopelessly outmatched by the Dutch, who were far wealthier and had a far larger seafaring population to draw upon : the Netherlands possessed several thousand seagoing vessels at a time when Portugal had only 300 at the most; and well over 100,000 Dutchmen had some experience of sailing, at a time when a Portuguese census listed only 6,260. Nor was the disparity only one of numbers : the Dutch were on average more robust physically, and their ships were larger and better built. By a coincidence unfortunate for the Iberians, the Spanish Armada was destroyed in its enterprise against England in 1588, just two years before the Dutch attacked Principe and Sao Tome, and by 1594 the Dutch were trying to enter the Pacific through the Straits of Magellan. For the time being, however, they were unsuccessful; and in the following year, Alvaro de Mendaña led a squadron of four ships from Callao. His Chief Pilot was Fernandes de Quiros, born in Portugal but a subject of the Spanish Crown. Together they reached at last one of the main centres of Polynesian civilization, the Marquesas.

The meeting should have been congenial. The Spanish thought the islands themselves most attractive, and their inhabitants even more so. But this did not prevent them from firing upon the Marquesans with cannon and arquebus, without any provocation at all. Crews of canoes bringing coconuts to the Spanish squadron were massacred, and their bodies strung up *pour encourager les autres*. By the time the Spanish finally sailed off on 5 August 1595 they had killed at least 200 Marquesans, without having had a single one of their own men killed or even seriously injured by the natives.[14] Further slaughter took place in the Santa Cruz group, where landfall was made in September. This time, Mendaña's soldiers deliberately killed as many natives as possible, in order to make it inconceivable for their Commander to leave any of them behind to form a settlement. Mendaña's response to this behaviour provoked a mutiny, and Mendaña himself died on 18 October.

In 1605 Quiros actually sailed as close to the coast of Australia as one could get without seeing it. But the Dutch were already on the way. In 1602 the Dutch East India Company was founded, channelling national effort into the assault on the Spanish Empire, and in 1605 they seized the main Spice Islands, although they were driven out the following year by a Spanish expedition from the Philippines. Meanwhile, a Dutch pinnace, the *Duyfken*, sailing from Bantam, coasted New Guinea on the south and west for over 800 miles, and followed the coast of the Cape York peninsula for some distance, without, however, realizing that Australia and New Guinea were separate islands. The experience was not rewarding for the Dutch: some of the *Duyfken*'s crew were killed by Australian Aborigines, whom the Dutch feelingly described as 'wild, cruel, black savages'.[15] It was nonetheless certain that other Dutch sailors would explore this unpromising coastline further, if only because it was found far more satisfactory to take advantage of the monsoonal winds by sailing 4,000 miles eastward from the Cape of Good Hope before turning north to the Spice Islands, than to follow the African coast, as had been the original practice. There was also of course the persisting challenge of the unknown, but presumably rich and perhaps even civilized 'Great South Land' to be explored and exploited.

The next Dutch landfall in the Pacific was, however, not on Australia, but on Tonga. In 1615 Jacob Lemaire and Willem Cornelis Schouten led two ships, the *Eendracht* and the *Hoorn*, on a voyage of exploration to the South Pacific, to try to find the rumoured rich continent of the south. They were further encouraged by the knowledge that they could always sail on to the East Indies and trade profitably there, if *Terra Australis* did not appear. The *Hoorn* was set on fire before it even rounded South America, but the *Eendracht* pressed on, with its crew increasingly ravaged by scurvy despite a relentless Dutch diet of beer, bread, butter and cheese. Schouten and Lemaire brought the *Eendracht* to the Tuamotus in April 1615. Their first contact with the natives was unfortunate: encountering a double sailing canoe, the *Eendracht* fired two shots across its bows to make it heave to, according to established European maritime practice. The natives were not aware of this particular law of the sea, however. Lemaire then despatched a shallop after the canoe. The natives fled and the Dutch fired on them again, although only with hail-shot, which apparently did not penetrate as deeply as the ordinary variety. Most of the natives then jumped overboard, and a dozen or so seem to have been drowned, despite attempts by the Dutch to save them. But goodwill was apparently restored when the Dutch took the survivors back to land and exchanged knives and beads for coconuts. The encounter with the Tongans was considerably more complex. The *Eendracht* reached Niuatoputapu, in the northernmost part of the Tongan group, on 11 April. The self-confident and sophisticated Tongans cheerfully swarmed on board the Dutch ship, trading briskly at the rate of five coconuts per handful of beads. Having sufficiently flattered the cupidity of the Dutch, the Tongans then attempted to storm the *Eendracht*, but were foiled by European musketry and, apparently, by the wishes of some of their number not to spoil a profitable trade. Business was resumed in any case on 12 April. More gifts were exchanged, and the Dutch played on their drums and trumpets to entertain the Tongans. On the thirteenth, the *latu* (chief) himself invited the Dutch to sail to the neighbouring volcanic island of Niuafo'ou, escorted by an armada of twenty-three sailing canoes and forty-five smaller ones, carrying in all about a thousand Tongans, with the chief's canoe sailing abreast of the *Eendracht*. Once out at sea, the chief's canoe rammed the Dutchman and the Tongan armada again attempted to board and seize the *Eendracht*, again being repelled by musket-fire and canister-shot. The same intriguing alternation between business and sport continued when the *Eendracht* reached Niuafo'ou : the Tongans exchanged flying-fish for beads, attempted to capture a Dutch shallop sent ashore for water and gave up after three or four of their number had been killed. The pattern was altered slightly at Futuna, in the Horn Islands, about 120 miles north-west of Niuafo'ou, where Schouten and Lemaire made landfall on 19 May. Here the natives began by warning the Dutch off, the Europeans opened fire and six natives were killed; and then on 22 May the representatives of the two cultures got down to bargaining and feasting, having taken the precaution beforehand of exchanging hostages as a warranty of mutual good behaviour. Pigs were eaten; sailors and islanders danced together; the *kava*-drinking ceremony was performed, the natives drinking and the Dutch observing; and the two races eventually parted, with every expression of cordiality, relieved to see the last of each other.[16]

This happy parting at Futuna was a tribute to the pragmatism of all concerned. The Tongans were naturally interested in the opportunity for a little aggravation, as a change from their peaceful existence, but had no wish to be massacred; and the Dutch were concerned only to do business and get on with the search for the more profitable shores of *Terra Australis*. They also were unencumbered by ethnic or theological preoccupations : Polynesians might seem better-looking and more sophisticated than Melanesians, but the Dutch were just as prepared to exchange nails and knives for nuts and bananas with the inhabitants of New Ireland, off the coast of New Guinea, after the preliminary fighting had been got through.

Terra Australis Incognita nonetheless still remained Incognita. Schouten and Lemaire had got no closer to the southern continent than had Quiros. The Governor-General at Batavia, Anthony van Diemen, accordingly despatched Gerrit Thomasz Pool in April 1636 to follow the coastline of Cape York as far as he could possibly go. He was also warned to treat the natives 'with great kindness, wary caution and skilful judgment'.[17] It was a most commendable and forbearing command, especially coming from one of the high officials of an empire which only thirteen years before had massacred the English traders at Amboyna, was attempting to do the same for the Portuguese in Ceylon and Brazil, and had in general shown itself more prompt than any other to base its authority upon the simple and totally implacable exercise of superior military force. The Dutch were murderous, but they were seldom prejudiced. It is therefore all the more unfortunate that Pool himself was murdered by New Guinea natives before he had any opportunity to display either kindness or caution. His expedition only got as far as Van Diemen's Land, on the north-west coast of Australia. In June 1639 van Diemen sent Abel Janszoon Tasman north to explore the coasts of Korea and China, and if possible loot the Spanish treasure-fleets on the way. This also was a failure, Tasman returning with forty-one men dead from scurvy and assorted maritime complaints out of a crew of ninety, having got to within 600 miles of Japan without seeing anything. He was, however, despatched again in August 1642 with two ships, the *Heemskerck* and the *Zeehaen*, to investigate the 'remaining unknown part of the terrestrial globe',[18] meaning more precisely the South Pacific and South Atlantic. Sailing far south, Tasman sighted the island which now bears his name on 24 November. The Dutch anchored and explored, but found nobody. They then sailed due east, reaching the north-west coast of the South Island of New Zealand, one of the most impressive but least welcoming coastlines in the region, on 13 December. They sailed north and into Cook Strait, looking for an anchorage. On 18 December, they saw smoke rising from beyond the dunes at the northernmost tip of the South Island. The Dutch launched two ship's boats. They were approached by two canoes from the mainland. Tasman ordered his crew to play drums and trumpets, as Schouten and Lemaire had done to entertain the Tongans. The Maoris went away, but on 19 December the Dutch were approached by eight Maori canoes. Tasman sent a cockboat from the *Heemskerck* to warn the *Zeehaen* not to allow too many natives to come aboard. The cockboat was rammed by one of the Maori canoes while returning to the *Heemskerck*, as the *Eendracht* had been rammed off Niuafo'ou, and four of the sailors were killed. The Dutch fired, but without hitting anything, and prepared to sail off. Some twenty-two canoes then came out from the shore, apparently heading for the ships. They were driven off by canister, but apparently only one of the Maoris was actually hit.

If the Maoris had intended to discourage foreign invaders, their efforts were successful. Tasman and his two ships sailed away. Their next and last visit to New Zealand shores was no more encouraging. They attempted to anchor on Three Kings Island, at the northernmost extremity of the North Island, on 4 January, but were deterred by the surf and the sight of thirty or more men of giant stature moving about on the highest hills, taking what seemed to be enormous strides while they brandished weapons and called out loudly in rough voices. The Dutch had had enough.

Tasman does indeed seem to have been almost uniquely averse to bloodshed. He can only have found the Tongans an immense relief. Here at least there was no question of fighting : after their experience with Schouten and Lemaire the Tongans had resigned themselves to the fact that there was no future in trying conclusions with the Dutch. The ships were visited by friendly Tongans who contented themselves with discreetly pilfering nails wherever practicable; the Tui Tonga himself entertained the foreigners ashore with a massive feast; and the Dutch noted approvingly that the island (Tongatapu) was cultivated like a garden, in best Netherlands style, with houses set in the midst of plantations rather than clustered in villages, and that the inhabitants most strikingly appeared to have no arms.[19]

The reception of Abel Janszoon Tasman by the Tui Tonga Tabuoji was the only important meeting between the Europeans and the Pacific peoples up to that date which had not involved bloodshed. Its amicable nature was due entirely to the simple fact that the Tongans were not silly enough to challenge the Dutch again. It was of course true that Tonga itself presented an unrivalled appearance of undisturbed tranquillity. Tasman was doubtless correct in his observation that the Tongans went unarmed. He also noted one of the reasons why they could afford to do this : law and order were rigorously maintained, and a native accused by the Dutch of having pilfered a pike was punished by having a coconut pounded against his head until it broke. What Tasman was not to know, of course, was that the Tongans were prepared to live peaceably at home because they could get all the fighting they wanted in Fiji, even if they were no longer so welcome in Samoa. This was, admittedly, likely to be a temporary state. A further division between temporal and spiritual authority had indeed already been made, about 1610, when the reigning Tui Haa Takalaua, whose line had been invested as mayors of the palace by the Tui Tonga Kau-ulu-fonua Fekai, found it expedient to create a third line, the Tui Kanokupolu, to take over the temporal power, reserving the sacred role for himself. It may be assumed either that the Tui Takalaua had wearied of the burdens of office, as legend has it; or that he sought to increase the prestige of his own line, just as that of the Tui Tonga had been enhanced, by handing over the actual work to an administrative dogsbody; or, most simply, that he felt that the position of the Tui Takalaua was becoming as precarious as that of the Tui Tonga had become half a century or so before, and decided to do something to avert a direct challenge to himself before it was too late. Meanwhile, the Fijians were extending their influence : Tui Lakeba, ruler of the largest island in the Lau Group, east of Viti Levu, arrived in Tonga with a large following at about the same time as Tasman, married the daughter of the Tui Tonga and established one of the major Tongan families, the *Fale Fisi* (House of Fiji).[20] It has been suggested that this readiness to welcome a people whom they recognized as more skilful and artistic in most respects than themselves did the Tongans no good. Sir Basil Thompson claims that what the Tongans learned from their hearty visitors was 'the cold-blooded treachery that will betray a brother to satisfy the thirst for blood; the brutal ferocity that spares neither sex nor age; the depraved lust that is gratified in outrage on the dead; [and] the foul appetite of revenge that will eat the body of a slain enemy.'[21] On the other hand, the Tongans also acquired from the Fijians by way of compensation the best weapons and woodwork in the Pacific; earthenware jars, which they had neither the knowledge nor the clay to make themselves, and a roaring trade in beautiful Fijian parrots. In any event, the Tongans were to make visits to Fiji themselves, of a kind to make the Fijians wish they had stayed at home.

European zeal to uncover the possibilities of the south had slackened for a time. The Dutch went to war with the Portuguese again in 1644, the year in which Tasman led the *Limmen*, the *Zeemeuw* and the *Bracq* along the west coast of Australia, as far as Dirk Hartog Island. Nothing of profit was found. This was enough to convince the States-General that it would be better for everybody if Australia were left undiscovered. Even if there were anything there of value, this would only serve to attract more and stronger rivals into the field. The Dutch had troubles enough already. They had, moreover, finally conquered Malacca by 1656 and could rest content with the wealth of the East Indies in their hands.

Sea power was in any case passing from the Dutch to the British and French. The reasons for this were partly physical : ships were getting bigger, but the Dutch coastline was always silting up and it was becoming difficult to build ships with draughts shallow enough to be able to use Dutch harbours but deep enough for stability on the high seas. The main problem was necessarily one of resources, however: the Netherlands had after all a population of only 2,700,000, while France by contrast numbered some 11 million people and England 5 million, with Scotland and Ireland providing another 1 million each. The successful seizure of Malacca in 1656 marked the furthest reach of Dutch ambition in the Pacific. It was followed eight years later by the formation of the French East India Company to see what opportunities for profit the Dutch might have left. Even more farsightedly, the English founded the Greenwich Observatory in 1675, to devise some means of solving the hitherto intractable problem of calculating longitude. In the meantime, the ocean began to swarm with assorted pirates and freebooters, attracted mainly by the hope of looting the Spanish treasure convoys. One of these, William Dampier, wound up in 1697 on the north-west coast of Australia, in the pirate-ship *Cygnet*. Returning to England, he suggested that a journey be made 'to the remoter parts of the East India Islands and the neighbouring coast of *Terra Australis*',[22] for the purpose of increasing British shipping and extending British naval power. The Admiralty were sufficiently convinced to send Dampier out on such a voyage in 1699, as commander of the *Roebuck*. The trip was both unhappy and unprofitable, although Dampier did at least prove that New Britain, New Ireland and New Holland were separate from Australia.

The Dutch had one more remarkable voyage of discovery to make, however. In August 1721 Jacob Roggeveen sailed from Holland with three ships, the *Arend*, the *Tienhoven* and the *Africaansche Galey*, in an attempt to discover the southern continent, a project initially conceived by his father. On 5 April 1722 they made landfall at Easter Island, where Roggeveen observed the great basaltic statues, at that stage covered from neck to ground with a long cloth. On the heads of the statues baskets had been placed, filled with stones painted white. The natives were seen to light fires in front of the statues and squat before them with bowed heads, bringing the palms of their hands together and moving them up and down. The Easter Islanders were friendly, though extraordinarily given to stealing things from the Europeans, even after Roggeveen had shot several of them as a deterrent.

The Tuamotus were next. Here the *Africaansche Galey* was lost, and a landing party was ambushed by the islanders, presumably annoyed when the Dutch fired into them to make them clear the beach. Ten

Dutchmen and an unrecorded number of islanders were left dead in
this exchange of courtesies. Things went off far more pleasantly at Tau,
the easternmost island of the Samoan group, which Roggeveen reached
on 15 June. The islanders were good-looking, friendly and eager to
trade. But Roggeveen was not sufficiently encouraged by this experience
to go on looking for *Terra Australis* : his men were tortured by scurvy,
and three or more of them were dying each day. The last Dutch bid
for the southern continent was abandoned, and Roggeveen headed west
for Batavia. Australia was not going to be Dutch after all.

If it was not going to be Dutch, it would necessarily have to be either
British or French; though until 1812 the outcome was uncertain. British
predominance on the high seas could have been lost to France on many
occasions during the eighteenth and early nineteenth centuries; and was
in fact so lost temporarily during the American War of Independence.
French seamen were indeed running wild throughout the Pacific in the
first half of the eighteenth century, despite an injunction from Louis XIV
between 1712 and 1716 against trading with the Spanish colonies.
During this period, 109 French ships made voyages into the Pacific, and
half the circumnavigations actually completed were achieved by Frenchmen.[23] Technology again speeded up the tempo of exploration. A Board
of Longitude was founded by the British in 1714, to deal with the most
serious technical problem still remaining in the way of long-distance
voyaging; the sextant was invented in 1731; and the invention of the
chronometer in 1735 finally provided the means with which to gauge
longitude accurately. The Pacific was at last wide open to European
incursions; and the Seven Years War gave the British an opportunity to
close it off for their own uses. Continued British raids against Spanish
treasure galleons sailing from Manila culminated in the seizure of
Manila itself in 1762. It was agreed under the terms of the subsequent
peace settlement that the Philippines should remain Spanish, but the
British had by this time completed plans to seize the Spanish possessions
of the Falkland Islands, at the other gate of the Pacific. So had the
French. Louis Antoine de Bougainville established a French settlement
on East Falkland in the first quarter of 1764. A British expedition was
despatched for the same purpose to West Falkland in September 1765.
However, the Spanish themselves persuaded Bougainville to sell his
settlement back to them for cash in 1766, and suppressed the British
settlement by an expedition from Buenos Aires in 1770. War between
Britain and Spain was averted by an agreement in 1774 that the British
should be allowed to put a garrison back on West Falkland, on condition

that the garrison was then withdrawn, leaving an inscription and a British flag to register London's claim to sovereignty over the islands.

This was only the first of a series of contests in the control of the South Pacific. In August 1766 Samuel Wallis in the *Dolphin* and Philip Carteret in the *Swallow* left Plymouth to obtain complete knowledge of the lands in the southern hemisphere. Bougainville sailed from St Malo with *La Boudeuse* and *L'Etoile* on 15 December of the same year to investigate the possibility of establishing a French colony somewhere in *Terra Australis*. The Pacific peoples had for all practical purposes lost control of their destinies already. Their future would be decided by decisions taken by alien races 12,000 miles away.

It happened by pure coincidence that this decisive phase of the European invasion occurred at a peculiarly critical moment in the development of the Pacific peoples themselves. Relations between Fiji and Tonga had become still more intertwined. In 1750 or thereabouts the Tongan chief Wakanimolikula was stranded in the eastern Lau Group of the Fiji Islands, and amused himself by participating in the local tribal wars. The results were highly significant. The Fijians had always adopted a strictly limited approach to warfare, seeking victory on the cheap through the employment of overwhelming numbers, treachery or guile. When these methods were not available, they preferred not to fight at all. The Tongans by contrast fought for fun. They were also far more advanced than the Fijians in the development of concepts like discipline and order. An immensely formidable ally had thus become available to any Fijian chief who entertained serious ambitions of conquest, and who could offer these *condottieri* from across the sea sufficiently attractive prospects of loot. Coincidentally, a family phenomenally endowed with the qualities that make for success in tyranny had just risen to power on the tiny island of Bau, about 350 yards wide, just off the south-east coast of Viti Levu. In 1760 the Bau chief Nailatikau swooped ashore on the neighbouring district of Ua-ni-vuaka, massacred or drove out the inhabitants, and began cultivating their territory according to the most enlightened agricultural principles. The survivors enlisted the assistance of the northern district of Verata in repeated attempts to displace the prospering and expanding Bauans. A hundred years' war had begun for the mastery of Fiji.

Tahiti itself was about to erupt in bloody internal conflict even as Wallis approached Matavai Bay in the *Dolphin* on 17 June 1767, having left behind the unsound *Swallow* before entering the Straits of Magellan. Wallis at least knew what he was there for : too sick to go ashore himself,

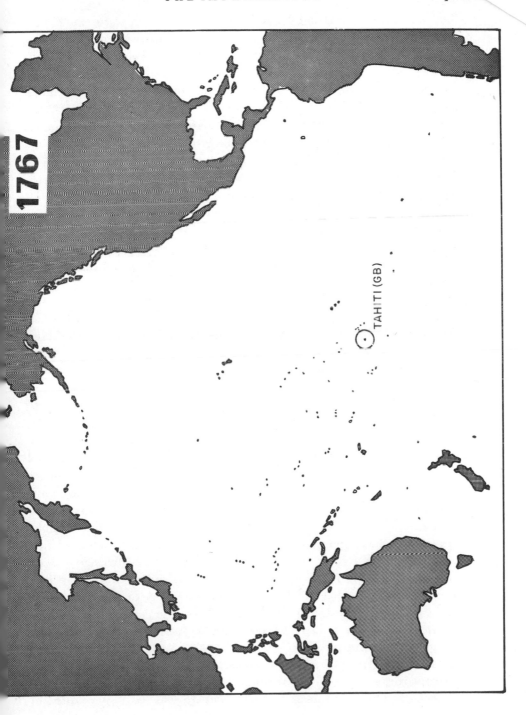

he despatched his second lieutenant, Tobias Furneaux, to annex the island in the name of King George III. The natives understandably attacked Furneaux and his landing party, but were repelled by the guns of the *Dolphin*. Wallis had, however, been particularly careful to avoid arousing the hostility of the islanders any more than was absolutely necessary : his bombardment achieved the maximum effect with the minimum of damage, killing only one native and wounding another. The exchange certainly seemed to leave no ill feeling on either side. Intercourse in every sense of the word flourished. After ten months of living hell in the service of the Royal Navy, Wallis's men were able to appreciate the attractions of a South Pacific summer, awesomely impressive and lushly beautiful island scenery, fresh fruit and vegetables and uninhibitedly accommodating girls with lovely brown bodies. Even people less deprived than British sailors of the eighteenth century have found Tahiti uncommonly attractive. It can only have appeared to the crew of the *Dolphin* as a considerable improvement on what would have been until then their most optimistic notions of Heaven.[24]

Wallis sailed out of Tahiti on 26 July 1767. Bougainville sailed in on 2 April 1768. He anchored by Hitiaa, on the eastern side of Tahiti Nui, while Wallis had anchored about seventeen miles away, to the northwest of the island. His visit was brief, lasting only thirteen days, but immensely cordial : the Tahitians had learned that it was unrewarding to challenge European guns, and Bougainville and his men appear to have been fully aware of all that the islands and their people might be able to offer to sailors in need of rest and recuperation. He was indeed sensitive enough to appreciate that European influence might well change the condition of the islanders for the worse, and found evidence of this already in the presence of syphilis, which he was satisfied must have been brought by the British, especially as the Tahitians themselves referred to it as *apa no peritane*, the British disease. Interestingly, responsible officers on both the *Dolphin* and *La Boudeuse* insisted that their ships were free from venereal disease when they reached Tahiti. In the nature of things, both claims can only be regarded as incredible, so one can assume that the Tahitians were treated within the space of a year to both the British and French varieties of the pox.[25]

They were also treated to both British and French sovereignty. Bougainville claimed Tahiti for France, just as Wallis had claimed it for Britain. The Tahitians were, however, too busy with their domestic power struggles to concern themselves with disputes between foreign pretenders. The pre-eminent *marae* of Papara was suddenly assailed by the elderly and formidable Vehiatua of Teahupo in the east; by the able and thrusting Tuteha in the west; and in the north by Tu of Te Porionuu, young, undersized, disagreeable, mediocre, cowardly, ambitious and cruel, according to his unenthusiastic chroniclers.[26] The defenders of the *marae* were either massacred, or driven right across the island, while Tuteha carried off the sacred red-feather girdle of supreme rank. However, the person still recognized as the greatest single chief on the island was the child Teriiere, who had fled from Papara with the slightly less sacred yellow-feather girdle. He sought refuge first at Haapape in the north, where he was threatened with the proximity of the incompetent but malevolent Tu, and then at Matavai Bay, where Wallis had anchored and where Cook was to arrive on 13 April 1769.

Cook had sailed to Tahiti for two purposes. One was simply to observe the transit of Venus. The other was to verify whether or not 'a continent, or land of great extent, may be found to the southward of the tract lately made by Capt. Wallis in His Majesty's Ship the Dolphin . . .'.[27] If *Terra Australis* did exist, he was to cultivate a friendship with the inhabitants, show them all possible respect, and take possession of convenient situations in the name of King George III. The prize would be control of the trade routes of the Pacific and the wealth of an unexplored continent.

The visit to Tahiti was successful, at least as far as the instruction to cultivate friendship with the natives was concerned. The Tahitians came out in their canoes with the same intentions of peaceful commerce with which they had welcomed Bougainville. Cook for his part had already prepared 'rules to be observ'd by every person in or belonging to His Majesty's Bark the Endevour, for the better establishing a regular and uniform Trade for Provisions &c with the Inhabitants of Georges Island'.[28] The trouble was that the islanders did not follow the same rules : visitors swarmed aboard the *Endeavour*, stealing anything on which they could lay their hands, despite the efforts of one of the Chiefs, classically named Lycurgus by Cook, to deter his people by throwing at them 'the first thing that came in his way'.[29] The meeting was marred by only one bloody episode : an islander pushed over a sentry and ran off with his musket; the commanding officer on the spot, a midshipman, gave the order to fire; and the marines, on one account at least, obeyed with enthusiasm.[30] However, they killed only one native, although a few others were wounded; and Cook did his best to reassure the Tahitians that the newcomers were in fact friendly.

They did indeed part with something like mutual respect : Cook recorded approvingly that the Tahitians were in general 'tall, strong and well shaped'; that they were 'a very cleanly people both in their persons and diat'; and that 'their features are agreeable and their gate gracefull, and their behaviour to strangers and to each other open affable and courtious and . . . free from threachery, only that they are thieves to a Man and would steal but everything that came in their way and that with such dexterity as would shame the most noted pickpocket in Europe'. He noted too, with admirable attention to detail, that : 'The young girls whenever they can collect 8 or 10 together dance a very indecent dance which they call *Timorodee*, singing most indecent songs and useing most indecent actions in the practice of which they are brought up from their earlyest Childhood, in doing this they keep time to a great nicety'; and that both sexes 'express the most indecent ideas in conversation without the least emotion and they delight in such conversation beyond any other'.[31] As a further guide to Tahitian mores, Cook took with him on his departure a Raiatean aristocrat and priest named Tupaia, as pilot, general informant and interpreter.

Tupaia had his weaknesses : Cook described him as 'a Shrewd Sensible, ingenious man, but proud and obstinate which often made his situation on board both disagreeable to himself and those about him, and tended much to promote the deceases which put a period to his life'.[32] Tupaia, in fact, failed to survive the journey back to England. However, his services as interpreter helped in some measure at least to mitigate the full shock of Cook's encounter with the New Zealand Maoris. The basic problem here was that the Maoris were a heartily aggressive people, whose taste for eating human flesh had not been modified by any previous experience of European weapons. Like the Tahitians, they found the British and French arriving on their shores almost simultaneously. Unlike the Tahitians, they saw no reason to encourage the visitors to come again.

The British once again arrived first, without being aware that the French were in the race as well. Jean de Surville had left Pondicherry on 3 March 1769, hoping to forestall any attempt by Cook to consolidate a British claim to Tahiti. His visit to New Zealand was in fact quite unintentional, as well as disastrous : sixty of his crew had died of scurvy, and de Surville felt compelled to try to find the lands discovered by Tasman in order to take on board fresh food and water, before attempting to go anywhere else. Cook had meanwhile sighted the northernmost point of New Zealand on 7 October. The first encounter with the natives occurred on 9 October, when Cook landed with a small party to try to talk with a group he had observed on shore. The Maoris promptly ran off, but returned to attack four boys whom Cook had left in charge of the boat. They were deterred only when one of their number had been killed by a musket-shot. Cook landed again the following day, and attempted to converse once more. The Maoris responded with what was obviously a war dance : they 'brandish'd Their Weapons, distort'd their Mouths, Lolling out their Tongues and Turn'd up the Whites of their Eyes, Accompanied by a strong hoarse song . . .'.[33] The natives were not friendly. Cook nonetheless got Tupaia to persuade some of the Maoris to swim over to him, where they received presents. However, one of the Maoris snatched a sword from a member of Cook's party, and was shot dead with ball, after being ineffectively peppered with smallshot. The other Maoris ran away, but returned to carry off the dead man's weapons, despite a further volley of smallshot, which wounded another three of them. The Englishmen noted that whereas 'it has allways been remark'd amongst Savages lett them be ever so much used to fire arms that as soon as they see a man or two fall that they immeadeately fall in to disorder and give way yet these People was so far from shewing any kind of fear that when they saw the man fall they immedeately had ye Presence of mind to attemptd it a second time'.[34]

They were indeed to 'attemptd it' several more times. Giving up hope of establishing any kind of friendly relations with this tribe, Cook sailed on. His next attempt to establish goodwill was even more unfortunate. He had resolved to try to kidnap some natives and take them on board the *Endeavour*, to try to gain their friendship by good treatment and presents. He accordingly detached a ship's boat to approach a Maori canoe. Tupaia called on the occupants to come alongside. Instead, they rowed away. A musket was fired over their heads to make them surrender. Far from doing so, they attempted to attack the Englishmen. Once again, Cook had to order his men to open fire, killing three of the Maoris and wounding another. The survivors were taken on board, treated with all possible kindness, and released the following day with presents and assurances of goodwill. Cook admittedly decided to move on, rather than test the effectiveness of his efforts to conciliate these difficult natives. Further attempts were no more promising. Some Maoris seemed prepared to trade peacefully, but their behaviour tended to become so unruly that they had to be driven off by guns fired harmlessly over their heads. On 15 October they tried to kidnap Tupaia's servant and were discouraged only after two or three had been shot dead. Cook was nonetheless surprisingly optimistic about the prospect of future dealings with the Maoris. He concluded in the first place that their behaviour followed a consistent pattern : they would first approach newcomers and either try to trade with them or alternatively invite them to come ashore and be knocked on the head; they would then attack with any means available until sufficiently convinced by gunfire that their opponents had superior weapons, but were prone to use them only with moderation and in self-defence; and 'ever after they were our very good friends and we never had an Instance of their attempting to surprize or cut off any of our people when they went ashore . . .'. He considered in short that on all the evidence 'it doth not appear to me to be at all difficult for Strangers to form a settlement in this Country. They seem to be too much divided among themselves to unite in opposing, by which means and kind and gentle usage the Colonists would be able to form strong parties among them.'[35]

Cook had found it frequently necessary when dealing with the Maoris to temper kind and gentle usage with applications of round-shot. De Surville, in fact, had far more congenial relations with the natives. Interestingly, the two ships were almost directly opposite each other on 12 December, with Cook on the eastern side of the North Island, and de Surville on the western. De Surville rounded the North Cape and came to the eastern coast, just as Cook was being blown out of sight of land. He anchored in Doubtless Bay on 17 December, sending his crew ashore, a few at a time, to collect fresh vegetables. The French were compelled by sheer physical weakness to remain in the bay for some weeks until they recovered their health. During this time, they received remarkably friendly treatment from the Maoris, who actually helped the enfeebled French sailors to fill their water-casks and gather plants. De Surville repaid this kindness with presents of pigs, fowl, seeds and a hatchet. Unfortunately, this amicable intercourse came to an end when some Maoris attempted to drag away a waterlogged dinghy belonging to de Surville. He promptly sent ashore a landing party, burned the Maoris' canoes and seized a chief who was taken on board and placed in irons to be carted back to France. However, the Maori died at sea a month later. De Surville himself was drowned while attempting to enter the harbour of Chilca, in Peru, where the condition of his ship had compelled him to seek shelter.[36]

Cook by contrast was only at the beginning of his triumphs. He had dealt most happily with the Tahitians; he had certainly acted with most commendable good sense and restraint in dealing with the far more difficult problems presented by the New Zealand Maoris; he had charted the actual shape of the New Zealand islands with quite amazing accuracy; and he was now about to acquire for Britain nothing less than the great southern continent itself. The *Endeavour* turned west on 31 March 1770. On 19 April land was sighted at Point Hicks, now Cape Everard on the Victorian coast. Ten days later, the *Endeavour* anchored in the shelter of Botany Bay. Native huts were observed on both sides of the bay as they went in. Cook landed with a small party, including Tupaia, to try to establish contact. Not surprisingly, the Aborigines were unable to understand Tupaia's assurances of goodwill, and attempted to oppose the landing by throwing darts, until driven off by repeated discharges of smallshot.

This was not encouraging. Nevertheless, although further encounters with the Aborigines were scarcely more rewarding, they served to convince Cook that these natives were not indeed a warlike people, but on the contrary 'a timorous and inoffensive race, no ways inclinable to cruelty'. Their houses were 'mean small hovels not much bigger than an oven' and their canoes 'as mean as can be conceived'. Indeed, he considered that the natives 'may appear to some to be the most wretched people upon Earth'. However, Cook continued, in an uncharacteristically Utopian vein,

> in reality they are far more happier than we Europeans; being wholy unacquainted not only with the superfluous but the necessary Conveniencies so much sought after in Europe, they are happy in not knowing the use of them. They live in a Tranquillity which is not disturb'd by the Inequality of Condition : The Earth and sea of their own accord furnishes them with all the things necessary for life, they covet not Magnificent Houses, Household-stuff &c. . . . In short they seem'd to set no Value upon any thing we gave them, nor would they ever part with any thing of their own for any one article we could offer them; this in my opinion argues that they think themselves provided with all the necessarys of Life and that they have no superfluities.

As for the land itself, Cook felt that : 'We are to Consider that we see this Country in the pure state of Nature, the Industry of Man has had nothing to do with any part of it, and yet we find all such things as Nature hath bestow'd upon it in a flourishing state.'[37] It was one of the more impressive historical ironies that the way of life of this timorous, inoffensive yet tranquil people, as Cook judged them, was to be affected over the next 200 years perhaps more gravely than that of any other indigenous people subjugated by Europeans, and that the land which he had found to be in the pure state of nature was to be made the site of one of the most affluent and probably one of the more materialistic civilizations upon earth.

All this can be traced from the moment when, on 22 August 1770, Cook took possession of the whole eastern coast of Australia, from latitude 38° south, in the name of George III. But the Pacific was still far from being anything like an English lake. The French were at sea again. In April 1771, three months before Cook had returned to England, Marion Dufresne sailed out of Port Louis with the *Mascarin* and the *Marquis de Castres*. One of the purposes of the voyage was to return to Tahiti a young native, Aoutourou, previously borrowed by Bougainville and introduced into French society. Aoutourou died before the expedition had got well past Africa, but Dufresne sailed on towards the South Pole, making landfall off the New Zealand coast on 25 March 1772. He eventually anchored in the Bay of Islands, near where de Surville had taken refuge three years before. Two chiefs came aboard the *Mascarin* and invited du Fresne to visit their village. He accepted and went ashore, with fifteen of his crew. A second party was landed the following day to cut wood. Both parties were attacked by the Maoris, massacred and apparently eventually eaten. Twenty-seven Frenchmen in all met their deaths.

This was by far the roughest handling that the Pacific Islanders had yet had the opportunity of administering to any Europeans. It has been suggested that the Maoris might have been seeking revenge for de Surville's rather ungracious, thought still bloodless, return for their kindness; it is certainly conceivable that Dufresne might have unwittingly broken some local *tapu*; but it is perhaps most likely that the Bay of Islands Maoris were only treating new arrivals in the customary Polynesian manner, and that the very different treatment accorded to de Surville and his men further north was due simply to the fact that the Maoris they met with there did not consider them worth eating in their present state, and were prepared to wait until their condition improved. There is also the simple tactical fact that Polynesian warfare consisted above all else in the practice of ambush : Dufresne walked right into one, while the more suspicious and less impressionable de Surville had probably been more on his guard. The survivors of Dufresne's expedition in any case took the expected revenge : in the first pitched battle between Europeans and Polynesians, twenty-seven Frenchmen stormed the fortified village of the Maoris, killed or drove off the defenders and burned their dwellings to the ground. Dufresne's second-in-command, the Chevalier du Clesmeur, then formally took possession of New Zealand in the name of Louis XV.[38]

Du Clesmeur's action was in fact never officially ratified in Paris. The next formal annexation in the Pacific was carried out by the Spanish, reaching out from the Viceroyalty of Peru to seize Easter Island, for fear that the whole Pacific might become a maze of British bases. Then, having secured Easter Island, the Spanish sent the frigate *Aguila* under Don Domingo de Boenechea to reconnoitre Tahiti. Don Domingo arrived on 8 November 1772 and remained until 20 December. The Spanish, by no means certain of the situation, treated the Tahitians with the utmost delicacy and respect, even incredibly succeeding in keeping Spanish men and Tahitian girls separate for the whole duration of the visit; the Tahitians, all too well aware what they might be up against, responded with friendliness and discretion.

Don Domingo sailed off to Lima on 20 December, leaving priests behind, and taking with him some young native men for instruction in the Spanish language and Christian principles. It was not his fault that he had anchored off Taiarapu, in the domain of Vehiatua, with whom he had his main initial contacts. The importance thus enjoyed by Vehiatua may well have urged the bellicose and pragmatic Tutcha to seize the eastern coastline, to secure for himself any benefits that might accrue from contact with the Europeans. He mounted an expedition against Vehiatua, taking with him as ally the poltroon Tu, more frightened of the devil Tuteha next door than of the older devil Vehiatua on the other side of the island. All went perfectly for Tu: the aged but resourceful Vehiatua destroyed the forces of the alliance, killing Tuteha himself, but was prepared to make peace with Tu, who prudently decamped for the mountains again, taking with him the sacred red-feathered girdle, which he had opportunely removed from Tuteha's body.

Meanwhile, Cook was at sea again: on 13 July 1772 he had sailed from Plymouth with the *Resolution* and the *Adventure*. His instructions were once again to investigate and survey the still imperfectly comprehended Southern Continent, and to take possession for Britain of any new islands he might discover on the way. Sweeping south from Cape Town the British expedition became the first to cross the Antarctic Circle, reaching 67° 15' South on 18 January 1773. The *Resolution* followed the general line of the Antarctic Circle until 8 March, when Cook turned north-east towards New Zealand, 'to injoy some short repose in a harbour where I can procure some refreshments for my people of which they begin to stand in need of'.[39]

From New Zealand Cook sailed to Tahiti, arriving on 16 August 1773. There he found Tu still apparently frightened of everything and everybody, but invested in the girdle of supreme authority, and for all Cook could make out paramount chief of the area.

This was exactly what Tu was eventually going to become; and one of the major reasons for his success was the fact that uncomprehending foreigners were prepared to treat him as if he enjoyed supreme power, at a time when he was the lowliest of pretenders. But this was by no means the only way in which European incursions were influencing the development of the Polynesian peoples. The Tahitians were certainly as hospitable as human flesh and blood could stand: Moorehead records that the women of the island were so generous that there were literally not enough sailors to go around.[40] On his second visit Cook noted a shortage of domestic animals which he attributed to the civil wars which had taken place just before his arrival; and the ravages of imported diseases were obvious. Venereal disease abounded, no doubt the contribution of both the British and the French, while the Spanish for their part had left a legacy of gastric influenza no less deadly to people who had had no opportunity to acquire any kind of immunity. The Europeans could hardly be blamed for the civil war, or for Tu's utterly unanticipated rise to power; so far their presence had merely acted as a catalyst. Nevertheless the capacity for survival of a society so marked already by the first light touches of European contact must have seemed doubtful.

In Tonga, on the other hand, Cook found nothing to inspire the slightest misgivings. Everything impressed him favourably. In the first place, the islands were incredibly beautiful and well cultivated. Cook felt as if he were transported to 'one of the most fertile plains in Europe ...nature, assisted by a little art, no where appears in a more flourishing place'. It was no wonder that 'joy and contentment is painted in every face' in islands whose people 'injoy every blessing of life'.[41] The Englishmen were unable to make up their minds whether or not the Tongans were better-looking than the Tahitians. They were, however, far less addicted to thieving, and were invariably mild and benevolent in their behaviour towards the visitors; these factors, combined with the extremely refined development of their arts, convinced Cook that they had achieved a higher state of civilization than the other Polynesians he had encountered.

Of course, had he been able to see beneath the surface, Cook might have been less enthusiastic. The Tongans had learned from their meetings with the Dutch a century before that it was necessary to respect European weapons. They did not therefore find it necessary to respect Europeans. Tongan boys mocked the anxiety of the English to acquire souvenirs by offering to exchange samples of Tongan excrement for nails and cloth. A local chief who entertained Cook, and whom Cook mistakenly took to be the Tui Tonga himself, treated the English with such 'sullen and stupid gravity' that Cook at first assumed him to be 'an edeot which the people were ready to worship from some superstitious notions'.[42] It was not a serious mistake. Cook was to make a far greater one four years later, when he imagined that these highly civilized and organized people were necessarily friendly. The warrior chiefs of Vava'u, the northernmost island of the Tongan group, were already beginning to assert their power, and the most ambitious of them, Finau Ulukalala, was acquiring authority greater even than that of the Tui Kanokupolu. Quite unknowingly Cook was to participate in one of the supreme dramas of Polynesian history.

There were other things that Cook could not have known at the time. As the *Resolution* headed south-east from New Caledonia towards New Zealand on the trip that was to take it home, Don Domingo de Boenechea was sailing west from Callao, back to Tahiti, naturally unaware that Cook had been there in the meantime. He was again commanding the *Aguila*, accompanied this time by a store-ship, the *Jupiter*. His mission was to recover the priests who had been left on his last trip and to claim Tahiti for Spain. De Boenechea himself died in the course of this expedition, but his successor, Don Tomás Gayangos, took the ships and the priests back to Callao, leaving behind a simple wooden cross dated 1774, proclaiming that Christ had conquered and King Charles III ruled in Tahiti.

Neither statement was of course true, as far as the Tahitians themselves were aware. Cook dealt with the problem in August 1777 by simply inscribing on the other side of the cross a memorial of the year (1767) on which Wallis had claimed the island for King George III, as well as the dates of his own visits in 1769, 1773, 1774 and 1777. It was, however, only by the narrowest of chances that the English had survived to reaffirm their claim to Tahiti. Cook had put into the island of Namuka in the Ha'apai group in May. He was greeted by the war-lord Finau Ulukalala, who had now extended his dominion to include Ha'apai as well as Vava'u. Finau may have tried to persuade Cook to come with him to Vava'u. In any event, Finau agreed to entertain the visitors at a colossal feast on Lifuka, the largest inhabited island of the Ha'apai group. The Englishmen settled down to enjoy a spectacle of athletics, dancing and general hilarity provided by some 10,000 Tongans, while the other chiefs consulted with Finau how best to massacre the visitors and seize their ships. Finau apparently favoured an ambush by day, when at least the Tongans would be able to see what they were doing. The others found this prospect too daunting and voted for a night attack. Angered by their failure to accept his advice, Finau refused to countenance the attack at all. This change of plans did not merely preserve the lives of the British expedition. It also brought to flashpoint the feudal rivalries smouldering in Tonga. Cook and his men sailed south to Tongatapu to witness the ceremony of the presentation of the first-fruits to the Tui Tonga Paulaho, at which Finau made the necessary obeisance to the sacred king. Cook, who had erroneously supposed that Finau had claimed to be paramount chief himself, accordingly treated him thereafter, as a contemptible impostor, to the great embarrassment of Finau and his kinsmen. There are few things more dangerous than an embarrassed Tongan.

Turmoil and disaster were in fact riding on the sails of Cook's ships on this last and tragic voyage. It was of course purely coincidental that the Europeans should have been making their new round of visits at a time when there was actual civil war in Tahiti; when the Vava'u warlords were in a mood to challenge the stability of the Tongan system and when there were local chiefs in Hawaii prepared to try again to impose on their group of islands the enforced unity which Kalaunuiokuu had failed to achieve in the thirteenth century.

Fighting may indeed have started even before Cook arrived, to bring to the Hawaiians their first contact with the world outside since the islands had been visited, presumably involuntarily, by Tahitian adventurers 500 years before. The situation was certainly confused. Hawaii itself was ruled by Kalaniopiu, who also controlled the eastern district of Maui; the rest of Maui, as well as Molokai, Lanai and Kahoolawe, was governed by Kahekele; Oahu was ruled by the venerable Peleioholani, who was disputing with Kahekele for the overlordship of Molokai; while Kauai and Niihau were ruled by Kaneoneo at the actual time of Cook's arrival off the southern shore of Kauai on 20 January 1778.[43] The local inhabitants adjusted with remarkable promptitude to this new experience : they apparently accepted that the Englishmen were gods, but nonetheless hastened to trade with them, seeking above all to acquire iron nails or anything from which they could be manufactured, as large and as sharp as possible. Cook and his men did in fact discover some much-worn iron nails already in the possession of the islanders, and assumed that these had probably been salvaged from fragments of wrecked Spanish vessels washed up on the shore.

Cook's ships then sailed north, having introduced the islanders to fire-arms and venereal disease, according to the invariable Pacific practice. They returned in November 1778. The chieftains had obviously decided in the meantime to try to enlist the help of the gods in the furtherance of their territorial ambitions. Kahekele, the rival of Peleioholani, sent the British a gift of a red-feather cloak, of the kind which Cook had un-successfully tried to purchase on his first visit. Kalaniopiu of Hawaii, who was by this time at war with Kahekele for the overlordship of Maui, visited Cook's ship with a retinue of chiefs, including his favourite Kamchameha, described by Cook's able and generally invaluable Second Lieutenant, James King, as having 'as savage a looking face as I ever saw, but nonetheless in disposition good natur'd & humorous, although his manner shewd somewhat of an overbearing spirit . . .'.[44] Other chiefs came to invite the sailors to desert and join in a civil war which had broken out on Kauai, as a result of which Kahekele's half-brother was to become ruler of the island.

This desire to make use of the gods and their weapons did not avert the tragedy of 14 February, when Cook was killed in an affray which followed his attempt to hold Kalaniopiu as a hostage until a stolen cutter was returned. This misconceived adventure led to the bloodiest and most disgraceful encounter between Polynesians and Europeans since Alvaro de Mendaña and his men had ravaged the Marquesas in 1595. It all began with a combination of simple human errors : Cook lost his temper; the English in general assumed too readily that the Hawaiians would not face firearms; and the egregious Lieutenant Williamson managed to misconstrue Cook's signals from the shore and left his Captain to be murdered instead of rowing in to rescue him. Cook and four marines were killed in the mêlée. By the time the fighting was over, two days later, rather more than thirty Hawaiians had been shot or bayoneted, an unspecified number were decapitated and their heads stuck on poles as the English had been wont to treat Scotsmen thirty years before, and about 150 of their dwellings were burned to the ground.[45]

Both sides agreed on treating the affair as a thoroughly unfortunate business. It would indeed have been a thoroughly fortunate one if the death of the world's greatest explorer had discouraged other Europeans from coming to Hawaii. But this was impossible, simply because of the extremely convenient location of the islands: Cook himself had noted that 'Spain may probably reap some benifit by the discovery of these islands, as they are extremely will situated for the Ships sailing from New Spain to the Philippine Islands to touch and refresh at'.[46] However, commerce in the Pacific was sufficiently slack for the islands not to be troubled by foreign visitors for eight years more. This is not to say that they were at peace. War continued, apparently leading to further fragmentation rather than unity. By 1780, Hawaii itself was effectively divided between Kalaniopiu and Kamehameha. King Kalaniopiu died in 1782, and was succeeded by his son Kiwalao. The latter, however, fell under the influence of his powerful and apparently wicked uncle Keawemauhili, who had hopes of enlarging his personal territories at the expense of Kamehameha and other chiefs of western Hawaii. His ambitions led to a battle in 1782 at Mokuohai, just inland from Kealakekua Bay, in which Kiwalao himself was killed.

This victory of Kamehameha and his allies led to a further territorial adjustment, Kamehameha holding the western and northern districts; Kiwalao's brother Keoua the south; and Keawemauhili the east. But this was only the most temporary of arrangements: Kamehameha launched an ambitious pincer attack against Keoua and Keawemauhili, striking at the former by land and the latter by sea. Both attempts failed completely. He tried again in 1785, and failed again. Hawaii remained divided.

By the contrast, Kahekele of western Maui appeared to be well on the way towards establishing hegemony in the other islands of the group. He had already succeeded in containing the attempts of Kamehameha's predecessor Kalaniopiu to extend Hawaiian control from eastern Maui. His other rival, old Peleioholani of Oahu, who was challenging Kahekele for the lordship of Molokai, died shortly after Cook's arrival, Peleioholani's son Kumahana was deposed and power seized by Kahahana, who may have been a protégé of Kahekele's.[47] In any event, Kahekele briskly invaded and overran Oahu, taking up residence himself at Waikiki. Meanwhile, Kahekele's half-brother Kaeo had established his own authority over the islands Kauai and Niihau and accepted a working alliance with Kahekele in which Kahekele was the dominant partner. Kahekele himself continued to support Keoua and Keawemauhili against Kamehameha, and successfully resisted an attack which Kamehameha made against Maui in 1786, for the express purpose of dissuading Kahekele from interfering in Hawaiian affairs. A classic feudal impasse had been achieved. None of the contending chiefs had the manpower or the superior military technology necessary to impose his authority over all the others. The breakthrough did not come from the resources of the Polynesian civilization itself. It had to come from outside. It was coming even as Kamehameha withdrew baffled from the shores of Maui.

Cook had suggested that Hawaii might be of the most immediate value to Spain, whose control of the American coastline extended as far north as San Francisco Bay. It might also have had some attractions for the Russians, circumspectly developing a fur trade in Alaska. But the importance of Hawaii in the eyes of foreigners lay chiefly in its convenient situation for ships needing to revictual or recuperate on the way to and from the Asian mainland.

The first requirement was thus something to stimulate commerce between the Americas and Asia. This was provided by the development of the fur trade. Cook's exploration of Antarctic waters opened new horizons to squadrons of sealers, who proceeded quite simply to butcher the animals to extinction, to the best of their ability. Moorehead quotes the example of two ships that managed to slaughter 45,000 seals in a season.[48] The most profitable market for the skins was Canton, and the most convenient stopover, in the central Pacific at least, was Hawaii. Two English ships, commanded by Captains Portlock and Dixon, were the first to call at the group for this purpose in 1786. They returned the following year, shedding the first beachcomber, the first white man to choose deliberately to live as a Polynesian, John Mackey. The American Douglas arrived in 1788 from the sealing station of Nootka Sound with the *Iphigenia* and the *North West America*. He happened to visit Kamehameha's domains in western Hawaii, and Kamehameha himself was told how the *North West America* had been constructed at Nootka Sound. Kamehameha promptly asked Douglas to leave him a carpenter so that he could have a similar craft built for himself. Douglas apparently declined. However, Kamehameha was not the only chief to have become convinced on remarkably brief acquaintance of the superiority of Western technology : only six weeks later Douglas saw a double canoe painstakingly schooner-rigged off the coast of Kahekele's dominion of Oahu. In any event, when Douglas returned in 1789 he let Kamehameha have something far more portentous than a carpenter : a swivel cannon, capable of being fired from the platform deck of a double canoe.

This was the start of what can only be described as an arms race which gradually involved all the major chiefs of the Hawaiian Group. It was given further initial impetus by a peculiarly savage and oddly coincidental exchange between Hawaiians and Europeans in 1790. Captain Simon Metcalfe anchored off Maui in the *Eleanora*, about the same time that his son Thomas anchored off the west coast of Hawaii in the *Fair American*. One of Simon Metcalfe's sailors was killed by the Maui islanders and a small boat stolen. He retaliated by first bombarding the nearest village, and then firing on canoes with cannon loaded with grapeshot, after he had encouraged the islanders to approach the *Eleanora* for trade. Simon Metcalfe thus killed well over a hundred islanders. Meanwhile, his son and four of his crew were being killed, and the *Fair American* seized, by orders of the Hawaiian chief Kameeiamoku, whom Simon Metcalfe had beaten with a rope's end on a previous trip. Soon afterwards Simon Metcalfe also arrived in Hawaiian waters, but sailed away without knowing what had happened to his son. He also sailed away without his boatswain, the Englishman John Young, who had gone ashore and had been kept there by Kamehameha for fear that Young might discover about the massacre and tell Simon Metcalfe.

Kamehameha now had a western-style ship, the *Fair American*, obtained for him by his tributary chieftain Kameeiamoku; a swivel cannon; and two Europeans to advise him how to use the gun and the ship, Young, whom he had taken prisoner, and Isaac Davis, the only survivor of the *Fair American* massacre. The Hawaiians were acquiring the destructive capacity of Europeans. Everything had changed.

It had changed elsewhere in the Pacific as well. Before 1789, the Pacific Islands still belonged for all practical purposes to the people living there. After 1790, it was clear that their destinies were in the hands of foreigners, subject to alien wills. The aliens of course were still far from having things all their own way : the Samoans massacred the crew of a boat sent ashore by the French explorer La Pérouse in 1787, thereby earning themselves over thirty years' respite from foreign intruders. However, a highly significant pattern of dependence was developing in the other islands. Cook had noted in his last visit to Tahiti that the natives had adopted the use of iron implements so extensively that they were forgetting how to make stone ones. In matters of warfare, they were becoming dependent not only on foreign weapons but on foreigners to service them. The first decisive intervention of this kind was made in Tahiti in 1790 by the *Bounty* mutineers, who had anchored in Matavai Bay, and whose guns enabled Tu to resist a challenge by the chiefs of Paéa and Ahurai and force them to submit to his authority.

Only sixteen of the mutineers had elected to remain in Tahiti. They

had been joined in 1789 by a dangerous drunk named Brown, left by
the fur-trader *Mercury*. Only a further ten beachcombers had settled by
then in Hawaii. But the avalanche was coming. The first whalers nosed
into the Pacific in the same year, still staying for the most part in
American waters. But two years earlier the first great experiment in
transportation to the Pacific had been launched. Singularly, there had
been no great rush to the great southern continent since Cook claimed
New South Wales for Britain in 1770. A Parliamentary Committee did
not begin to consider the prospect of actually settling the new colony
until 1779. Nothing had been done four years later, when James M.
Matra, who had been one of Cook's midshipmen, sent to the British
Government 'A Proposal for Establishing a Settlement in New South
Wales', where, he said, 'the climate and soil are so happily adapted to
produce every various and valuable product of Europe'.[49] Matra's own
idea was to resettle American Loyalists, driven out by the Revolution.
The Government decided instead to relieve the overcrowding on the
convict hulks in the Thames. The decision was taken in 1786. Eleven
ships sailed in the first fleet on 13 May 1787, taking with them 800 convicts, at least two-thirds of them professional criminals, who could hardly
be considered anything but a total liability to their own country. About
a third of the total shipment were women. It was recognized that there
might not be enough of these for colonizing purposes : Lord Sydney, one
of the originators of the project, accordingly proposed 'the sending of
unmarried men to carry off the beautiful women of Otaheite [Tahiti]
as wives, so that Botany Bay might be peopled with beings that would
have been an ornament to human nature.'[50] This might have seemed
unlikely, considering what the fathers would have been like. However,
the enchanting prospect of a mulatto Australia was dismissed by
Governor Phillip, on the grounds that the Tahitian women would merely
pine away in misery in New South Wales. But it was inevitable that the
new colony should look to the Pacific for trade, if not for sex. In the
first place, it was believed that the hinterland of the country might be
impossible to reach, let alone develop; in the second, the colony did not
become self-supporting in food until 1820.

The answer was obviously to import livestock from the islands. In
1793, Captain George Vancouver, commander of a British naval
squadron in the North Pacific, despatched the storeship *Daedalus* south
to Tahiti 'to take on board such hogs, goats, fowls &c . . . as may be
likely for the purpose of being serviceable to the said colony'.[51] The
Tahitian pork trade had begun. The former island paradise had become

enmeshed in the economic system of the man-made hell of New South Wales.

Vancouver had plans for Hawaii as well. Kamehameha had renewed his plans for conquest in 1790, joining with Keawemauhili of western Hawaii in a second invasion of Maui while Kahekele was absent in Oahu. The defenders were massacred. Kamehameha seized Lanai as well as Maui, and attempted to establish a claim to Molokai. The balance of power in the group had thus altered completely. It swung back again almost at once. Keoua of southern Hawaii turned furiously on Keawemauhili, who had seemingly betrayed him by aligning with Kamehameha, killed Keawemauhili himself, and marched into Kamehameha's Hawaiian territories. Kamehameha returned from Molokai and met the invasion in a murderous but indecisive battle at Hamakua. Keoua, disturbed by alarming volcanic displays more than by Kamehameha's assaults, retired to the south, but still kept the territories of the dead Keawemauhili, as well as his own domain of Kau. Meanwhile, Kahekele had recovered his forces and reconquered Molokai and Maui.

This might have gone on forever. It did not do so, simply because of the alien element which had entered Hawaiian politics of power. Kamehameha now deployed a fleet of canoes against Kahekele again, but this time supported them with his foreign sloop, the *Fair American*, and with double canoes armed with cannon operated by Davis and Young. Kahekele and Kaeo also had cannon and foreign experts to fire them, but not in the same quantity. The challenge was turned back, and the initiative again lay with Kamehameha and his alien gunners.

Keoua was the next obstacle to be smoothed away. Two of Kamehameha's allies induced Keoua to meet with Kamehameha, apparently to divide the authority of Hawaii between them. Keoua accepted the bait and was murdered on the meeting ground by another of Kamehameha's allies, Keeaumoku. Kamehameha himself may or may not have been directly responsible for the treachery. It was in any case normal Polynesian diplomatic procedure, and Keoua appears to have had the gravest expectations beforehand that he would not survive the negotiations. The outcome was of course Kamehameha's establishment as the supreme chief of Hawaii. The only question was how long the rest of the Group could resist his ambitions. Vancouver had meantime been earnestly trying to arrange a peace between Kahekele and Kamehameha based on the existing territorial divisions. However, in spite of his insistence that firearms should not be made available to the

Hawaiian chiefs, Vancouver equipped Kamehameha's tame beach-comber and gunner John Young with rockets and hand grenades 'to be used only for the protection of Kamehameha'; rigged one of Kamehameha's largest canoes with a full set of sails, sloop-fashion; and actually had his carpenters construct a foreign-style vessel for Kamehameha's use. He may also have promised Kamehameha that the British Government would send him a man-of-war laden with European articles as a present.

What Vancouver was after in return was of course simply the cession of Hawaii to Britain. He got something like it on 25 February 1794. Vancouver himself reported that Kamehameha had made 'the most solemn cession possible of the Island of Owhyhee to his Britannic Majesty . . . and himself with the attending chiefs unanimously acknowledged themselves subject to the British crown'.[52] It is most likely that the Polynesians, who were never silly, encouraged Vancouver to believe this, as the best way of extracting from him firearms, or at least the promise of getting them. They themselves, according to their own historians, had no intention of conceding any territorial rights to the British Government, but had accepted only what amounted to British protection of the dominions of Kamchameha.

These were about to be extended dramatically. Kahekele died at about the same time as Vancouver and Kamehameha concluded their mis-understanding. His dominions fell to his half-brother Kaeo, overlord of Kauai, and his son Kalanikupule. Fighting between these two began almost at once. Kaeo had almost succeeded in overrunning Oahu when Kalanikupule was rescued by foreign intervention. Two British ships, the *Jackal* and the *Prince Lee Boo*, and an American ship, the *Lady Washington*, had put into Honolulu harbour. The Englishmen provided guns, ammunition and nine sailors, enabling Kalanikupule to win a decisive victory. Kaeo was killed. The *Lady Washington* sailed off to Canton after its captain and several of the crew had been shot by the Englishmen, possibly accidentally, during the victory celebrations. Kalanikupule then murdered the captains of the two British ships and seized the vessels to serve as the spearhead of a renewed challenge to Kamehameha. However, the survivors recaptured the ships and sailed to Hawaii, where they warned Kamehameha of Kalanikupule's intentions. Kamehameha took the initiative himself, invaded Oahu and destroyed Kalanikupule's forces at the battle of Nuuanu. Kalanikupule was eventually captured and appropriately sacrificed to the war god, Kukailimoku. That left only Kauai and Niihau still unconquered. Kamehameha despatched an invasion fleet to Oahu, only to see it swamped by rough seas. He was in any case temporarily distracted by a revolt against his own rule on his home island of Hawaii.

However, if the struggle for supreme power in the Hawaii Group now entered a relatively quiet phase, events were beginning to follow a similar pattern in the South Pacific, for the Polynesian system was now being racked by every imaginable kind of strain. Most of these pressures derived directly from the European intrusions. In the political and military spheres, for example, feudal strife had been virtually endemic in most of the islands even before the eighteenth century brought a confrontation of cultures, but its effects had always been mitigated by the inherent obstacles to tyranny imposed by a feudal or oligarchic system, and particularly by the fact that no one chief could reasonably hope to defeat all his peers in battle. European firearms changed all this, virtually guaranteeing victory to whoever possessed the most guns. It was not that the flintlocks or even the muzzle-loading cannon of the period were so vastly superior to Polynesian weapons in their destructive capacity: English or French sailors armed with muskets were probably less favourably placed in this respect *vis-à-vis* the Polynesians than Spanish adventurers of a century or more earlier, invulnerable in their armour and irresistible with pike or rapier.[53] But the Polynesians did not yet realize this. Firearms did not so much kill people as cause them to panic and thus fly into situations where they could be killed off more readily by traditional Polynesian weapons. The effect was the same, however: any chief who possessed firearms had the means of slaughtering opponents until he had attained supreme power, or as much of it as he was allowed to enjoy by the Europeans who provided military aid.

This in itself was certain to make Polynesian wars immensely more extensive and bloody than they had ever been before: they were fought for higher stakes, with more fearful if not precisely more destructive weapons. Here the Polynesians necessarily bear most of the responsibility for their own destruction: no doubt they did not fully comprehend the consequences for their own society of European-type warfare, but they were certainly at least as anxious to get guns as the Europeans were to let them have them, at the appropriate price. Disease, however, was another matter. Anti-erotic moralists might have felt that no people deserved more to be scourged by venereal and other diseases than the Polynesians. And yet the pre-European experience of the island races would seem to suggest that enthusiastically cultivated eroticism and general high living, tempered with infanticide, socially approved murder, a dash of cannibalism, a considerable amount of small-scale warfare and the barest minimum of disagreeable physical labour, were the ideal recipe for health, happiness, social stability, profound religious experience and great cultural achievement in both the plastic and dramatic arts. The Europeans had certainly changed all this. Wallis and Bougainville had brought venereal disease; Vancouver had brought dysentery; the Spanish had brought influenza; and now private enterprise of all kinds was bringing guns, and mercenaries to use them.

Not only the human environment was being imperilled directly by the presence of the Europeans. Cook had introduced into Tahiti cattle, horses, pigs, and assorted poultry. Captain Tobias Furneaux, who accompanied Cook as commander of the *Adventure*, had brought goats, probably the most indiscriminately destructive of farm animals. Vancouver similarly introduced into Hawaii cattle, goats and geese. The intention in every case was simply to ensure that the Pacific islands would produce a greater quantity and variety of the commodities that Europeans wanted. Economic colonization had begun.

Bringing things into the Pacific was, however, less obviously destructive than taking things out. What might be termed the extractive aspect of economic colonization was still at an early stage of development. But the pattern of the nineteenth century had been established before the end of the eighteenth. Sealers and whalers from the ports of Britain, France and the United States, having virtually exterminated their prey in European waters, were moving increasingly into the Pacific. In Hawaii, Simon Metcalfe had in 1790 begun the sandalwood trade with China that was to bring famine and dependence to the people of Hawaii and the well-nigh total exploitation of the sandalwood resources of Fiji. Destructiveness of this kind was of course not in itself deliberate: it was merely a by-product of commercial enterprise. The intentions of the missionaries, on the other hand, were precisely to destroy every significant aspect of Polynesian civilization. The by-product in this case was the progressive depopulation of the Pacific islands.

The whole missionary phenomenon is of course both complex and extraordinary. It is, to begin with, a peculiarly Christian problem: Islam is the only other major proselytizing religion, and the fundamental simplicity of Islam has meant that it can be spread just as convincingly and accurately by soldiers as by theologians. Christian propagandists by contrast relied heavily on techniques of intellectual or emotional persuasion, involving direct repudiation of the traditional values of their prospective converts. The Christian missionary thus tended to appear

as the ultimate cultural chauvinist, especially when he first descended on
the Pacific peoples in the nineteenth century. His function was in no
way to comprehend the values or life-styles of the people he approached,
but rather to convince them that their own values guaranteed that they
would be unhappy for ever after they were dead, however happy they
might be while they were alive. The consequences of this kind of teaching
were certain to be doubly unfortunate. As C. Hartley Grattan sums the
matter up, the missionaries hated "nudity, dancing, sex (except mono-
gamous marriage), drunkenness, anything savouring of *dolce far niente*,
self-induced penury, war (except in God's name), heathenism in all its
protean manifestations, and Roman Catholicism.[54] This litany could have
been made more oecumenical, perhaps, by simply substituting the
words 'believers of any persuasion other than their own' for 'Roman
Catholicism'. The missionaries accordingly hated everything which in
the opinion of most people, and of the Pacific islanders in particular,
made life worth living. More seriously, they refused to recognize the
fact that it was really difficult to find other ways of filling up one's days
in a tropical climate. For example, one simply could not physically
work twelve hours a day, whether one wanted to or not, as people could
be made to do in English factories. No more could one spend the time
in systematic and intense thought, as the English were to find out themselves when they tried living in the tropics. The missionaries were, in
fact, to the extent that they succeeded in their endeavours, to leave the
Polynesians with nothing to do except pray and sing hymns, keeping
their eyes resolutely closed to beauty, in the hope of avoiding the wrath
to come. They were inviting them to die out. The Polynesians survived
only to the extent that the missionaries failed.

It was indeed the missionaries themselves who looked like dying out
first. The London Missionary Society had been established in 1795. It
was, as Moorehead points out, an essentially lower-middle-class, non-
Establishment body whose principal objective may be described as that
of imposing on foreign peoples values spectacularly rejected by the
British ruling class at the time.[55] The missionary ship *Duff* arrived in
Matavai Bay in March 1797, to unload four dissenting clergymen and
thirty-five artisans, servants, wives and children. They were at least
assured of safety there: Tu himself might have had no intention in the
world of accepting Christian beliefs, but he certainly believed that power
grew out of the barrel of a gun, and that the more he encouraged
Europeans to come to Matavai Bay the more European military technology he would have at his disposal for the defence of the hegemony

which he was securing in Tahiti, against all traditional probabilities. His main allies, the *Bounty* mutineers, had been recaptured by the *Pandora* in 1791. The missionaries would provide a valuable European presence, supplementing the three castaway sailors still in Tahiti.

By contrast, the decision to land nine artisan missionaries in Tonga was distinctly unfortunate. Finau Ulukalala had died in 1790. He had been succeeded in Vava'u by his younger brother, known conveniently as Finau Ulukalala II. The title of Tui Kanokupolu, by now the most influential office in Tonga, had been secured for Mumui of Tongatapu by his son Tukuaho, an adventurer of the same ambitious order as both the Finaus, with a reputation for ferocious ill-treatment of his victims remarkable even for a Tongan aristocrat. Tukuaho succeeded his father in 1797. He was then himself murdered by Topou Niua, an ally of Finau, on 21 April 1799, on the occasion of the offering of the first-fruits to the Tui Tonga. This assassination provoked in turn an extraordinarily savage civil war between Finau and Tupou Niua on the one hand, drawing their support from their own islands of Vava'u and Ha'apai, and the traditionalist supporters of the murdered Tui Kanokupolu, based mainly in Hihifo, the western part of Tongatapu. Three of the missionaries were killed by members of the traditionalist forces for quite non-political reasons; the new Tui Kanokupolu, Tukuaho's eldest son Tupou-malohi, was driven into exile in Fiji; and the year 1800 ended with the traditionalists still entrenched in Hihifo, beyond the power of Finau and Tupou Niua to expel them.

The consequences of this affair were considerable, quite apart from the obvious fact that Tongan society had been torn apart and Tongan subjects slaughtered for the first time in something like 600 years. The first was that warfare, by making husbandry impossible, was producing the same kind of ecological chaos in Tonga as Vancouver's cattle were to produce in Hawaii, and Cook's hogs in Tahiti; the second was that Tonga and Fiji were thrown into contact again, by the flight of the Tui Kanokupolu; the third was that the same kind of political impasse was reached in Tonga as had been reached in Hawaii and Tahiti: the dawning of the nineteenth century saw Kamehameha baulked before Kauai, Finau similarly stymied by the entrenchments of Hihifo, and Tu sustaining a precarious hegemony solely on the guns of the Europeans who occasionally sailed into Matavai Bay. The Polynesian warlords could attain their ambitions only at the price of becoming foreign puppets. The process could hardly be altered. All that was now in question was what it would leave of the Pacific peoples and their ways of life.

III

The Conquerors

The epicentre of Western influence in the Pacific at the turn of the nineteenth century was necessarily New South Wales. Over 4,000 Europeans were established there and on Norfolk Island by the end of the eighteenth century. In October 1800 Governor King sent 'six yards of red bunting and twelve pounds of Australian-made soap' as a present to open commercial relations to Tu of Matavai Bay, now styled by his friends His Majesty King Pomare of Tahiti. The immediate result was 'a very timely supply of 31,000 pounds of excellent salt pork . . . procured at a trifling cost of $2\frac{1}{2}$d per lb'.[1] This was certainly of vital commercial importance to New South Wales. It was of even more urgent moment to Pomare. The arrival of the *Porpoise*, the ship despatched by King, came literally in the nick of time to save Pomare from being bundled out of Tahiti by his feudal rivals. Even the paltry three or four muskets which he obtained on this occasion were enough to sustain his power until the brig *Venus* arrived with a more plentiful supply of firearms. These were provided by the merchant adventurers Charles Bishop and George Bass, who were less reluctant than King to let the islanders have what they obviously wanted most in exchange for their hogs. The arms trade even included pieces of artillery, as in Hawaii : Pomare purchased a swivel gun for the price of ten hogs.[2]

The economic relationship naturally encouraged King to think in terms of a political relationship. The British Government had awarded Phillip and his successors in New South Wales jurisdiction over 'all the islands adjacent in the Pacific Ocean, within the latitude aforesaid of

10° 37' South and 43° 39' South'.[3] This was certainly understood by King to include Tahiti: the vessel sent to Matavai Bay to collect the first shipment of pork was also instructed to arrest and bring back any deserters from British ships who could be found on Tahiti. In 1801 King appointed one of the missionaries in Tahiti to be Justice of the Peace, and issued proclamations warning the captains of British merchant ships calling at Tahiti to respect the missionaries and give the natives no cause for offence.

King took these measures in his capacity as Governor of New South Wales and its dependencies. Pomare's nominal sovereignty counted for nothing, since the realities of the situation were only too obvious: his authority in Tahiti depended absolutely on the willingness and availability of Europeans to defend it. There was after all a certain incongruity in the idea of Tahitian independence, when the territory had already been claimed by Wallis and Cook for Britain, by Bougainville for France and by Domingo de Boenechea for Spain.

In 1800 it had appeared to King rather as if the French might be preparing to settle the problem for ever by taking over the whole South Pacific. Napoleon had sent out two ships, the *Géographe* and the *Naturaliste*, ostensibly to study the coast of the Australian continent. The expedition could hardly have had any purpose at the time other than a strictly scientific one, but the crews seem to have been convinced that the real object of the enterprise was to spy out the land for future French occupation, and one can only presume that final French victory in a renewed struggle with Britain would have been followed by French landings on part at least of Australia.[4] King himself had no doubt that this was a reasonable expectation. The British Admiralty, to be on the safe side, sent Matthew Flinders in the *Investigator* to look for suitable landing sites in Van Diemen's Land and along Bass Strait. In August 1803 King despatched the *Lady Nelson* and the *Albion* to Van Diemen's Land to forestall any renewed French bid. Such a possibility was temporarily averted by the British naval victory off Trafalgar in 1805. However, it was clear that, with the shipbuilding resources of the European continent available to him, Napoleon would in a few years be able to construct new fleets strong enough to overwhelm the British by sheer weight of numbers. Indeed, by 1810 Napoleon felt strong enough at sea to consider sending a squadron to seize Port Jackson, counting, with some justification, on the support of the convicts exiled there. He changed his mind, however, and in 1812 French hopes of victory were betrayed permanently by the decision to invade Russia.

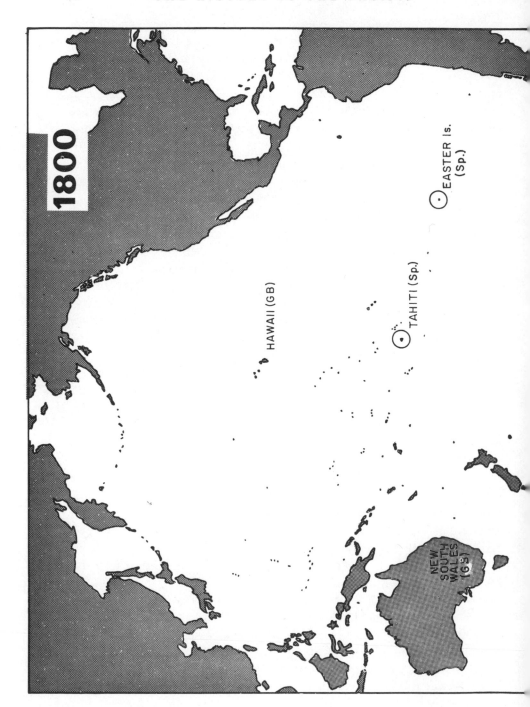

1800

EASTER Is. (Sp.)

HAWAII (GB)

TAHITI (Sp.)

NEW SOUTH WALES (GB)

But the defeats of 1814 and 1815 called a halt only to French projects of expansion in continental Europe. They positively encouraged a diversion of French ambitions overseas. French whalers had been venturing into the Pacific ever since the turn of the century. Four ships were actively working in the South Pacific in 1817. In the same year, the Government of the Restoration despatched Damblart de Lamastre to the Indies, de Kergariou to China, and Louis Claude de Freycinet on a voyage of circumnavigation. Nobody could be certain where the French were going to show up next. Nor did the French pose the only threat, for by now the Americans and especially the Russians were also arriving in the Pacific in increasing numbers.

Meanwhile, the situation in the islands had developed in a peculiarly irrational way. Pomare had died in 1803. His son and heir, Pomare II, had been thrown out of Tahiti altogether by a rebellion against his shaky rule in August 1808 and forced to flee to the small westward island of Moorea. This might have meant the end of the dynastic pretensions of the Pomare family, had the rebels only been prepared to continue trading with the Europeans in Matavai Bay, exchanging hogs for guns, as the Pomares had done. Instead, they turned on the European traders and officials who had kept the Pomares supplied with arms, and seized the first ship to come into Matavai Bay, the schooner *Venus* owned by Bishop, Bass and Co. The *Venus* was promptly recovered by the next arrival, the *Hibernia*, and the Europeans now resumed trade with Pomare in the Leeward Group, where he had set up his court, accompanied by the missionaries who had fled with him from Tahiti.

Pomare II was as yet no more a Christian, even in the technical sense, than Pomare I had been. He was, however, at least equally prepared to seek power and profit as a client of Western colonialism. He could thus be regarded as a promising convert, in contrast with the distressingly anti-European rebels. The missionaries accordingly importuned the Australian authorities to increase their supply of guns to Pomare. Their hopes were fulfilled: Pomare accepted baptism in 1812; in November 1815 he defeated his main rivals at the battle of Feipi, relying on his musketeers and on a swivel gun mounted on a canoe and operated by an Englishman; and the first overlord of Tahiti showed his appreciation by ceremonially burning the old idols of his people and constructing a Christian cathedral some 700 feet long. Despotism had been established in Tahiti, thanks to the New South Wales pork traders, with a little help from the missionaries.[5]

Despotism was being established meanwhile in Hawaii as well, in a situation still more confused and fraught with peril for the independence and natural development of the Polynesian peoples. Kamehameha had been forced to abandon a plan to invade Kauai in 1803 when the island of Oahu, where his forces were assembling, was swept by what was probably bubonic plague. He had nonetheless managed to assemble by 1810 a fleet of about forty-two European-rigged sloops and schooners, led by the 175-ton ship *Lelia Byrd*. Confronted with what amounted to something like a Western-type navy, the ruler of Kauai, Kaumualii, agreed to acknowledge Kamehameha as his sovereign, while continuing to govern Kauai himself as a tributary kingdom. Kamehameha for his part referred to himself in a letter to George III as 'subject to' the King of England. The British still did not officially recognize any relationship other than one of cordial friendship, but the captains of non-British ships visiting Hawaii assumed that the group was effectively a British protectorate.

The question of who ruled in or over Hawaii was indeed made more obscure by Kaumualii's submission. Kamehameha had established a system of appointing representatives or viceroys to enforce his rule over the various islands of the Group, apart from Kauai. Most were native-born chiefs. However, two of the most important viceroys were Europeans, John Young, who governed Hawaii itself between 1802 and 1812, and Oliver Holmes, who held office in Oahu. Hawaii was no longer being ruled entirely by Hawaiians. Having depended on Europeans to gain him power, Kamehameha was now coming to depend on Europeans to exercise the power they had ostensibly won for him.

Problems associated with the European presence in the Group became suddenly more acute in 1816. The sandalwood trade had swollen to enormous importance, and 1,000 tons had been shipped to China in 1812. The implications for the Hawaiian people were distinctly unfortunate. As soon as Kamehameha realized the commercial significance of sandalwood, he established a royal monopoly over the trade; undertook to pay for his requirements from the foreigners by supplying them with quantities of sandalwood; and organized the Hawaiian people to abandon farming and fishing and concentrate their energies on cutting down their sandalwood groves to supply the foreign market. One predictable result was famine, which Kamehameha attempted to mitigate by periodically ordering both chiefs and commoners to turn to and produce food, just as he attempted to moderate the wholesale exploitation of the sandalwood reserves by placing *kapus* or religious prohibition on young trees. Even more serious, however, was the prospect of direct foreign intervention in the luxury trade. Russia had emerged from the Napoleonic wars as apparently by far the greatest power in continental Europe and Asia. Its influence in the world outside the two continents was held back only by British command of the seas. Russian explorers and traders set out to establish their own claims to recognition as a maritime power in the Pacific. Alexander Baranov, the governor of the Russian American Company, had established commercial relations with Kamehameha in 1807, and in 1815 he sent out Georg Anton Scheffer to investigate the possibility of setting up a permanent Russian trading station in the Group. After first visiting Kamehameha, however, Scheffer began separate negotiations with Kaumualii of Kauai in early 1816, and on 21 May of that year secured Kaumualii's signature to a document providing: that Kaumualii accepted Russian protection for himself and his kingdom; that the Russian American Company should have exclusive rights to the sandalwood trade with Kauai; that the Russians should have half of Oahu as well; and that the Russians should let Kaumualii have 500 men to take the island from Kamehamcha.[6]

This was the most direct challenge possible to Kamehameha's authority. Scheffer went rather prematurely direct to Oahu and raised the Russian flag at Honolulu. Kamehameha promptly ordered him to leave, under threat of force. Scheffer retired to Kauai and raised the Russian flag again above a fortress overlooking Hanalei on the north-east coast of the island and defended by cannon.

It might well have seemed that the Russians were bent on creating a Pacific empire, as well as European, Asian and American ones. But Kamehameha's fears were allayed by the arrival of a Russian warship, the *Rurick*, under the command of Lieutenant Otto von Kotzebue, who assured him that Scheffer was acting quite contrary to the wishes of Tsar Alexander. Russia's rulers characteristically dream widely, but act circumspectly. Alexander could hardly maintain stability in Europe, look after Russian interests in the eastern Mediterranean, preserve Spanish authority in the Americas, expand Russian enterprise in California and rule the Pacific all at the same time. He could indeed do none of these things without some measure of co-operation from the British, who he believed had extended a protectorate over Hawaii. Nothing could have seemed less intelligent to the authorities in St Petersburg than a dispute with Britain over Hawaii. Kamehameha accordingly ordered his dissident tributary Kaumualii to expel the Russians from Kauai; Kaumualii agreed, having apparently already realized that Scheffer was a greater challenge to his own authority than Kamehameha; and the Russians were driven out, literally by force, in 1819.

This was Kamehameha's last success. The old despot died in May 1819. He was undoubtedly the most sophisticated and resourceful of the pocket-Napoleons who were rising throughout the Pacific in response to the combined attractions of Western capitalism and Western military technology. He was, of course, the product of the most sophisticated and resourceful of Polynesian civilizations. His rise to power certainly contrasts impressively with the helpless dependency of the Pomares upon their European patrons, and with the carnival of butchery being performed in Tonga and Fiji. In the former group, Finau Ulukalala II had at last found an answer to the fortresses in which his surviving opponents had been able to hide from his vengeance. He had seized an English privateer, the *Port-au-Prince*, in 1806, and massacred most of its crew, preserving the remainder to help him to use the ship's guns against his enemies' fortifications. His success was total, if temporary. Tupou-malohi, son of the murderous and murdered Tui Kanokupolu, paid homage to the usurper Finau, in return for being allowed to survive in retirement on Ha'apai. The last fragment of the Tongan system had apparently been shattered. However, the traditionalists gained a partial revenge, worthy of Renaissance Italy. Tupou-toa, younger brother of Tupou-malohi, managed without much difficulty to persuade the sanguinary Finau II that his fellow-usurper Tupou Niua was not to be trusted. Finau accordingly permitted his ally to be clubbed to death by his tribal enemies, thereby himself earning the hostility of Tupou Niua's fellow-chieftains on Vava'u, who first swore their unfailing allegiance to Finau, then built a gigantic fortress on Vava'u and prepared to resist him to the death. Finau attacked them with 5,000 warriors, 50 canoes and 4 cannons, but induced them to surrender only after he had sworn to take no revenge upon them. As soon as they had surrendered, however, Finau, in accordance with what had by now become standard Tongan practice, broke his vows, and after butchering some of the leading chieftains of Vava'u set eighteen of the others adrift in leaking canoes to experience the ignominy of death by drowning.[7]

Finau himself died in 1811, having, according to Basil Thomson, 'in his short life caused more bloodshed and human suffering than the aggregate in the whole of Tongan history before his time'.[8] He died just before he was able to efface 900 years of Tongan history by abolishing the office of the Tui Tonga. This was finally accomplished by his son Moengangono, who reigned briefly as Finau III. But the centre of political authority had meantime shifted to Ha'apai, where Tupou-toa, the contriver of the death of Tupou Niua, had managed to attract around him the great warriors of Tonga. Tupou-toa became nominal Tui Kanokupolu on the death of his brother Tupou-malohi, about the same time that Finau III also died, and attempted to invade Tongatapu. He managed to sustain some kind of authority over the southern islands until 1820, when he died in his turn, and what had once been the most orderly of Pacific nations relapsed again into anarchy.

The Tongans had managed to reduce themselves to chaos almost without any help from the Europeans. The Fijians had expanded their natural chaos with considerable help from outside, but help which as yet hardly posed any kind of threat to Fijian independence. But Fiji, too, had been sucked into the vast network of the sandalwood trade, with ships coming from New South Wales, India and the United States, and Fijian chiefs yielded as Kamehameha had done to the attractions of profit and exploitation. The visitors for their part were as ready as elsewhere in the Pacific to exchange military aid for trading advantage. In 1808 seventeen heavily-armed sailors from three ships agreed, in return for a cargo of sandalwood, to help Tui Bua on Vanua Levu to carry out a massacre of the Tacilevu people which probably surpassed anything done in that line before in Fiji. Far more important, however, had been the arrival in Bua Bay a few months earlier of an American deserter, Charles Savage, with the crew of the *Eliza*, and a collection of muskets and munitions. Having been persuaded to leave Bua Bay for Bau, in eastern Viti Levu, Savage was welcomed there by the Bauan chief Naulivou, anxious to extend the boundaries of his tiny state, contained ever since 1760 by the peoples of Verata to the north and his suspicious ally Rewa to the south. The warriors of Verata were the first to discover the new power which had come to the service of Bau when they were massacred by Savage's sharp-shooting at Kasavu and Nakelo. Savage was not the only European ally of Bau: most of his colleagues from the *Eliza* had shipped off again on other vessels, but he was joined by about twenty other beachcombers attracted by the excitement and by the rumours of 40,000 Spanish dollars of which Savage was supposed to know the whereabouts. Savage himself did not last long. He was abandoned by the Bauans in the course of a raid on Vanua Levu, drowned by the locals, carved up, cooked, eaten and his bones made into sail needles. No European was absorbed more completely into Fijian culture. But Savage had changed the course of Fijian development.[9] His gunnery had broken the power, if not the spirit, of Verata; Rewa collapsed into the role of a tributary of Bau, shattered by dynastic rivalries; and the chiefs of Bau set off on the road to unity by conquest already followed by the Pomares and Kamehameha.

The main protection of the Fijians lay, as with the Tongans, in their reputation for ferocity. Only Europeans prepared to identify themselves with local ways were prepared to set foot in Fiji. Even the murderous merchants who had so quickly dominated affairs in Tahiti left the Fijians comparatively to themselves, and the exhaustion of the sandalwood trade in 1813 gave the Fijians almost twenty years' freedom from foreign intervention in which to do what they liked to themselves.

A similar name for ferocity had all this while kept to a minimum European presence in the largest of all the Polynesian islands. The Maoris of New Zealand attacked and ate Dutchmen, French and English with impressive consistency. Their most striking exploit came in 1809, when they captured and massacred almost everybody on board the ship *Boyd*, which had stopped to pick up spars on the way from Sydney to London. But even without this deterrent there was apparently little to attract European interest in New Zealand. The islands were as remote as it was geographically possible to be, the shoreline was generally daunting, and the climate was cold and wet, even by European standards. Commercial prospects were similarly unappealing. The tall New Zealand trees looked as if they would make excellent spars and masts, but their wood was extraordinarily hard to cut and work, and there was considerable effort involved in dragging the trees over rough ground to beaches where they could be floated out to the waiting ships. New Zealand flax too 'appeared for a while to be the solution to the rope problem of the Royal Navy';[10] however, although tough and strong, it was also brittle and swelled excessively when wet. New Zealand hardly seemed to be worth the trouble.

It could seem otherwise only to the missionary societies. The Maoris certainly appeared in unusual need of conversion: they had to be persuaded in the first place that eating people was wrong. They also represented something very close to virgin territory: it could hardly be said that the Maoris had been corrupted by friendly intercourse with Europeans, as missionary zealots might think that the Tahitians and Hawaiians had been corrupted: the obvious fact was that European captains kept as far away from New Zealand as they practicably could. There was also, paradoxically, the factor of comparative safety: at a time when Tonga and Tahiti were rocking with civil war and ambush and massacre raged endlessly around the coastline of Fiji, the intelligent, attractive and highly-organized cannibals of New Zealand seemed rather more promising people to live among than their relatives in the more familiar islands.

The first permanent white settlement in New Zealand was established in the Bay of Islands in 1814 by Samuel Marsden, the senior chaplain in New South Wales. Marsden was fearless, indefatigable, humourless, domineering and pre-eminent even in the appallingly sadistic climate of New South Wales for his belief in the salutary effects of flogging people. Estimates of the pre-missionary white population varied : Marsden himself claimed to have encountered six runaway convicts; another Englishman, John Nicholas, said that he had met only two other Europeans of any description. By 1815, again according to Marsden, the white population in the Bay of Islands had risen to twenty-one, all associated with the Church Missionary Society. The number had grown to about forty-five by 1819, and appears to have varied between twenty-odd and fifty-odd for the next five or six years.[11]

A community of this size was not likely to make much impact upon 150,000 Maoris. Ethically, and perhaps theologically, they made no effect at all. Understandably, it was the missionaries who yielded to the pressures of life in Maori New Zealand, rather than the other way about : the first baptism was not recorded until 1825; the missionaries seem to have spent much of their energy, if not their time, in denouncing one another for, and presumably practising, sodomy, fornication and drunkenness; and the Maoris appear to have found the evangelists most useful as minor sources of supply of firearms.

The missionaries excused themselves for trading muskets with the Maoris on the grounds that they had to eat. The consequences of this commerce were appalling beyond anything that could reasonably have been imagined. However, the role of the missionaries in the destruction of the Maori race was only marginal in this area. Maori ingenuity contrived the catastrophe. Hongi Hika, the predominant chief in the Bay of Islands area, mild-mannered, dignified, nice to missionaries, had induced Marsden to send him to England, ostensibly to assist in the preparation of a grammar of the Maori language. Having distinguished himself for his aplomb in London society, Hongi returned by way of Sydney, where he exchanged the gifts he had received en route for some 300 muskets. With these he set out on a campaign of slaughter throughout the north and centre of North Island unmatched in the history of the Pacific. The exact extent of the bloodshed is of course impossible to ascertain, but Hongi's wars were probably responsible for the deaths of at least 5,000 men in battle by the time of his own belated death in 1828. An overall figure of 40,000 plus can be taken for all deaths resulting from war between 1821 and 1840, by which time an uneasy peace had settled on the country as a result of general exhaustion. It is of course a little difficult to imagine at first exactly why the Maoris should have turned on one another so insatiably and so destructively. Land was certainly not an important factor: the New Zealand Maoris were free to enjoy a share of arable land per head vastly greater than that available to any other island people, and more than adequate for rational human purposes. The explosive factor seems to have been simply the desire for status, or more accurately personal honour. Maori society had enabled tribal antagonisms to develop more widely and over a longer period than in any other area of the Pacific, because the sheer size of the country had hitherto made it impossible for any one ruling family to impose its authority on the others as had happened in varying degrees in Hawaii, Tonga, Tahiti and even Fiji. Nor could these antagonisms be easily settled by going to war, because the fact that all the contenders were armed with the same weapons of limited destructiveness meant that war was likely to be a chancy and inconclusive business. A tribe armed with muskets, however, could wipe out five centuries' accumulated resentments easily, by destroying the objects of its resentments. This of course ensured that any survivors of the massacre would have acquired more grounds for resentment in a matter of hours than they had in all previous history, and would be looking for muskets and allies with which to even the score.

The process is quite comprehensible. What is more difficult is to relate the enormous casualties in the Maori tribal wars to general Pacific experience. In spite of the Fijians' reputation for ferocity, for example, it was exceptional for more than half a dozen or so warriors to be killed in any of the pitched battles between Bau and Verata, although it was not unusual for hundreds more to be put to death in the subsequent festivities.[12] Even the bloody and protracted dynastic struggles in Tonga were not characterized to anything like the same extent by wholesale massacre in the field.

The explanation almost certainly lies in the fact that the Fijian and Tongan wars of the early nineteenth century, like the Hawaiian conflict, were fundamentally pragmatic struggles to satisfy dynastic ambitions. Honour as such was hardly involved. There was, therefore, ample opportunity and justification for changing sides, coming to terms or simply bolting the camp. Other factors contributing to maximize bloodshed in

New Zealand and limit it elsewhere in the Pacific were geography and military skill. The Hawaiians fought with considerable distinction in terms of administration, strategy and the employment of new techniques; but even Kamehameha was forced to abandon any notion of a seaborne invasion of Kauai. The area in which he could fight was limited, practically speaking : he could not kill people he could not get at. The Fijians could get at each other without great difficulty, but they were truly serious only about the spoils of war, not the actual fighting.

War by itself could never be a serious challenge to the survival of a Polynesian people. Not that war ever came by itself : famine was an absolutely inevitable associate, simply because men could not farm and fight at the same time, and men who were killed in the fighting were not going to be available for the farming. All this the Maoris could be said to have brought on themselves. But it was the Europeans who were responsible for introducing two far more lethal factors into the situation. These were simply trade and blankets. The Maoris, like the other Pacific islanders, and unlike the Australian Aborigines, realized in the very first stages of contact with the Europeans that they possessed goods and services which the foreigners not only wanted, but in the nature of things simply had to have, and that they were in a position to trade with the foreigners on terms that seemed favourable to themselves. It might not be absolutely necessary, though it would usually be commercially necessary, for the foreigners to get their cargoes of sandalwood timber or flax. It was absolutely necessary for them to get food, water and whatever they might require for running repairs to their ships, and the Maoris were usually present in sufficient numbers and organization to ensure that the foreigners would not be able simply to take what they had to have. The Maoris, like the Tahitians, thus traded with the Europeans very largely on their own terms. But the sheer favourableness of the commercial situation brought its own form of disaster. In Hawaii, famine spread because the fields went untilled while the men hacked down the sandalwood groves. In New Zealand, the Maoris were impelled by their own cupidity to leave their healthy hilltop villages (pa) and move down to the much less healthy coasts and estuaries, where they worked harder than ever before to supply the new market. They were thus adopting a way of life which would lessen their physical resistance to the unfamiliar diseases which the Europeans were bringing with them. This dangerous situation was made far worse by the efforts of the missionaries to alter the Maoris' style of dress. John Butler, the new leader of the Bay of Islands missionary station, who consoled himself for his inadequacies in that role by taking to drink, looked forward to the day when 'they will all be clothed, and in their right mind, sitting at the feet of Jesus and hearing His holy word'.[13] The most effective way of getting them clothed was to sell them blankets. The missionaries began actively to cultivate this form of trade in 1830, after the drawbacks of the musket trade had become all too evident. The blankets were soon to prove the more deadly. Maoris began acquiring these and other articles of European dress as symbols of prestige, as quickly and in as great a quantity as possible. Status and sophistication came to be indicated by the sheer number of blankets one could load oneself with, in season or out. One was therefore loath to remove these wrappings for any purpose, least of all that of washing. The impeccably fastidious and hygienic Polynesians thus began to encumber themselves with filthy blankets which they wore day and night, wet and dry, hot and cold.

The consequences were impossible to ignore. The fact of depopulation was evident to Maoris and Europeans alike before the end of the 1830s. Its extent was in question only because of the impossibility of obtaining anything like precise estimates of Maori population. There were probably at least 200,000 Maoris in the country in 1769. Seventy years later, the number had fallen to not more than 125,000.[14] The causes were not sexual promiscuity, which was nothing new to the Maoris, not drunkenness, which was still virtually unknown; nor even twenty years of horrific wars. The causes of depopulation, in short, did not derive basically from contact between the Maoris and the bad Europeans. They derived from contact with the good ones. It was the evangelizing missionary and the law-abiding trader who in the main induced the Maoris to adopt a mode of life guaranteed to expose them to famine and epidemic. The supreme crisis of the Polynesian peoples was at hand. The question being posed by the end of the first half of the nineteenth century was literally whether they would live or die.

The crisis of survival in fact extended throughout the Polynesian Spearhead. The challenge was clearly twofold. The impact of European technology, capitalism and religion was imperilling the very existence of the island peoples. The impact of European political ambition was imperilling their independence. Populous, united, strategically situated Hawaii remained the area most obviously exposed to the political threat. Kamehameha had been able to disembarrass himself of the Russians, thanks to their belief that Hawaii was some kind of British protectorate, but American interest in Hawaii was growing and the Americans seemed less likely to respect a relationship which the British themselves were none too concerned to press. The domestic situation was once again inopportunely confused. Kamehameha I had died in 1819 and had been succeeded by his son, the allegedly dim Liholiho, as Kamehameha II. The new King's mother, the dowager Queen Kaahumanu, announced at his coronation that she was to share authority with him in the capacity of *kahina-nui* or special counsellor. This was apparently acceptable to Kamehameha II himself. However, the rule of the Kamehameha dynasty was by no means acceptable to all the chiefs in the group. The French captain Louis de Freycinet, who had visited the islands in 1819 on a scientific expedition, was told that the chief Kekuaokalani for one wished simply to overthrow the royal house and slaughter every European on the islands. De Freycinet, as befitted an officer of the restored Bourbon monarchy, sternly lectured the Hawaiians on the horrors of rebellion and civil war, and assured them that the flag of France would always be disposed to maintain the Kamehameha regime in order and tranquillity. De Freycinet insisted that this did not represent any challenge to the alliance which he understood to exist between Hawaii and Great Britain: he could indeed assure Kamehameha II of French support precisely because France was also an ally of Great Britain.

This was in August. In November Kamehameha and Kaahumanu struck at the main social obstacle to the establishment of a European-oriented despotism. The traditional *kapu* were formally abolished, and the power of the priesthood thus directly challenged. The traditional fabric of Hawaiian society had already been weakened too much for effective resistance; Kekuaokalani made his stand in western Hawaii and died fighting a hopeless battle against the army of the royal reformers. Hawaii was open to the future.

It began to take shape the following year. Missionaries poured in from the United States, 100 women and 84 men in all, in twelve descents between 1820 and 1848. In the same year, John C. Jones was officially appointed as United States Agent for Commerce and Seamen to represent American interests in the kingdom. In 1822 a further earnest of British interest arrived in the form of the six-gun schooner *Prince Regent*, which the British Government had instructed the authorities in New South Wales to build for Kamehameha I as a gift back in the tense times of 1815. In the meantime, the royal pair had jointly taken steps to deal with the continuing threat to their rear presented by Kaumualii of Kauai. Kamehameha II visited Kaumualii, and confirmed him in his position as tributary but sovereign king of Kauai and Niihau; and the matriarchal Kaahumanu married Kaumualii. She also

married Kaumualii's son Kealiiahonui. Never can dynastic problems have
been more effectively and thoroughly resolved.

There was still the problem of determining the exact nature of British
intentions towards Hawaii, and the extent to which the British could be
relied on to protect Hawaii from the cupidity of other foreigners, assuming that they did not want it for themselves. Kamehameha II responded
to the gift of the *Prince Regent* by begging leave to place the whole of
the Group under the protection of Great Britain. In 1823 he set out to
approach the British directly as he had approached Kaumualii, sailing
in November for Portsmouth in the British whaler *Aigle*, taking with him
in his retinue his viceroy, Governor Boki of Oahu.

It was Kamehameha II's last exercise in personal diplomacy. He was
received by the British Foreign Secretary George Canning in London,
but died of measles in July 1824 before he could have an audience with
George IV. Kamehameha's favourite wife Kamamalu, who had accompanied him, had already died of the same complaint. The responsibility
for completing the mission fell on Governor Boki. He was fully competent to handle the task. Boki told George IV that Kamehameha had
wished the British sovereign to watch over Hawaii; that he acknowledged George IV as his landlord and superior; and that he wanted the
British king to help him if foreigners of any other nation came to take
possession of his lands.

The British were far from unresponsive. Canning had already suggested that George IV should approve sending a British warship to
convey the remains and retinue of Kamehameha II back to Hawaii,
'an attention perhaps the more advisable as the Governments both of
Russia and of the United States of America are known to have their
Eyes upon those Islands'.[15] The King apparently told Boki that he
would not take possession of Hawaii for his own, but would 'watch
over it, lest evils should come from others to the Kingdom'.[16]

This was reassuring, if not exactly specific. The real significance of
George IV's words was spelt out in the instructions issued to Captain
Lord Byron of the 46-gun frigate *Blonde*, who was entrusted with
returning the Hawaiians to their home islands. Byron was reminded
that the King was entitled to claim sovereignty of the islands both by
right of discovery, and by the cession to Vancouver performed by
Kamehameha I. However, these rights were not to be asserted against
any domestic authority. On the other hand, Byron was to take the
islands under British protection if any other foreign power were to
assume sovereignty over them in any way. In other words, the British

were determined neither to take over Hawaiian affairs themselves, nor to allow anybody else to do so. It was a policy which might prove a little too delicate to operate successfully if more aggressive powers entered the field.

The situation with which Byron had to deal was indeed more than the British had bargained for. Kaumualii of Kauai had also died in April 1824. It had been his intention that Kauai and Niihau should fall in their entirety to Kamehameha and his heirs. Kaumualii's death had been followed by a rising in Kauai, led by chiefs dissatisfied with the distribution of lands, but the rebellion had been crushed before the news of the deaths of Kamehameha II and his wife reached Hawaii. Byron sailed into Honolulu harbour on 6 May 1825 to find a peaceful but leaderless nation.

It was obviously expected that Byron would present the islanders with some clear and probably official constitutional guidance when the national council of chiefs, accompanied by the British consul and some American missionaries and merchants, met in June. He was, however, careful to suggest only that the modified despotism stabilized by Kamehameha I should be continued. On the other hand, he strongly opposed the notion that the American missionaries should draw up a code of laws for the people. But American influence was not to be checked so easily. Kaahumanu, now acting as regent, was formally admitted to the Church in December 1825, and she immediately proposed that the Ten Commandments should be adopted as the foundation for the laws of the land. This was apparently acceptable enough to the chiefs, but it was vigorously opposed by the foreign and technically Christian traders, who feared that it might lead to an extension of missionary authority, making things more difficult for themselves.

The traders had their own notions about the kinds of law most urgently needed in Hawaii. The chiefs had for years been accumulating debts which they had undertaken to pay off with cargoes of sandalwood. The claims of the traders amounted to some $200,000 by 1826. Two American warships consequently arrived that year to compel Kaahumanu to acknowledge 'the debts due to American Citizens, to be Government debts'.[17] A law was imposed requiring every able-bodied man to supply a specified quantity of sandalwood, or cash or goods to the value of four Spanish dollars. Each woman was required to provide a mat or material valued at one such dollar. Hawaii had acquired its National Debt.

The American warships also secured what amounted to a treaty of commerce, friendship and navigation, granting American traders most-favoured-nation right in Hawaii. The treaty, again like the Vancouver cession, was never actually ratified by Congress, but was repeatedly appealed to successfully by American citizens carrying on business in Hawaii. The Hawaiians were in fact simply being made to dance to foreign tunes. Their international status was consequently becoming anomalous in the extreme. A French ship, the *Comète*, landed three Roman Catholic priests on Hawaii itself in July 1827. They had achieved sixty-five baptisms by mid-1829. The Protestant missionaries complained to Kaahumanu, who forbade the priests to teach their religion in 1830. In 1831 they were formally banished and native converts were actively persecuted. However, another American warship arrived the following year, once again to enforce payment of the claims of American traders, and to advise Kaahumanu to call off the persecution of Roman Catholics. Nevertheless, sanctions against the new religion were re-applied in 1835 by Kamehameha III, and when another priest, this time a British subject, arrived in 1836 he was promptly ordered to leave. However, a French warship, the *Bonite*, arrived opportunely the day before the priest was due to leave, and her commander, Captain Vaillant, took the opportunity to impart to the King and chiefs 'a sense of the power and greatness of France'.[18] He succeeded to the extent that Kamehameha III agreed to leave the Roman Catholic proselytizers undisturbed and positively to welcome any other French citizens who might wish to come to his kingdom. Vaillant sailed home to report to Paris. On the same day that he left Honolulu, Lord Edward Russell sailed in with the British man-of-war *Acteon*. Russell was a little less circumspect than the French. His purpose was to impose on Kamehameha III a treaty which would safeguard the interests of British subjects wishing to reside and trade in Hawaii. Kamehameha objected to the terms of the settlement, but promptly submitted on being assured that if he did not do so 'there was an end to a good understanding between the two Governments'.[19] Russell sailed away, and the clerics whom Kamehameha had wished to deport sailed back. Disregarding the assurances that he had given Vaillant, Kamehameha immediately ordered them to leave again. His renewed attempts to extirpate Catholicism and French influence were again frustrated by the arrival on 8 July 1837 of the British warship *Sulphur*, followed two days later by the French warship *Vénus*, commanded by Captain du Petit-Thouars.

The game of theological musical chairs continued. The British and

French warships forced Kamehameha to agree to let the clerics remain in Hawaii, on condition that they left at the first opportunity. This time it was the French who secured the extra bonus of a treaty allowing French citizens free right of entry and according them most-favoured-nation treatment. Kamehameha responded six months later by formally banning the practice or teaching of Roman Catholicism throughout his kingdom. The ball was back with the French.

But this time Kamehameha had gone too far. He had seriously underestimated the strength of the French. Napoleonic France had perforce left the world outside Europe relatively untroubled, but France of the Restoration and the July Monarchy was sweeping the high seas for prestige and profit. French armies had invaded Spain and North Africa; French naval squadrons had seized Vera Cruz and were blockading Buenos Aires; and in July 1828 instructions were sent from Paris to Captain Laplace of the frigate *Artémise* to visit Tahiti and Hawaii to 'make it well understood that it will be altogether to the advantage of the chiefs of these islands of the Ocean to conduct themselves in such a manner as not to incur the wrath of France'.[20] The death-sentence had been pronounced on Polynesian independence.

It was, of course, not simply the Kamehameha and Pomare dynasties with which the French were concerned. Their major fear was that the American missionaries in Hawaii and the British missionaries in Tahiti might in fact be seeking, under the pretext of religious zeal, 'to establish at those points in the Ocean the exclusive influence of their nations and to monopolize to their profit the commerce which can be carried on there'.[21] The fact that French commerce was not active in the Pacific only made it the more necessary to defend whatever French interests were involved there. From this point of view, the expulsion of two French missionaries from Tahiti in 1836, coupled with the theological tug-of-war raging in Hawaii, could only indicate that the Pacific islanders were not prepared to accord French authority the same respect that they accorded British and American. There were more tangible grounds for concern as well. The British obviously intended to close the continent of Australia against any foreign penetration. It was easy to imagine that they intended to do the same with the huge islands of New Zealand, provided only that one was prepared to attribute the most sinister and expansionist motives to British foreign policy, as the French of course were. James Busby had been sent from New South Wales to the Bay of Islands in 1833 to exercise the duties of British Resident. He had no effective authority, but he had taken direct action in 1835 to frustrate the ambitions of a singularly gullible French adventurer, Baron Charles de Thierry, who had appointed himself 'Sovereign Chief of New Zealand'. Busby encouraged thirty-five North Island chiefs to sign a declaration of independence to forestall any pretensions by de Thierry. De Thierry appealed repeatedly to the French Government, pointing out the advantages that New Zealand could provide as a base for French power in the Pacific. It was also unquestionable that British interest in New Zealand was multiplying: a drift from the Australian colonies to the far more congenial climate and fertile soil of the islands across the Tasman had been accelerating since 1833, due first to the discovery that whale oil could be gathered profitably and easily in Cook Strait, and afterwards to the apparent failure of the Western and South Australian settlements.[22] The white population of New Zealand had passed the thousand mark by 1838. The number was not perhaps impressive, except for the fact that it was made up almost entirely of people of British stock. This certainly helped to confirm the impression, already sufficiently clear in Paris, that the British were literally taking over the Pacific. Australia was wholly British; Sydney had already become a major city, and was by far the major outpost of European culture and commerce in the Pacific proper; and the number of visits to various islands by British warships to show the the flag and protect British interests far exceeded those made by the French or Americans. France accordingly acted to restore the balance; but, as in the eighteenth century, it acted just a little late..

The French lash fell first on Fiji. In October 1838, Dumont d'Urville led the corvettes *Astrolabe* and *Zélée* to Lakeba, seeking revenge for the massacre of the crew of the *Aimable Joséphine* four years before. It was really too late for justice, as the rebel chiefs of Bau who had been responsible for the massacre had themselves been put to death by Naulivou's heir, young Cakobau in 1837. The discerning Cakobau, however, saw the need to placate the formidable avengers. Verani of Viwa had been the chief most directly responsible. The Bauans accordingly guided the French to Viwa, having first warned the inhabitants to clear out; the French landed and burned an empty town, carrying off as token of their victory one singed pig; and the warlords of Bau had something else to laugh about in the years to come.

The French descent on Viwa would not have been comical if d'Urville and his men had found anybody to kill, but there was no comic relief to soften the impact on Tahiti when Cyrille Laplace brought his frigate *Artémise* to Tahiti, requiring Queen Pomare to grant complete freedom

of movement and worship to Roman Catholics. Laplace did not need to
use the force his instructions empowered him to employ, simply because
Pomare's authority was too weak anyway for her to be able to challenge
any outside pressure. Laplace then swept on to Hawaii. Arriving there
in July 1839, he demanded, under threat of immediate hostilities, complete freedom of worship for Roman Catholics, a salute to the French
flag from Honolulu's shore batteries, and payment of an indemnity of
20,000 Spanish dollars. To give symbolic point to the affair, Laplace
marched ashore with 120 marines and 60 sailors, all bearing arms, to
attend mass. In conclusion, he exacted a commercial treaty from
Kamehameha III, providing that 'no Frenchman accused of any crime
whatever shall be judged otherwise than by a jury composed of foreign
residents, proposed by the Consul of France'[23] and that French mer-
chandise should neither be prohibited nor subject to a duty of more
than 5 per cent.

Nobody could pretend to believe any more in the independence of
states whose legislators were intimidated by foreigners in this fashion.
The only question was which foreign power was going to take formal
possession of territories that no longer possessed any legal integrity.
British interests were presumably most clearly at stake, since commercial
enterprise in Tahiti had been developed overwhelmingly from New South
Wales, and Hawaii was more or less a British protectorate, even though
commercial development there was by now entirely American. However,
at the time, there were special reasons why the British Government and
in particular the Foreign Secretary Lord Palmerston, turned a blind eye
to French activity in Fiji, Tahiti and Hawaii. Fiji was no-man's-land;
Australian enterprise was turning its back on the Pacific, with the
opening of the Victorian hinterland; and the decision had already been
taken to steal a march on the French in New Zealand.[24]

The French Government was well aware of this. De Thierry had
been bombarding Paris with proposals for a French annexation of New
Zealand, but the French deliberately did nothing until after the British
had granted Edward G. Wakefield's New Zealand Company a charter
to colonize New Zealand as a private venture. They even waited until
the British Colonial Office had sent Captain William Hobson out to
treat with the Maoris for the recognition of British sovereignty over all
or part of New Zealand, after which he was to proclaim himself
Governor. The emigrant ship *Comte de Paris* and its escorting corvette
Aube left France at the same time that Hobson was securing the
signatures of the North Island chiefs to a treaty accepting Victoria as

their sovereign and himself as their Governor. Hobson then claimed British sovereignty over the South Island without waiting for signatures, and sovereignty was additionally declared over deserted Stewart Island, perforce without any signatures at all. New Zealand was well and truly annexed by the time the French ships arrived in July and August. Hobson's annexations had indeed been far more complete than the British authorities had bargained for : by an impressive error, the boundaries of the new colony had been drawn from 47° 10′ South to 34° 30′ North, 4,700 miles further north than intended, to include Fiji, New Caledonia, the New Hebrides, the Gilbert and Ellice Islands and the Marshalls.[25] A legal foundation had accidentally been provided for any future pretensions by New Zealand towards imperial domination of the South Pacific, if anybody prepared to take them seriously.

Nobody was disposed to be provocative at the time. The annexation had been carried out simply because it provided a welcome relief all round : the Australians were anxious for their expanding economic interests to be secured; the Maoris were partly in a state of shock from the impact of the wars and the accompanying depopulation, and partly concerned to develop their own commerce with the foreigners; and the Protestant missionaries were anxious to get the islands annexed by Britain, before they could be annexed by a French Government which would favour Roman Catholic proselytizers. In fact, the French Government had excellent reasons for not contesting British annexation : New Zealand was literally as far away from France as one could physically get; the islands could not possibly be defended against a British attack based on Australia; there was no significant French economic interest to be considered, any more than there was really anywhere else in the Pacific; and it was in accordance with international practice to expect that French forbearance over British designs on New Zealand would be requited by British forbearance over French designs on less conspicuous but more digestible islands in the area.

The Polynesian islands indeed fell like ninepins before foreign pressure over the next few years. Incongruously enough, the next manifestation of foreign domination took the form of a vigorous declaration of independence. The Laplace intervention had helped to convince American capitalists that they had to take some action to protect themselves from further incursions by the French Government in Hawaii. They had already effectively secured control over the internal affairs of the island. Then, on 8 October 1840, they persuaded Kamehameha III to establish a constitutional monarchy, under which law-making power was to be vested in a Council of Chiefs, including the king and the *kahina-nui*, and a representative body elected by the people. However, the King was also to have a cabinet of eight ministers to advise him. All were Americans. In 1841 Kamehameha signed a contract allowing the American firm of Ladd and Company to finance its operations through capital stock open 'to subscription to American, English and French capitalists',[26] the contract to be null and void unless the governments of the three countries concerned acknowledged the sovereignty of the Hawaiian Government. One of the partners of the firm, Peter A. Brinsmade, approached the American Secretary of State, Daniel Webster, in 1842, to sound out official United States thinking on Hawaiian independence. An official mission with plenipotentiary powers was despatched from Hawaii in the same year, consisting of Sir George Simpson, the Governor of the Hudson's Bay Company, the Reverend William Richards, the American 'chaplain, teacher and translator' to Kamehameha III, and the king's Hawaiian private secretary, Timothy Haalilio. Richards and Haalilio were to go to Washington and then meet up with Simpson in London, after which they would go in company to Paris. Richards had a trump card. The new British Foreign Secretary Lord Aberdeen had decided in October that while Britain should not seek a paramount influence in Hawaii 'no other Power should exercise a greater degree of influence [there] than that possessed by Great Britain.'[27] Richards could therefore credibly threaten Webster that he would place Hawaii under British protection unless he obtained the desired recognition of independence. Webster, congratulating Richards on the fact that 'Yankees are shrewd negotiators', agreed that the interests of all commercial nations required that the Hawaiian Government should not be interfered with by foreign powers; and that the United States were more interested in the fate of Hawaii and its Government than any other nation could be, simply because the great majority of ships visiting Hawaii belonged to the United States. Everything was discussed in uncomplicated commercial terms. Webster agreed to appoint a salaried consul in Hawaii as an indication that the United States recognized Yankee-guided Hawaii as an independent state. He did not consider that a formal treaty was necessary.

Nevertheless the manner in which Webster had chosen to recognize Hawaiian independence seemed to Lord Aberdeen reason why Britain should do the opposite. Aberdeen suggested that the United States were in fact trying to acquire colonies indirectly, by exerting an influence over the Hawaiian Government in favour of American interests and to the injury of British. Webster himself wrote to Everett, the American Ambassador, denying that the United States wished to exercise any undue influence in Hawaii, and hoping that no suspicion of a sinister purpose of any kind on the part of the United States would deter the British and French Governments 'from adopting the same pacific, just and conservative course towards ... this remote but interesting group of islands'.[28]

In the meantime, the plenipotentiaries had gone to France. There the Foreign Minister Guizot assured them without hesitation that France would grant them the desired recognition. In fact the Hawaiian mission arrived just after news had reached Guizot of the success of France's latest Polynesian venture. Abel du Petit-Thouars, now Rear-Admiral, had been briefly instructed to sail from Valparaiso in France's most impressive warship, the *Reine Blanche*, and seize the Marquesas. He was able to do so at first in May 1842 without any difficulty, by giving presents to some chiefs and assuring others that he would protect them from any vengeance they might have incurred by plundering an American whaler. However, resistance broke out when the Marquesans realized what had happened and the French were forced to establish blockhouses to maintain their colonial presence.

There was, of course, no material French interest to justify the seizure. The significance of the Marquesas lay solely in the fact that they provided harbours from which French naval power could be exercised in the Pacific without fear of observation by the British. But the Marquesas were only the beginning of French compensation for the loss of New Zealand. While du Petit-Thouars was subduing the Marquesans with the pride of the French Navy, d'Urville in the corvette *Aube* was visiting Tahiti, partly to check up on the treatment accorded French priests and traders by the latest representative of the Pomare dynasty, Queen Pomare Vahine IV. This lady was the daughter of the Christian but debased Pomare II, and successor to her brother, Pomare III, who had died in 1827 at the age of seven.[29] The real reason for d'Urville's presence was that a number of chiefs opposed to the Pomare line had apparently invited French intervention to avert an unspecified 'deceitful plot against us'.[30] Textual evidence suggests that the appeal had in fact been written for them by a Frenchman. It did not really matter. The French knew what they were doing. Admiral Buglet wrote to Queen Pomare assuring her that France had no intention of seizing her possessions, and that the *Aube* was there only as a demonstration of the goodwill of the Orléans Monarchy. Meanwhile, d'Urville heard the usual complaints from the French residents. Du Petit-Thouars arrived in September 1842 in the *Reine Blanche*, trained her sixty guns on Papeete, and demanded payment of an indemnity of 10,000 Spanish dollars within forty-eight hours, on penalty of French occupation of the strategic points of the island. Queen Pomare was in no condition to deal with the situation, as she was about to give birth; the French residents were not going to pay an indemnity to stop the island from becoming French; and the same chiefs who had signed the remonstrance seeking French intervention now invited du Petit-Thouars to establish a protectorate over the group.

Island after island accepted French protection and the Tricolour. The islet of Wallis on central Oceania was next, in November 1842. The mission station of Futuna succumbed at about the same time. But the French were after far bigger game. Du Petit-Thouars detached Captain Laferrière in the *Bucéphale* to land some Roman Catholic missionaries on the huge and quite unknown island of New Caledonia. During his visit, Laferrière managed to induce fourteen local chiefs to acknowledge the sovereignty of Louis Philippe over the island. French commercial and territorial presence in the Pacific was still minuscule compared with British, but strategically the French were making impressive gains.

It was thus not surprising that the Foreign Minister Guizot should have been perfectly happy to recognize the independence of Hawaii, once assured that Tahiti at least would never be anything except French. However, events had overtaken the negotiators. The balance had been upset again. Lord George Paulet arrived in Honolulu in the frigate *Carysfort* in February 1843 in the middle of violent legal disputes between a number of British residents, including the consul Richard Charlton, and the Hawaiian Government. The self-appointed British acting-consul, Alexander Simpson, coincidentally a cousin of Sir George Simpson, whom he detested, appealed to Paulet to take steps to defend British interests. Paulet did so, by demanding that 'fair steps' should be adopted to arrange disputes involving British subjects, and that Kamehameha III should recognize Simpson as acting-consul in Charlton's absence. Relying on Paulet's support, Simpson presented new demands, including one for an indemnity of 100,000 Spanish dollars. Kamehameha III then gave the game away : he offered Hawaii to the British, doubtless hoping that they might some day decide to give it back. For the second time, Hawaii was provisionally ceded to Great Britain The British flag was hoisted over Honolulu on the very day on which Kamehameha I had granted the deed of cession to Vancouver, forty-nine years before. A 'Queen's Regiment' of native soldiers was organized; laws against fornication, introduced in deference to the sentiments of American missionaries, were abrogated; and the three schooners possessed by the former Hawaiian Government had their native names changed to *Victoria, Albert* and *Adelaide*. Hawaii was British.

It remained so for only five months. On 26 July, Paulet's commanding officer, Rear-Admiral Thomas, arrived from Valparaiso in the frigate *Dublin*; revoked the deed of cession, in the conviction that this would be the desire of the British Government, which had not yet had time to send him instructions; and formally recognized Kamehameha III as an independent sovereign. The British flag was hauled down; the Hawaiian flag was hoisted; and Hawaii belonged to itself again, or more accurately, to the representatives of American business interests advising Kamehameha III.

Events entirely outside their control had thus conspired to make the Richards-Simpson-Haalilio mission a success, apart from the fact that Haalilio died on the return voyage. The British and French were not prepared to quarrel with each other over Hawaii, and the Americans lacked the power to quarrel with either. They were all three prepared to leave the Group to its own devices, as the safest means of ensuring that it would fall under the authority of none of them.

Anglo-French relations were in any case more strained than either government found convenient as a result of the French protectorate over Tahiti. The chiefs were still no more united in affection for the Pomare dynasty than they were before. They were, however, becoming increasingly at one in their resentment of the French intervention. The situation was exacerbated by the arrival from New South Wales in 1836 of the new British consul, the Francophobe George Pritchard, sent to investigate the situation. Pomare herself began to appeal to the British in Sydney to restore the authority the French had taken from her. There being a reasonable expectation that the French Government would no more ratify the action taken by du Petit-Thouars than French, British or Spanish Governments had ratified similar actions by zealous servants in the past, Pritchard continued to recognize Queen Pomare as sovereign, disregarding the French officials left behind by du Petit-Thouars. All that this achieved was to make matters worse: du Petit-Thouars returned to Tahiti in 1843, having learned that the protectorate had been ratified by the Government in Paris, and hoisted the French flag over all the important points on the island. Queen Pomare appealed once more to be relieved of the protectorate. However, du Petit-Thouars, believing that his government would have preferred an out-and-out annexation in the first place, declared Pomare deposed, confiscated her property, and took possession of the island in the name of King Louis Philippe of France.

This was a showdown. Pritchard struck his flag; the terrified Queen fled for protection to a British warship; and the captain forwarded to France her appeals against du Petit-Thouars's latest move. Improbably enough, Pritchard had guessed right. The race for bases between Britain and France had developed to a point at which war would be difficult to avert, and this at a time when Louis Philippe was actually hoping to achieve a *détente* by visiting Queen Victoria. Equity, of course, could not begin to enter into the situation : nobody could deny that the occupation of Australia and New Zealand had given the British control over territory and resources far greater than would be available in all the rest of the Pacific lumped together. This was already fully appreciated in Sydney, where speakers at public meetings as well as in the Legislative Council were pretending to act as the consciences of the British people, calling on Great Britain not to back down before the challenge of France.[31] On the other hand, it could have been said that British territorial holdings in the Pacific were only commensurate with the vast preponderance of British material interests; that no other country had been able to establish any significant prior right to either Australia or New Zealand; that the British Government had twice renounced possession of Hawaii, where British interests were second only to American; that France had already collected New Caledonia and assorted islets as compensation for New Zealand; that British economic interests were overwhelmingly predominant in Tahiti, and Cook and Wallis had established substantial prior rights of possession; and that British public and official opinion was exasperated by French depredations in Latin America and North Africa, all the more so because these had as usual followed earnest assurances that nothing of the kind was about to happen. All in all, it was the turn of Paris to withdraw its arm. Guizot decided not to ratify the annexation, and the protectorate relationship was restored.

All this shilly-shallying was not agreeable to the more enthusiastic of the British colonists in Australia and New Zealand. Spokesmen for the New Zealand Company had referred as early as 1841 to New Zealand as a predestined Britain of the South, the hub of its own empire. Sydney merchants had proposed that a colony complete in all respects should be established in New Caledonia to checkmate Laferrière's claims for France. They similarly began to favour the colonization of fertile and comparatively peaceful Samoa, as soon as it was learned in 1845 that Roman Catholic missionaries had arrived there, thus providing an excuse for French intervention.

These Australasian pretensions were symptomatic of the weaknesses of the big British colonies, rather than of any real hopes they might have had for the future. Geographical remoteness was apparently already having its effects. The New Zealanders, like other island peoples, were simply losing touch with the realities of the world outside. They were becoming not unlike the Samoans, who were to explain to Sir Peter Buck that the human race might have started in the Garden of Eden, but the Samoans had always lived in Samoa. It was, of course, relatively simple for a euphoric colonial journalist or politician to overlook the fundamental differences between what Britain was and what New Zealand could ever possibly be. The resemblances were obvious, if specious : they were both island communities, of about the same size, and in very similar locations in their respective hemispheres. The very simple difference was that Britain was a great European nation, barely twenty miles off the coast of the continent to which it belonged, while New Zealand was 1,500 miles away from anywhere. Its white population was still tiny even by Pacific island standards. It was impossible in practical terms to imagine how New Zealand could ever acquire a population large enough to defend itself against any existing power remotely interested in the Pacific islands, let alone defend the island dependencies which New Zealanders were already interested in acquiring. The newspaper *Southern Cross* nonetheless looked forward in 1844 to 'the onward march of civilization over and through the vast extent of the Great South Seas'.[32] Its prophecy was in fact not wholly ill-founded : there was plenty of marching in progress or threatened in the Pacific already, though the presence of civilization would have been hard to detect in the manoeuvres taking place. Every motive for expansion was present : organized religion, commercial enterprise, racism, greed, political ambition, diplomatic prestige, strategic preoccupations. In Hawaii, yet another exploratory French bid for annexation had been headed off by the United States in 1843, with the tacit approval of the British, who hastened to conclude a commercial treaty with Hawaii in the following year. This Hawaiian merry-go-round could hardly go on for ever : the British, French and Americans might be content for the time being to respect the formal independence of the island kingdom, since a takeover attempt by any of them would provoke an unwanted crisis; but every month that the British and French withheld their hands from Hawaii only helped to guarantee that it would eventually fall under American political domination, as it had already fallen under American commercial domination. Nothing could indeed check this, short of a successful war by a European power against the United States, or the break-up of the American Union itself : the monstrous growth of the former British colonies had already outstripped the remaining British presence in the Americas, had already achieved predominant influence in Latin America, and would at some time gain control of resources and numbers which would enable the United States to challenge the powers of Europe and Asia.

But the American shadow did not yet extend further south or west than Hawaii. It was the French who were the most obvious menace to Polynesian independence in the South Pacific. In 1844 French Marist missionaries began to arrive in Fiji. The Tongans appealed to the Governor of New Zealand to extend British protection over their kingdom. The appeal was unsuccessful. In 1845 the Catholic Church set up mission stations in Samoa. Its arrival coincided with that of the adventurous German firm of Johann Godeffroys of Hamburg. Apparently unconcerned, the British Government prepared to discourage New Zealand imperial ambitions by framing the Act providing for a government of New Zealand in such a way as to correct the weird geographical errors of November 1840. But the British colonists were themselves beginning to provide one of the most serious of all challenges to the continued existence of the island peoples. One of the major problems facing European colonists in tropical territories had always been to persuade the native population to do their work for them in the way in which they wanted it done. There were indeed places where the problem hardly arose : India and New Zealand, for example, had large, long-established and sophisticated populations producing eminently marketable commodities which they were fully able and willing to make available to the Europeans on a more or less rational market basis. In other cases, such as in South Africa or the Americas, it was practicable to ignore, exterminate or expel the native populations, because the climate and conditions were such that Europeans could undertake the labour of production themselves. However, there were other territories where Europeans found the climate too enervating to encourage them to work themselves, and where the native population simply could not be induced to work profitably for their overlords either. The preferred answer to this problem had been the slave trade. Basically, this involved finding people who were accustomed to farm labour in hot climates and transporting them under conditions of servitude to European-owned plantations. It was, of course, officially no longer legal, but business enterprise will always produce a commodity to meet a demand. The Australian climate was certainly often most uncomfortable for Europeans to work in, and the Australian Aborigines could not be induced to settle down to routine plantation labour; so enterprising squatters in New South Wales began to import Melanesian islanders as station-hands, at an average wage of £2 per year.

It was obviously going to be a difficult business. The Polynesians, who were both experienced, if not always enterprising, agriculturists, and sophisticated by European standards, were not going to be induced to work in outback New South Wales or the Queensland canefields for anything that their putative owners would be prepared to pay them. Melanesians, on the other hand, living on generally far less favoured islands and without Polynesian experience of European ways, could more easily be lured into the Australian colonies. But not all Melanesians were safe to approach, even with the best intentions: in 1847 the New Caledonians massacred every missionary they could catch and forced the rest to flee the island. This, of course, was bound to bring the French back, and the British Government was duly bombarded with requests from Pacific island potentates seeking British protection, as well as offers by the New Zealand Government to take on the job. The Reverend Walter Lawry hastened from New Zealand to Tonga and Fiji and persuaded both Tupou and Cakobau to seek New Zealand protection. The New Zealand Governor, Sir George Grey, urged that the British Colonial Office should consider annexing both island groups, and asked further that a British warship should be sent on a goodwill visit to Samoa to forestall any French ambitions there. Meanwhile, Bishop Selwyn founded a Melanesian Mission in Auckland, to prepare to extend New Zealand-based Anglican ecclesiastical influence over the rest of the South Pacific. Selwyn indeed had gone so far as to visit New Caledonia after the massacre of the Catholics, accompanied by the Australian Captain Erskine.

So the race was on again. Selwyn's visit had genuinely alarmed the French, ever ready to believe that there were no limits to British rapacity. Once again the Tricolour swept over the Pacific. Two French warships descended on Hawaii, and French landing parties continued to loot, burn and destroy until the shattered Hawaiians reaffirmed the sub-

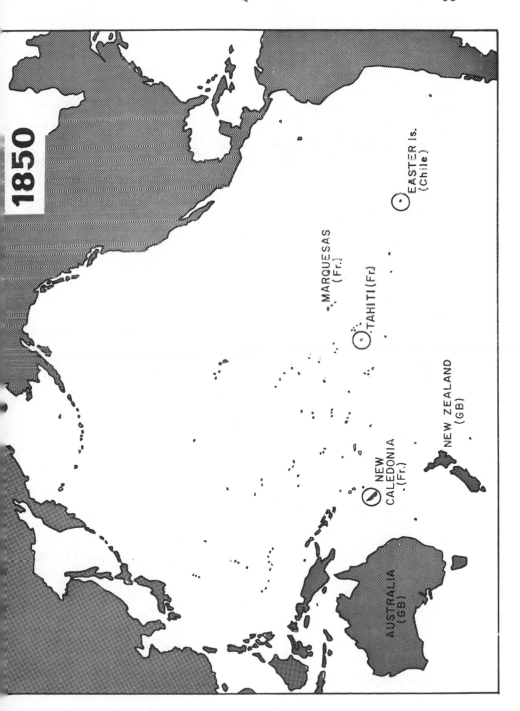

missions they had made to Laplace ten years earlier. Plans began to be formulated in Paris to develop Tahiti as a penal colony, in spite of the vehement and singularly hypocritical protests of the British, who had only stopped using New South Wales in the same way nine years before, were still sending convicts to Tasmania, and were to continue transportation to Western Australia until 1868. Nobody could have taken the British objections seriously. In any case, the new regime of Louis Napoleon was of a kind which could be counted on to produce an annual crop of political prisoners, whom it would naturally wish to deport as far away from France as possible. The only real question was whether it would be to Tahiti or New Caledonia.

French influence in the South Pacific was therefore certain to expand, provoked to some degree by the wild ambitions of Australian and New Zealand clerics and colonial administrators. Meanwhile, a sudden and unpredictable shift in power among the island peoples themselves was about to take place and to render the situation still more uncertain. Cakobau of Bau could now deploy probably the largest land and sea forces ever available to any island ruler. In 1849 he set off against Verata with no less than 129 huge canoes, the best vessels in the biggest fleet in the Pacific. Unfortunately, the Bauans' efficiency matched neither their technology nor their numbers. The campaign broke down; a storm disorganized the Bauan forces; and Cakobau retired baffled. This indeed was becoming his normal experience. The tyrant of Bau was finding it impossible to force his subjects to pay tribute. Tyranny was becoming distinctly unprofitable. Cakobau appreciated that one of the main unifying elements among the anti-Bauan groups, apart from the all-important reluctance to pay up, was Christianity. He accordingly declared war against Christianity in 1850. This campaign did not succeed either. Nevertheless, when Cakobau succeeded to a throne of increasingly dubious value in 1852, on the death of the scruffy and senile old Tanoa, he promptly organized another mighty fleet of eighty canoes carrying 12,000 warriors against the Macuata tribes, who had just eaten their Bauan governor. A Macuatan war-canoe was captured and its crew of thirty cooked and eaten; but Macuata itself remained inviolate and unpaying.

The example of these fiascos naturally induced other coastal tribes to desert the Bauan empire and defy Cakobau. This was hardly surprising, but it had implications which went beyond the shores of Fiji itself. The Bauan tyranny had imposed a partial system of order on Fiji, which had perhaps helped to maintain its independence: Europeans were content to leave a moderately effective native imperium alone, especially if it was both corrupt and ferocious. The collapse of Bau on the other hand could only lead to chaos in Fiji, which would benefit nobody.

The Tongans were only too aware of this situation. The first imperialists of the Pacific were about to enter the power game again, extending their authority into Fijian affairs in an extraordinary reversal of national roles. Anarchy in Tonga had given way to relative calm by the mid-century. Tupou-toa, the murderer of Tupou Niua and effective warlord of Tonga, had died in 1820. He was succeeded by his son, the immensely able and discreet Taufa'ahau, who was also approved as Tupou-toa's successor by Finau IV of Vava'u. Tongatapu itself remained independent and in chaos, but by 1833 Taufa'ahau had united the rest of the group under his rule as King George Tupou I. Taufa'ahau had shown his practical wisdom in 1837, when he despatched young Prince Ma'afu, whose claim to the throne of a united Tonga was about as reasonable as his own, to take command of the Tongan community in Fiji, whose numbers had increased considerably during the Tongan 'Time of Troubles'. This at the same time appeased Ma'afu by enabling him to set himself up as a virtually independent chief in his own right, and also assured some control over a large and potentially dangerous group of émigrés. Ma'afu proved to be an ideal choice. His royal lineage, personal *mana* and superb diplomacy soon persuaded the Tongans in Fiji to accept him as their national leader. This, of course, created a new situation. The Tongan émigrés had already become a problem with which the Fijians, divided as they were now among the Bauan tyrants, their opponents and the utterly disorderly tribes of the interior, were quite unable to deal. Tongans in Fiji had always loafed, swaggered, brawled and thieved, but this had not been a serious matter before, because the Fijians appreciated these forms of behaviour, and because there had never been very many Tongans in Fiji at any one time. But the Tongans were now numerous, organized and led by a leader on all the evidence more competent than Cakobau himself. Ma'afu gradually and discreetly began to extend Tongan authority along the coast, drawing on the allegiance of the anti-Bauan groups. His position was strengthened still further when King George Tupou, having brought the civil war in Tongatapu to an end at last, began to despatch Tongan preachers to Fiji to spread Christianity and Tongan influence. The religion which the European imperialists had brought to the Pacific was now serving the ends of the oldest native imperialism. In 1835 George Tupou made his boldest move. He visited the desperate Cakobau en route to Sydney, expressed his concern over the situation in Bau and its dominions, and suggested in the most indirect way possible that Tonga might be prepared to help the Bauans do what they seemed unable to do for themselves.

Another unsuccessful campaign, this time against Kaba, helped to make Cakobau even more receptive when the Tongan king visited him again on his return from Sydney. George Tupou told Cakobau casually how the United States commercial agent Williams had spoken of the desirability of civilized men getting together to wipe Bau from the face of the earth, a task which in his opinion a single warship could accomplish in the time it took a man to smoke a good cigar. Tupou suggested that one way out might be for Cakobau to become Christian. The tyrant of Bau saw the theological issue clearly. To remain true to the faith of his ancestors would mean getting blown to pieces by European gunnery; becoming Christian would mean that the Europeans might tolerate him a little longer, and might also secure him Tongan assistance in murdering his victims. Christianity triumphed, and the new faith became known throughout Fiji as the Faith of Cakobau.

In fact this apostasy gave other Fijians further reason to unite against Cakobau. Fijian traditionalists joined with political rivals and simple enemies of Bau to resist the tyrant. But the tyrant now had allies. Thirty large canoes sailed under George Tupou's command to Lakeba, with 2,000 warriors. They were there joined by Ma'afu, with another nine canoes and 1,000 more fighting men. In company with 2,000 Bauans, who had literally come along for the meal, they assaulted the rebel stronghold of Kaba. Fijians on both sides, observing that the Tongans attacked in disciplined ranks and actually kept on attacking even after some of them had been hurt, contrary to accustomed Fijian practice, concluded that the newcomers were gods and not men and left them to it. Organized resistance to Bau had been broken.

But it had been broken by the Tongans, and broken only to establish a basis for Tongan control over the Fiji group. Ma'afu now established himself at Lomaloma, took possession of Vanua Balavu and began waging aggressive wars in Vanua Levu, allegedly in defence of Christianity. Cakobau's situation was desperate. It was not merely that the Tongans, whom he had appealed to to protect his empire, were now dispossessing him of it. He was also in debt to the United States to the tune of some $45,000, representing the value of articles of war and luxury which he had obtained from American traders in return for promises of land which he did not possess or had been unable to deliver. Nor was it a propitious time for native potentates to become involved with foreigners. Annexation was in the air again. The obvious determination of Louis Napoleon to seize New Caledonia had panicked the easily-panicked Australians and New Zealanders. Sir George Grey insisted that New Zealand had a claim to New Caledonia under the terms of the Treaty of Waitangi. He suggested as a further precaution against expansion by France that 4,000 Maoris should be sent to occupy Tahiti as fellow-Polynesians and British subjects. But attempts to represent New Zealand, with its European population of 28,000, as the Britain of the South Seas were received sympathetically neither in London, where the British Government was concerned with establishing an understanding with France to counter possible Russian moves in the Near East, nor in Sydney, where the New Zealanders were told that the British and French Governments would have to be left to settle their colonial problems themselves. The French indeed settled the problem their own way in 1853 by annexing both New Caledonia and the Isle of Pines. However, the crisis with Russia had by that time brought Britain and France effectively together, and the Australians at least had transferred their anxieties from French ambitions in the South Pacific to Russian and American domination in the North. Australia could always find some foreign threat to worry about.

So could Cakobau. The French occupation of New Caledonia was characteristically unabashed. The huge island represented the only French colony apart from Algeria where ordinary Frenchmen could be expected to farm and settle. The French colonial administration duly set aside one-tenth of the mountainous and unwelcoming interior of the island as a reserve for the original inhabitants, estimated to number about 100,000, and proceeded to chase them into it. Meanwhile, American warships tended to visit Fiji, and inquire about the state of Cakobau's finances. Other Europeans arrested and hanged a Bauan chief, merely for having murdered, dismembered and eaten his wife. Independence had become an empty dream.

Cakobau was not beaten yet, however. Affairs in Fiji had clearly reached a stage at which the British Government could not refrain from taking some interest. William Pritchard was appointed British Consul for the Group in 1857. The frantic Cakobau saw a way out. He persuaded the responsive Pritchard to draw up a deed of cession under which Fiji would pass to the British Crown, in return for the Imperial Government's discharging the American claim for $45,000. It was not, however, going to be so easy. Cakobau had described himself in the deed as 'Chief of Bau and its dependencies' and as possessing 'full and exclusive sovereignty and dominion'[33] throughout the group. This, at least, was very obviously not true. It was also bitterly challenged by the Tongans, both George Tupou and Ma'afu, who correctly saw Cakobau's acceptance of British sovereignty as simply a means of avoiding having to accept Tongan sovereignty. George Tupou was said, with some exaggeration, to be 'dead with crying because of the cession'.[34] Ma'afu promptly set off on another campaign of conquest to seize as much of Fiji as possible before the cession could be ratified. He invaded Macuata, subdued Beqa and Kadavu, and appeared with his fleet off Bau itself. Pritchard intervened at this stage. The situation was not simple : Cakobau was appealing for British protection, on the grounds that most of his allies and half the Fiji Group had been conquered by the Tongans, who were thus possessing themselves of land which had been ceded to Britain; while Ma'afu, insisting that he was merely educating the Fijians in correct religious and political behaviour, suggested that he could run Fiji himself in a manner far more satisfactory to Europeans than the 'old savage' in Bau. Pritchard compromised by persuading Ma'afu under the guns of the British warship *Elk* to renounce all political claims to Fiji, which Pritchard himself would attempt to govern for the time being. George Tupou meantime hedged his bets by appealing to Queen Victoria for a treaty of commerce and amity between Tonga and Britain, as well as a British guarantee of Tongan independence, which at the time hardly seemed to be threatened by anybody.

At the best of times the British would hardly have wanted to take Fiji. Recent events made certain that they would not accept it as a gift. Pritchard was sharply censured for his pretentions to extra-consular powers and the very notion of cession was rejected. The fact was that the British already had extremely grave native problems on their hands. Relations between whites and Maoris had come to a crisis in New Zealand, just twenty years after the signing of the Treaty of Waitangi. The Maoris had signed the Treaty in something like a state of shock, trusting that it would somehow secure them in the possession of their own land. This would have been difficult at any time to reconcile with the inevitable settler demands for more territory. The situation was also complicated beyond measure by the fact that land was traditionally held by the Maoris as a perpetual trust for all members of the tribe. It was thus often impossible for a European lawyer to discover who actually owned the land and was therefore legally entitled to sell it. European duplicity and Polynesian greed were of course not to be baulked : land was sold to the settlers with appalling speed, whether anything like a clear or acceptable title could be proved or not. Moreover, the Maoris had no satisfactory means of seeking redress politically. Under the constitution of 1852, the Maoris, who provided half the revenue of the colony, were largely excluded from voting by the provision that tenure of land under traditional Maori law did not give the right to vote. Less than a hundred Maoris voted in Auckland at a time when the white population numbered 28,000. The position was confirmed by a decision of the British Government in 1859 that Maoris would not be eligible to vote unless they actually held land under a European title.

The Maoris had already begun to take counsel of despair. In 1858 the Waikato and Taupon tribes joined in a movement to establish a Maori king or land protector, in whom would be vested the sole right to dispose of Maori lands. The New Zealand authorities nonetheless were unwilling to deny the right to sell land to any Maori or group of Maoris who had a title acceptable in European terms. The first clash came in Waitara in the North Island in 1858; by 1860 war was raging in Taranaki and 400 Imperial soldiers had been brought over from Australia with three warships to assist the New Zealanders. It was a humiliating situation for the Britain of the South Seas.

It also added a new element to the Fijian imbroglio. The outbreak of war in New Zealand helped to confirm the British Government in its view that it did not need any more small, clamorous groups of colonists at the other end of the world, unable to cope with their own problems and unwilling to pay adequately to have them solved by Britain. On the other hand, the war in New Zealand was inducing more and more colonists to move to Fiji, in company with Australians who had found the hardships of life in New South Wales and Victoria sufficient reason to try their luck in another of the 'islands whose useless luxuriance is waiting the advent of our race'.[35] A dominant white settler community was accordingly likely to be established, which would lead eventually to annexation just as surely as a similar development on a far larger scale in Hawaii could be expected to have that result. But there was a factor present in Fijian politics which did not apply in Hawaii. In spite of having already renounced all political ambitions in Fiji, Ma'afu decided in 1861 to launch another assault against the power of Bau. He was supported by George Tupou, who now demanded that Cakobau pay him $60,000 for services rendered in the war against Kaba. Ma'afu was deterred temporarily when the French corvette *Cornélie* arrived and demanded the arrest and trial of one of his most formidable chieftains, Semisi, on the grounds that he had flogged and otherwise ill-treated Roman Catholics. Semisi was carted off by the French to hard labour in New Caledonia, and Cakobau was granted a respite while the Tongans again considered among themselves how far they could go without provoking European intervention. George Tupou claimed openly that it was as right for Tonga to rule part at least of Fiji as it was for France to rule Tahiti and Britain to rule India and New Zealand. On the other hand, there were now several hundred Europeans in Fiji, who might object to being disturbed by Tongan invasions; and there was still the question of Cakobau's debts, which he was even less likely to be able to repay if his dominions were entirely snatched from him by the Tongans. George Tupou's position was clear enough : Tongan authority should be extended over Fiji at the earliest opportunity, but only as far as this could be done without risking a collision with the Europeans. Ma'afu was summoned to a meeting of the Tongan parliament in 1862 to co-ordinate plans. His views were, of course, basically the same as George Tupou's; nevertheless he professed a desire to settle down and enjoy a peaceful life, and retired to Vanua Levu as a judge on a stipend of £80 a year. But it was one thing to renounce territorial ambitions in Fiji when at home in Tonga, and quite another when the spoils were within reach of one's hand; Ma'afu was no sooner back in Fiji than he began planning again to dispossess Cakobau. Nor was George Tupou any less ambitious. In 1863 he sent commissioners to enquire into Tongan claims to land in Fiji. The territories in question comprised all Lau and Rambi, Taveuni, all the coastal chiefdoms of Vanua Levu, the Yasawas, Beqa and Nadroga : had George Tupou's claims been met it would have meant an extension of Tongan authority over nearly all the peripheral islands of the Group, as well as the western coast of Viti Levu and the eastern coast of Vanua Levu. It would also have demonstrated Cakobau's total helplessness to resist any other demands the Tongans might care to make.

But Cakobau was lucky again. The United States threatened to hold Tonga responsible for Cakobau's debts if he were prevented from paying them by Tongan incursions. George Tupou and Ma'afu compromised, and the Tongan king was content with Moala, Matuku, Vanua Levu, and Rambi, while Ma'afu was formally established as governor of the Tongan possessions in Fiji, with his headquarters at Lomaloma.

This arrangement was not likely to be permanent. Cakobau was still hoping that the Tongans would eventually go away and leave him to exploit Fiji in peace. Bau indeed was still the major Fijian metropolis, and Cakobau himself the predominant chief in the Group, apart from Ma'afu. The Tongans for their part had reason enough to believe that it might not be convenient for long to maintain an empire in Fiji. European interference in the Pacific was reaching perhaps its most violent and destructive stage. Having massacred between 2,000 and 3,000 of their native population since 1840, the Australians had decided to develop the practice of importing natives from the Pacific islands to work in the heat and humidity of Queensland. Other British settlers in Natal, in South Africa, had found a solution to their labour problem by entering into an arrangement with the government of India to bring over indentured Indian labourers; 100,000 Indians had been moved to South Africa in this way by 1890. The Australians had considered the same idea, but had decided against it when the British Government had insisted that Australia should pay the salary of an emigration officer in India, who would be responsible for selecting suitable candidates for Queensland. The enterprising Sydney trader, Captain Robert Towns, instead sent the schooner *Don Juan* to persuade Pacific islanders to work in Australia at a wage of 10 shillings per month, with the assurance that they would be returned to their homes after a year.

Towns himself was insistent that no force should be used in this enterprise : natives were to be freely hired, not shanghaied. Obviously the Kanakas thus brought back to Australia could have no idea in the world what they were letting themselves in for. On the other hand, they did go on board the blackbirders' schooners as technically free men; and most of those who were returned to their island homes seemed to feel that they had gained in wealth and prestige over their less-travelled compatriots, who had not seen the world and earned the white man's money. Certainly, they appear to have found the work sufficiently familiar and the conditions sufficiently congenial during their exile; and there was also from time to time the additional and enjoyable excitement of joining their white bosses in a weekend massacre of the local Aborigines, as on the Bellenden Plains in 1868. Life in Queensland was not too different from the New Hebrides or inland Fiji : the Kanakas do not seem to have experienced much visible cultural shock.

This was not the case with the communities from which the blackbirders did their recruiting. Inevitable clashes occurred between those tribes who were prepared to co-operate and those who resented any foreign interference, as well as between the latter and the blackbirders themselves. Community ways of life were disrupted by the departure of able-bodied men and their subsequent return as discontented *déracinés*.

The numbers were not large, considering the total population of the Pacific islands : some 2,017 Kanakas had been taken to Queensland by 1868, and 2,500 to Hawaii by 1885. However, the blackbirders necessarily took their recruits from available coastal communities, where the effect of the population loss was often enormous; and the situation was made far more serious by the ferocious depredations of the Chileans and Peruvians, uninhibited by any of Captain Towns's concern for the appearance, at least, of fair dealing. Their victory over Spain in the war of 1863 had awakened the Andean republics to a sense of the importance of sea power, and to the fact that the eastern islands of the South Pacific lay at their mercy. Chile had also acquired the nucleus of what was to become over the next twenty years one of the really efficient navies of the world and the most formidable fleet actually operating in the South Pacific. By 1864, Chilean and Peruvian blackbirders were operating as far west as Tahiti itself; the French had intervened to check their depredations in Gambier and the Pomutus; they had lifted 280 people in one sweep from the Penrhyn Islands; and they had virtually destroyed the culture of Easter Island by removing 1,000 people to suffer in the mines of the Andes.

Meanwhile in New Zealand what had been once the second largest Polynesian community in the Pacific was rapidly declining. Notwithstanding frantic appeals by Governor Sir George Grey for troops from all the Australian colonies, as well as for Sikhs from India, the Maori Wars had been a singularly limited affair, fought with remarkable mutual regard and with remarkably small loss of life. It was, of course, the case that where personal honour was not too seriously involved, Polynesian battles were never traditionally fought to the finish. Nor, except possibly in the Tongan conquests in Fiji, were they fought as part of a co-ordinated plan of campaign. Maori resistance was thus essentially a matter of local, isolated stands by individual tribes, in their own fortified villages, which were simply abandoned when the soldiers could no longer be kept out. The horrors of storm and sack were thus generally avoided. Such tactics certainly prolonged the war, because the Maoris could usually get away to fight again, but they meant that the colonial authorities were not seriously challenged by an enemy who never united sufficiently to gain even local superiority. In any event, the population balance had now swung overwhelmingly against the Maoris. Some New Zealanders certainly decamped to Fiji, where rivalry between Bauan and Tongan imperialists, and the respect both showed for European gunnery, ensured that white settlers would be left in safety. But far more immigrants poured into the colony. At least 5,000 entered as military settlers, attracted by promises from New Zealand provincial governments of up to fifty acres as a free gift, on the clear understanding that the political power of the Maoris would be finally broken. A far greater increase, however, came as a result of the fortuitous discoveries of gold on the west coast of South Island in 1864 and in the Thames Valley in the North Island in 1867. By the end of that year, the white population had indeed risen to 219,000, an increase of 300 per cent on the figure for three years earlier. The Maori population had declined in the meantime to 38,500, a fall of 30 per cent.

This enormous demographic change had striking consequences. The economic development of the colony since 1840 had been largely in Maori hands. The Maoris had done most of the felling of timber, most of the building of houses, most of the construction of roads. They had also produced most of the food for the settlers. Maoris owned dozens of flour mills and had virtually a monopoly of coastal shipping trade around the North Island. In the middle 1850s, proportionately more Maoris than Europeans could read and write. Numerically, as well as economically, they were the dominant people until about 1858. The Maori Wars changed all this. The wars were about the land issue, and the land issue was settled in the eyes of the Europeans by the Native Land Acts of 1862 and 1867. As early as 1863, the New Zealand Attorney-General had considered that the Treaty of Waitangi could be disregarded as a guarantee of Maori land rights, claiming that legislation should always prevail over the Treaty. Doubts were raised, not altogether without foundation, as to whether the Treaty could be regarded as having legal force at all. Force solved the legal issue in any case. Three million acres of land in all were confiscated during the wars. The British Government had attempted to restrain the colonists, by ruling that land could be confiscated from rebels but could not be taken simply as compensation for the costs of the wars. The New Zealanders got round this by simply extending the concept of rebellion. Tribes who took up arms against the government naturally forfeited their land. But so did tribes whom the government considered as having failed to co-operate in the appropriate manner. But this was only the beginning. The amended Act of 1867 attempted deliberately to destroy the whole distinctive nature of Maori society by enforcing the individualization of titles to land. It was assumed that by this means the traditional Maori community system would be destroyed; Maori social status would become assimilated to European; and a defeated and seemingly dying race would become absorbed into an expanding European society. With the economic basis of their society destroyed, it was deemed safe to extend full political rights to the Maoris. The 'worst act of injustice ever perpetrated by a New Zealand Government'[36] made it feasible for the same government to perform a striking act of justice. In 1867 the Maori Representation Act granted full manhood suffrage to the surviving Maori population, at a time when such political privileges had not yet been granted to white New Zealanders. Indeed, Maoris who temporarily held land under both traditional and European titles found themselves favoured for a while with two votes. Four Maori seats were created in Parliament, three in the North Island and one in the South. Even the sudden outbreak of civilian massacres in the still-continuing Maori Wars did not seriously interrupt these efforts to ease the last years of a dying race. Committees to organize village schools for the Maoris were initiated in 1871, the year in which fighting effectively stopped after possibly 1,000 Europeans and 2,000 Maoris had been killed; and half of the three million acres confiscated were returned eventually to the Maoris. It must, of course, be noted that instruction in the Maori schools had to be in English, and that schools were provided at all only if the Maoris were prepared to pay half the cost of constructing the school and a quarter of the teacher's salary, which few of the impoverished Maori communities were in a position to do; and the land was returned to the Maoris in the confident expectation that it would fall back into European hands soon enough. The New Zealanders were never a simple people.

The British Government was certainly less impressed by the remarkable generosity with which the New Zealanders extended more than political equality to the defeated Maoris, than by the expense and trouble in which the wars had involved Britain itself. Ten British battalions had been sent out to New Zealand to restore peace to the colony. The colonials had regarded this as so much their right that the decision by the British Government finally to withdraw the Imperial forces had been followed by warnings that New Zealand might stay neutral in future British wars. In fact, New Zealand was to show itself consistently more enthusiastic than any other part of the Empire to get into any war in which Britain became involved; but this was not known in the 1860s. The main lesson of the Maori Wars for the British was that New Zealanders were a liability as far as relations with native races were concerned, and only too capable of getting themselves into further scrapes from which Britain would have the trouble of rescuing them. There was certainly no reason to imagine that the New Zealanders had any qualities which would justify handing over other island peoples to them. The New Zealanders, for their part, with their population rapidly increasing, unlimited land available to them, and the Maori problem soon to disappear with the last of the Maoris, immediately regained all their former expansionism and euphoria. In one sense, expansionism was an appropriate mood. The last strongholds of independence among the island peoples were certain to fall before the end of the century. The New Zealanders had some reason for their anxiety that the last of the islands should fall to them.

They had indeed far more cause for concern than they were aware of at the time. The Asian island kingdom which was to prove the most feared and also the most dangerous menace to the Western colonial empires was preparing itself for its role as a great power. Japan had maintained effective if not quite complete isolation for over two centuries, since 1639. This withdrawal had not been motivated solely by xenophobia or a concern to preserve Japanese culture and traditions. Either would certainly have been justified: their first 100 years of contact with Europeans had brought the Japanese economic distress, as well as making them acquainted with the 'Inquisition, religious fratricide, imperialism and slave trade'[37] which appeared to be the main characteristics of Western civilization. But the Japanese had a more practical reason for seeking to exclude Europeans: the missionaries were showing increasing interest in interfering in Japanese politics, and the merchants were obviously ready to sell firearms to disaffected elements prepared to take up arms against the government. Only the Dutch were allowed to retain some commercial links with Japan, as the Dutch had shown goodwill in 1637 by bombarding the anti-government forces during the Christian Rebellion of Shimabara.

These links remained very slight, however: by 1715, only two Dutch ships and thirty Chinese junks were allowed to visit Japanese ports annually. Attempts by other foreign powers to establish or renew contacts made little impact. The British vessel *Argonaut* and the American *Lady Washington* and *Grace* made calls in 1791. The Russians sent a serious expedition in 1792 under Lieutenant Adam Kirillovich Laxman. The visitors were, in fact, treated considerately, but were allowed to leave in peace only on the understanding that they never came back. It was not until 1852 that the Russians made a decisive approach, as distinct from occasional surveying expeditions and piratical raids. They were impelled now by a dual concern, to secure ports to service Russian sailing to and from Alaska, and to acquire supplies in Japan to assist in the colonization of Siberia, before Japan itself fell completely under the control of either the British or the Americans. It happened that the Americans had also decided to approach Japan, partly for commercial reasons but also to ensure supplies of coal for their ships in the Pacific. President Fillmore despatched Commodore Matthew C. Perry in 1851 with a letter to the Emperor of Japan proposing that 'the United States and Japan should live in friendship and have commercial intercourse with each other'.[38] Perry took the long way round, across the Atlantic, round the Cape of Good Hope and on to Singapore, Hong Kong and Shanghai. Meanwhile the Russian frigate *Pallada*, under Vice-Admiral Evfimii Vasilievich Putiatin, had left Kronstadt for Portsmouth on 19 October 1852 to collect another ship and some artillery before going on to Japan.

Perry arrived first. The *Susquehanna, Mississippi, Plymouth* and *Saratoga* entered Uraga Bay on 8 July 1853. The Japanese, confused by this show of strength, were at least convinced that they were militarily unprepared to challenge the newcomers. Most would have preferred to have neither war nor trade with the Americans. They were, however, warned by Perry that 'the President desires to live in peace and friendship with your imperial majesty, but no friendship can long exist unless Japan ceases to act toward Americans as if they were her enemies'. Moreover, although Perry explained that he had visited Japan with only four of the United States' smaller warships, he designed, 'should it become necessary, to return to Yedo in the ensuing spring with a much larger force'.[39] He left at the end of July. The Russians arrived, also with four ships, on 21 August. Perry returned in February 1854. By this time, the Japanese had reached some decisions. They would explain to the spirits of their ancestors that the exchange of goods was a universal practice, and that the Americans should be allowed to obtain coal, wood, water and foodstuffs. For their part, they would 'construct new steamships, and especially powerful warships. . . . Openly these will be called merchant vessels, but they will in fact have the secret purpose of training a navy. . . . Our defences thus being strengthened, and all being arranged at home, we can act so as to make our courage and prestige resound beyond the seas'.[40]

This, of course, was for the future. In the meantime, Japan would adopt an appropriately low profile. A convention was signed with the Americans at Shimoda on 31 March 1854, under which the two nations agreed to live in permanent and perpetual peace, and the Americans were to be allowed to purchase coal, wood, water and provisions. The negotiations with the Russians were more prolonged, and may perhaps have been more profitable to the Russians, at least in the short ruun : they received all the rights and privileges extended to other nations, as well as obtaining from the Japanese a clear-cut definition of the frontiers of the two empires.[41] This achievement was all the more remarkable in that the Russians had adopted a generally more relaxed approach to the Japanese. Where the Americans had threatened to do to Japan what they were doing to Mexico, and tended to yell at the Japanese, 'calling the whole race savages, liars, a pack of fools, poor devils',[42] the Russians were content to patronize the Japanese with tolerant politeness, while joyfully describing in their diaries the repulsive appearance, absurd clothes and stupid faces of the Japanese, and the impossibility of their ever acquiring any military skills. At least the Japanese were concerned to do something about the last deficiency : in 1856 the Shogunate asked the Dutch to provide instructors for a modern navy; in 1857 the first Japanese steamship was built; the French agreed to assist in the construction of a dockyard in 1865; delegations were sent to Britain and France in the same year to study military techniques and administration; and in 1868 the old monarchy was restored to help the people 'fulfilling their wishes, to attain their full blossoming'.[43] The Emperor assured his people that this would be achieved by calling on the knowledge of the whole world to assist the restoration of Japanese national power. A national revival without precedent was taking place. A Japanese sun was rising over the peoples of Asia and the Pacific.

IV

The Colonial Ocean

The 1870s were creating a new world order, as surely as the last decade of the eighteenth century or the middle decades of the twentieth. Diplomatically, the whole structure of international power relations had been altered by the emergence of the United States after the American Civil War as the greatest military and naval power in the world. Any hope of containing the growth of American power by either a break-up of the American Union or the formation of a combination of Latin American states under French protection had been lost. Britain had failed to go to war with the United States at a time when foreign intervention would have ensured the secession of the Southern Confederacy. France had been unable after 1865 to secure Maximilian's regime in Mexico and at the same time safeguard its own position in Europe. This, indeed, was overturned six years later by military defeat in war with the German states. Until such time as the growth of Russia could alter the scene again, the United States and a united Germany loomed as the prospective great world powers of the coming century.

The Germans were already in the Pacific, if only in the form of the trading establishments of Godeffroys of Hamburg in Fiji and Samoa. The Americans had been in the Pacific virtually from the start, completely dominating the economy and most of the administration of Hawaii and developing commercial interests in the South Pacific, especially in Samoa. Neither Germans nor Americans had yet shown any signs of following the British and French into annexation. But technological change was making annexation virtually a necessity for any nation wishing to develop or even defend its commercial interests on the high seas. Nothing had been as effective in bringing native potentates to a sense of realities as the appearance of a foreign man-of-war under full sail. The British, French, Americans and Russians had thus been able to make their presences felt at literally the other end of the world. But new developments in naval technology had paradoxically limited very seriously the mobility and range of navies. Wooden sailing-ships could be kept at sea for virtually as long as their crews could stand it. They could never run out of fuel, because they used none; and their running repairs were normally of a kind which the men on board could carry out effectively in any convenient bay. Iron steamships were quite different. Their range of operation depended on the amount of coal they could carry in their bunkers, and any mechanical breakdowns or other repairs they might need could often be dealt with only by a fully equipped dockyard.[1] Bases had become a practical necessity, and particularly so in an area like the Pacific, where ships were liable to be operating at enormous distances from any of the continental land masses. The British and French were already tolerably well provided with bases, especially after the French incursions in Indo-China. It could only be · expected that the Germans and Americans and probably the Russians as well would start acquiring whatever strategic islands might be left.

This again raised the insoluble problem of the huge British colonies of Australia and New Zealand. Colonial and metropolitan attitudes were almost impossible to reunite. The British Government believed correctly that the fate of the Australasian colonies depended finally upon the fate of Great Britain itself. Any war in which the colonies might be threatened by a foreign power would have to be fought mainly with the resources of the British Isles, presumably in and around continental Europe. British victory would mean that the threat to the colonies would ultimately be removed, whatever might have happened to them in the meantime. British defeat would mean that the colonies would be at the disposal of anybody who wanted them, again no matter what they might have done on their own behalf in the meantime. It was possible for circumstances to arise, as indeed they did arise, in which the fate of the Pacific colonies and Australia would be almost irrelevant to the overall British strategic plan. It could hardly be irrelevant to the people who had to live in that part of the world. The conclusion was unavoidable. If the Pacific colonies could not defend themselves against a foreign invader, and if the British might find it difficult to defend Australia and New Zealand and at the same time fight a great power nearer home, at the other end of the world, the only solution was to ensure that no great power could get near enough to the Australasians to threaten their shores. The French were dangerously close already. The only way to stop other and worse dangers was quite simply to place under the British flag all the remaining independent territories of the Pacific.

There were other reasons as well. The huge military and political upheavals of the 1860s had produced economic upheavals in their train, rendered worse by the simple fact that no techniques had yet been devised to mitigate the effects of changes in the movement of international trade. The American Civil War, for example, had provided a great stimulus to those parts of the world which could produce commodities formerly exported by the blockaded Southern Confederacy. Most important of these was cotton. Plantations were developed in Hawaii and Fiji. Australians in particular rushed north to establish a new area of white economic supremacy. About 830 white men and women had moved to Fiji by 1867. Their number had grown to 2,500 by 1868, 2,000 of these being Australians.[2] In New Zealand, too, the pressure for northward economic expansion was increasing. This again was due not to the economic dynamism of New Zealand itself, but its reverse. The New Zealand economy was entering upon an agonizingly long period of depression, which was to end only with the transformation of the colony from a primarily manufacturing community to an almost wholly agricultural one. Prices of the main exports, wool and meat, fell after 1865. Despite the extraordinarily rapid growth in population, 75,000 people actually left the colony, mainly for Australia, between 1862 and 1870. As early as 1861, unemployed labourers in Dunedin had petitioned the Government to find them jobs in the other islands of the South Pacific.

The rulers of these islands were well aware of the dangers of their position. The Maori Wars, the ruthless French annexation and development of New Caledonia as a penal colony, and above all the Australians' callous treatment of the Aborigines, were all pointers to the probable fate of Fiji, Tonga or Samoa. Ma'afu and Cakobau agreed on a division of authority in Fiji. The various Tongan dominions and satellites grouped themselves in the Lau Confederacy, governed by Ma'afu theoretically, at least, on behalf of George Tupou. In 1867, Cakobau was formally crowned King of the Bau Dominions with a zinc crown manufactured at a local workshop and valued at 10 shillings, which he donned to the irreverent applause of the Europeans who filled every post in the new constitutional monarch's cabinet. Bauan Fiji became in effect a white settler dominion : Cakobau was compelled by his European ministers to go and fight wars, invariably unsuccessful, in Viti Levu, in defence of settler interests and land claims; all-white juries in Fiji acquitted white murderers, while native Fijians were shot out of hand for trespassing on settler property, as well as being excluded from social functions such as the Suva regatta; and the San Francisco-based Central Polynesian Land and Commercial Company began to insist that Cakobau should hand over 200,000 acres to them in quittance of his assorted debts.[3] Meanwhile, 3,000 islanders from the New Hebrides were brought to Fiji by blackbirders to serve on the settler plantations, in view of the unwillingness of the Fijians to work for hire and to order; and the Europeans further extended their control over Cakobau's kingdom by monopolizing the newly-formed elected assembly.

But, while Cakobau's position had become farcical, Ma'afu's had not : the Tongan Governor and his tough, disciplined warriors maintained an orderly and efficient administration over the Lau Confederacy. Nevertheless it was evident to George Tupou that this could no longer be counted on safely as a mere extension of Tongan authority. The crash was coming in Fiji, and any attempt to maintain Tongan imperialism there could only guarantee confrontation with the far more powerful foreign imperialisms. Accordingly, Ma'afu was ordered in 1868 not to involve Tonga at all in Fijian affairs; and the cord was finally cut in 1869, when all Tongan territorial claims in Fiji were formally ceded to Ma'afu. Another period of Tongan imperialism had come to an end.

It had not come to an end at any wish of Ma'afu's. As Governor of the Tongan dominions in Fiji, he had had a good chance of succeeding to George Tupou's throne. As merely Chief of the Lau Confederacy and viceroy of King Cakobau, he could have no hope of ruling the Tongan empire at all. He could indeed have no doubt whatever that George Tupou had abandoned his designs on Fiji because Fiji was just too hot to handle. Economic crisis was now joined to political chaos. The price of cotton had begun to fall with the end of the American Civil War. International trade was then disrupted further by the Franco-German War in Europe. The ever-resourceful Cakobau attempted to stave off financial calamity by selling the people of Lovoni to planters at the inflated price of £1,500 a head. Ma'afu meanwhile refused to help Cakobau in the footling wars he engaged in at the command of the settlers; rigidly maintained order in his own manor, using his Tongans to break up even European demonstrations that disturbed the peace; refused to accept Cakobau's son as heir to the throne of Fiji; collected an arsenal of 200 guns; and waited for either annexation or a *coup d'état*.

It was not only in Fiji that things had got out of hand. In Samoa for the past thirty years or so there had been an intermittent struggle for power between rival families and rival districts. An attempt had been made at a compromise by conferring the royal title of Malietoa on two contenders, Talavou, a son of Vai'inupo, who had held the title until his death in 1841, and Laupepa, who might be described as a kind of nephew of Talavou. However, in 1868, Laupepa's supporters declared him the sole holder of the Malietoa title. Talavou's supporters countered by establishing a rival confederation with its headquarters at Mulin'u, a promontory north of Apia harbour. The Laupepa faction then expelled the confederation from Mulin'u. Talavou was successful in re-establishing himself in Mulin'u, but not in forcing Malietoa Laupepa to accept the confederation as a central government.[4]

Fighting continued in desultory Samoan fashion for four more years. Meanwhile, the economic situation deteriorated even more seriously than it had in Fiji. European speculators had been encouraged to develop plantations in Samoa as well, to cash in on the high prices for cotton temporarily provided by the American Civil War. As always, the commercial sense of the Polynesians, which had made their initial dealings with the Europeans so easy and rational, led to their undoing. The Samoans were all too willing to sell land to keep up their cash incomes while they were fighting, and to obtain guns with which to do the fighting. The result was that the American Central Polynesian Land and Commercial Company, which already claimed 200,000 acres in Fiji, now claimed a further 300,000 acres of Samoa, or about half the kingdom. Once again, some order had to be imposed. In 1873 an arrangement was reached at Mulin'u under which authority was invested in a council of seven chiefs, the Ta'imu.[5] The Samoans now looked for a suitable outsider to draft a constitution which would be acceptable to the various foreign interests with claims on Samoa. The man appointed was Albert B. Steinberger, an obscure special agent of the United States State Department, who naturally had contacts with the Central Polynesian speculators. Steinberger proved himself adept in following the Samoans rather than leading them. His main constitutional innovation, the creation of a Lower House or Faipule, a congregation of village representatives, had already been conceived by the Ta'imu. It was Steinberger's initiative, however, which resulted in a note from Malietoa Laupepa to the US Government expressing a vague hope for American protection.

This was not likely to pass unnoticed. The Americans certainly had the greatest claims on Samoa, if one could believe them, but Johann Godeffroys had also purchased some 25,000 acres, and Germany too was therefore directly concerned. The New Zealanders were frantic. Julius Vogel proposed in the New Zealand Parliament and in letters to the Colonial Office that Samoa should pass under British protection; that Fiji should pass under British protection; that New Zealand should be granted authority to extend the sway of Britain in the Pacific, and to this end should open negotiations with the Ta'imu before Samoa fell under German or American rule; and finally that all territory in the South Pacific so far unappropriated should be appropriated for and on behalf of New Zealand, which would thus become the headquarters of British possessions in Polynesia, with the Governor of New Zealand becoming Governor-General of the Polynesian Islands.[6] Vogel was not alone in his demands. It would have been fair to say that, relatively speaking, the Australian colonists already had more land of their own to deal with than any other people in the world, and that they had shown little concern for the welfare of the unfortunate previous occupants of the continent; but these factors did not restrain the governments of New South Wales and Queensland from demanding, as they had already done ten years before, the annexation of all of the island of New Guinea which had not already been claimed by the Dutch.[7]

The Gladstone government in London was unresponsive to all these suggestions. The British did not want any more colonies anyway; the experience of the Maori Wars was a strong argument against attempting to impose colonization upon any native people who had not clearly asked for it; and they did not believe that either the Australians or the New Zealanders had shown themselves to have reached a stage of development at which they could be trusted with the administration of subject peoples.[8] Nor was London able to share the frequently expressed hopes of the Australians and New Zealanders that any problems of administration would be solved in the near future by the demise of the native peoples concerned. At the same time, the Gladstone government attempted to do something about the position of Fiji as the headquarters of the slave trade in the Pacific by passing the Pacific Islanders Protection Act to halt blackbirding, and despatching five cutters to the South Pacific to see that the Act was enforced. The difficulty was, however, that the Fijians had by now decided that annexation was positively essential as the only alternative to settler domination, bankruptcy or war. Cakobau renewed his offer to cede Fiji in 1874. He was aided by a providential change of government in Britain. Disraeli's Conservatives were more sympathetic to the imperial idea than Gladstone's Liberals, although it was improbable that even Gladstone could have left Fiji as it was for much longer. A deed of cession was finally signed by Cakobau and Ma'afu on 10 October 1874 ceding full sovereignty to Queen Victoria, who was to prescribe and determine the form of constitution and the maintenance thereof. Cakobau retired with considerable satisfaction to the enjoyment of a yacht and a pension of £1,500 a year, continuing to hold court in Bau until his death from asthma in 1883 and exacting tribute from places in Viti Levu 'whence before Cession he could only have levied with great difficulty'.[9] Cokabau's career might be regarded as an encouraging proof of the fact that the wages of sin can be uncommonly generous if one has a little luck. Ma'afu enjoyed himself perhaps even more, because in a more sophisticated style, in his retirement. His stipend was not so great, only £600 a year, but he supplemented it with rents from his holdings in Lau and by going into debt.[10] As an administrator he remained indispensable to the British authorities, something which could never have been said of Cakobau. The last of the Tongan lords of Fiji had possessed in the highest degree the qualities of efficiency, opportunism and maturity characteristic of his people.

Even if annexation did not exactly solve Fiji's problems, it at least meant that somebody else would have to worry about them. There was also a general feeling, and it was a reasonable one too, that annexation by a distant British Government was better than exploitation by rapacious British colonists closer at hand. Hilaire Belloc's cautionary lines :

> Always take a-hold of nurse,
> For fear of meeting something worse

were appropriate here. In Samoa, the Ta'imu soon began to feel that the Fijian solution might be appropriate for their own country. Steinberger's constitution had given Samoa its first king in 1875, when Malietoa Laupepa became head of state for a four-year term, to be succeeded thereafter by a candidate from the other royal lineage of Sa Tupau. Steinberger himself became premier and chief judge. An analagous situation had developed in Tonga, where the local chairman of the Wesleyan Church, Shirley Waldemar Baker, had made himself supreme lawgiver by framing constitutions for the country which were comprehensible only to himself, in the English and Tongan versions alike.[11] Nevertheless, Steinberger had provided Samoa with a genuine 'modern'

Samoan government, just as the regime of George Tupou was at least being administered by and for Tongans, however much the legislative process might be in the hands of Shirley Baker. But European pressures were far more powerful in Samoa than in Tonga. Clashes had developed between the interests of Godeffroys and the Central Polynesian speculators; local settlers suspected Steinberger of planning to disregard their interests in favour of those of either or both of the foreigners; and in December 1875 Steinberger was arrested and deported by Captain C. E. Stevens of HMS *Barracouta*. The Ta'imu and Faipule then signified their dissatisfaction with this high-handed military intervention in support of settler interests by deposing Malietoa Laupupa. Stevens intervened again, sending a landing party to restore the King. Heavy fighting took place, and Stevens was eventually dismissed, along with the British and American consuls, for a disregard of Samoan independence really remarkable even by nineteenth-century Pacific standards. However, the message was clear : Tonga might be able to maintain a limited independence, because of the peculiar nature of its people, and the lack of European commercial interest in the Group itself; but the process of European and American commercial penetration which had led to the annexation of Fiji and made a farce of pretended Hawaiian independence was likely on every account to produce the same result in Samoa.

The familiar pattern began to shape itself again. The Samoans, like all the other island peoples confronted with foreign imperialism, were convinced that they could preserve a measure of independence only if one great power were willing to protect them against the encroachments of the rest. As usual, Britain was the first choice, being both comparatively familiar and distant. Little positively bad was known about the British, while a great deal that was bad was known about the Australians and French, and the Germans, as yet largely an unknown quantity, did not inspire confidence. An appeal was made in 1877 to Sir Arthur Gordon, the Governor of Fiji, to grant Samoa the benefits of British protection. The occasion was hardly propitious : Gordon was coping with the aftermath of a pulmonary epidemic in Fiji, which had followed immediately on the announcement of British annexation and had wiped out a third of the estimated population of the Group, resulting in a depopulation which Gordon was trying to rectify by bringing in indentured labourers from India. The Maoris were clearly dying out; the Fijians were on the wane; the Aborigines were disappearing from the Australian scene; and Gordon was uninterested in offering protection to another native remnant, presumably due to become defunct in its turn. Meanwhile, the New

Zealand bleating for colonies continued unabated. Vogel was asking the Australian colonies to co-operate with him in contriving the annexation of New Guinea, as part of a plan for taking over the rest of the South Pacific. Grey insisted, not for the first time, that New Zealand should have the New Hebrides as well. New South Wales and Queensland were unimpressed by New Zealand pretensions; but both colonies proposed in 1878, and again in 1879, that the British Government should annex the eastern half of New Guinea.[12] In this climate of rampant expansionism, Gordon suggested that Samoa should be annexed by Britain. The Samoans understandably declined the offer, as their whole purpose was to avoid being annexed by anybody, and appealed to the Americans, who claimed to own half of their country already. Washington, however, was disposed to move very discreetly in the South Pacific, in view of the virtual certainty that it would soon have occasion to annex Hawaii; the Americans accordingly also declined to offer Samoa protection, entering instead into a Treaty of Friendship and Commerce in return for the use of Pago Pago as a base for the United States Navy.

This was, of course, a signal for action on the part of the both the British and the Germans, who paradoxically were becoming as concerned over New Zealand imperialism as the New Zealanders were for far less cause over German.[13] Both great powers now imposed on Samoa Treaties of Friendship and Commerce in return for base facilities, as the Americans had done. The bases were not in fact likely to help the strategic interests of either party, although there was no doubt that the Germans had by now sufficient interest in Samoa to justify some naval presence there: by 1880 there were no less than twenty-one German commercial stations in the country, recruiting labour to serve on German-owned plantations.

One effect of the Anglo-German intervention which might have seemed beneficial was that Samoa now had a king again, by foreign decree: the rather pliant Malietoa Laupepa was re-installed at Mulin'u, with Tupua Tamasese Titimaea as vice-king. He was soon to be faced with dynastic and international problems difficult enough to understand, let alone solve.

The first complication was provided by the French. It might be said that the French were more impressive as conquerors than as colonizers. French cruisers had made their country's flag feared throughout the Pacific over the previous eighty years, and the French annexation of Tahiti had been a salutary example of Gallic determination in the face of international opinion. But the development of Tahiti as a colony had been something else again. English missionaries had already left the Tahitians without any legitimate reason for living, and the situation had ameliorated only slightly under the domination of the priests. For their part, French colonists who had Algeria just across the Mediterranean to go to were hardly likely to leave for Tahiti except to escape their families or the police. French officials regarded Tahiti quite reasonably as the most unrewarding place they could be sent to in the French Empire. The result was a carnival of incompetence. Until 1883 the Group was officially under the authority of the French Navy, an arrangement which destroyed virtually all the authority and prestige of those traditional ruling forms which had survived the impact of the missionaries. The old institutions were simply ignored, and no effort was made to introduce the Tahitians to new ones. True, cannibalism and bloodshed were effectively checked by the French naval regime; but the fact was that an intelligent and enterprising people who had flourished before the European intrusions had fallen in numbers during this period of enforced peace to about 10,000 by 1860, from an estimated 35,000 in 1780, and perhaps five to six times this number before the arrival of the Europeans. Naval authority was replaced by a civilian administration in 1883. This, however, did not produce any marked improvement in efficiency. Fifteen governors had been sent out to Tahiti during the thirty-six years of naval administration. Only two had actually sought to perform any administrative functions: de la Richerie (1860–3) who had proposed a series of reforms, and his successor, de la Roncière (1863–9), who annulled them. But under the civilian administration thirty-one governors were sent out in forty years. None was in office for long enough to do anything effective. Indeed there is every reason to believe that they were sent out to Tahiti, not in order that they should do anything positive there, but rather that they should not do anything harmful in more important posts. The sole function of Tahiti was to serve as a place where the dregs of French officialdom could do the least harm to France, or to provide jobs for needy or undesirable relations. Ministerial posts flourished in Tahiti, even when there was nothing to administer. France was contributing nothing but neglect to the ocean it had so ambitiously sought to rule.[14]

The same was true of the Marquesas, where one of the centres of Polynesian civilization was literally dying out. But the French colonial scene was not entirely lacking in dynamism. The end of the Second Empire had only given impetus to the plan to develop New Caledonia at the other end of the Pacific as a penal colony. The Paris Commune had filled French prisons with enemies of the state whom the state proposed to remove as far away from itself as possible. At the same time, the emigration of free colonists to New Caledonia was stimulated by government action allowing immigrants to land where they liked and to occupy as much land as they liked, in a deliberate attempt to establish a stable and efficient community of large landholders. Any prior claim that the natives might have had to their own land was set aside by simply sending soldiers to chase them into the hills. The system was successful as far as imposing French rule on the territory went, but hardly so in any economic sense. A resolute policy of this kind applied to a huge area needs large numbers of soldiers, and any large French official undertaking seems to require enormous numbers of administrators. By 1876 the European population of New Caledonia comprised 2,753 colonists and 3,032 soldiers and officials.

The news that French convicts were coming to the South Seas predictably brought violent reactions from the New Zealanders and Australians, and their anxiety reached a peak in 1881, when it was discovered that the French were considering settling the New Hebrides with convicts shipped from New Caledonia. New Zealand politicians and clergy, objecting to the French convicts even more because they were Catholics than because they were criminals, suggested the usual remedy : New Zealand should annex the New Hebrides.

Meanwhile the Australians had found still another cause for concern : the Queensland Government had received in 1884 a succession of memoranda from the Commandant of their local Defence Forces, Major General Harding Stewart, raising a number of disturbing considerations. The Russians had built up a formidable Asiatic Squadron; they were improving communications across Siberia in order to supply it the more easily; Russian ships had been visiting Japan and the United States, clearly with the intention of using Yokohama and San Francisco as bases from which to attack the British Empire in the Pacific; and they were actually going so far as to allow their officers to marry English and American ladies, so as to be in a better position to learn the secrets of Australia's scarcely impressive shore defences. Their obvious intention was to mount a series of attacks against Brisbane, Sydney and Melbourne; and the exploits of the Chilean Navy in the War of the Pacific against Peru and Bolivia had shown what could be achieved by small, fast steamers mounting heavy guns.[15] The Queensland Government had already suggested on at least four previous occasions that Britain should annex New Guinea, to prevent that territory from being used as a base against Australia. In 1883 an Intercolonial Conference was held, consisting of representatives from the Australian colonies and New Zealand, to consider the situation. There was, of course, no real evidence that the Russians were coming to New Guinea. On the other hand, German merchants, who had been pushing into the interior of the island with extraordinary daring and resolve, were petitioning Bismarck to annex the island to the German Empire. The Germans, admittedly, were not the Russians, but the principle was the same: in the eyes of the Australians and New Zealanders, no part of the Pacific was safe in anybody's hands except their own. The Queensland Government took direct action: a magistrate was despatched in a police cutter to Port Moresby to annex the whole of Eastern New Guinea to the colony of Queensland. The British Government refused to sanction this move, however. Nor did it respond favourably to the New Zealand demand for the New Hebrides, renewed yet again on the assumption, proclaimed by Prime Minister Atkinson in Wellington, that the white race was destined to possess all the Pacific islands. Indeed, London and Paris sought to remove an area of dispute of real interest to neither of them by mutually undertaking to respect the independence of the New Hebrides, so that neither of them would have to worry about the other taking it, as they had previously done over Hawaii. New Zealand then turned again to Samoa. New Zealand agents persuaded the easily led and understandably desperate Malietoa Laupepa to appeal to Queen Victoria through the governments of both Fiji and New Zealand, this time seeking annexation. The Queen of Rarotonga also expressed concern, this time about the proposed French convict transportation programme, during a visit to New Zealand, and again indicated that she would be happy to accept British protection, exercised by New Zealand.

A series of great power hammer-blows once more brought an end for the moment to these aspirations of colonial imperialism. In 1884 Bismarck peremptorily annexed New Britain, New Ireland and the northern province of Eastern New Guinea, as part of his programme for German colonial expansion. In the same year, he sent the corvette *Marie* to Samoa, where Laupepa and Tamasese were compelled to sign a treaty effectively recognizing German authority, despite their appeals to the British Government. Laupepa then despairingly asked the New Zealanders to arrange to have a British warship sent to protect Samoa against the German intrusion. The British were in fact sufficiently concerned this time to take some action on their own account. The warship *Miranda* was sent to Samoa, albeit from Sydney, and without consulting the New Zealanders; Commissioner Romilly proclaimed a British protectorate over the south coast of New Guinea and the adjacent islands in October; and Commodore Erskine in HMS *Nelson* did it all over again on 6 November, apparently unaware that Romilly had taken possession of the lands concerned already.[16]

This, of course, did not affect what was going on in Samoa, where the Germans were applying an active policy of divide and rule. They vigorously persecuted Laupepa, driving him from Mulinu'u, while encouraging Tamasese to set himself up as a rival king. Two Samoan chiefs went to New Zealand to appeal directly for the country to be annexed by Wellington, while Laupepa himself begged the Americans to cover Samoa with a protectorate. Britain, Germany and the United States all sent commissioners to Samoa to try to agree on a peaceful solution, but without considering it necessary to consult the New Zealanders, who were given as a consolation prize the Kermadecs, which nobody wanted, to keep them quiet.

Meanwhile, the Germans had defeated Laupepa, whom they deposed and deported, appointing Eugen Brandeis to exercise effective authority in Samoa as premier to Tamasese. Polynesian control over the Pacific islands had virtually come to an end. But there was still one last tragic farce to be played out before the last independent native kingdoms fell before the new wave of great power imperialism. The coronation of King Kalakaua and Queen Kapiolani in 1883 had been perhaps the most magnificent in the history of royal Hawaii. As such, it was an accurate reflection of the startlingly unrealistic aspirations of the young King. Kamehameha the Great had never aimed to do more than unite Hawaii. Kalakaua was aspiring to nothing less than what he called the 'Primacy of the Pacific', with Hawaii at the head of a 'Union of Asiatic Nations', at a time when he held his own powerless throne entirely by the good graces of a grim community of United States businessmen, attracted to Hawaii only by the prospect of exploiting the island's sugar plantations. There is no telling just how far Kalakaua's ambitions might have extended. His first step was comparatively modest, however : in 1886 the Hawaiian king sent John E. Bush as a special envoy to Laupepa to propose the formation of some kind of association of states between Samoa and Hawaii. Federation was, of course, in the air at the time, but there was something distinctly improbable about a political association between two native states, neither of which had any effective control over its own affairs, domestic or foreign – two states, moreover, whose sole point of contact, historically speaking, was that both had originally been colonized from the Marquesas. Kalakaua nonetheless invited the

Samoans to agree to a convention with Hawaii, with a view to uniting the two kingdoms in a political confederation. This was immediately rejected by Bismarck, on whose orders Laupepa had just been sent into exile.

This setback apparently made no impression on Kalakaua. The Hawaiian Minister in Washington was instructed to represent Samoan as well as Hawaiian interests in the American capital. Kalakaua then looked about for a ship in which he could make a royal visit to Samoa to establish communications with his partner in the 'Confederation'. An old steamship, the *Kaimoloa*, was fitted up as a royal yacht. The next problem was to find a genuine Hawaiian crew. For want of better material Kalakaua manned the *Kaimoloa* with the inmates and graduates of a native boys' reformatory. Once out of harbour, his crew of juvenile delinquents predictably mutinied, and the voyage to Samoa was off.[17] Equally predictably, the United States businessmen who ran Hawaii took steps to ensure that Kalakaua's follies were brought to an end. A misnamed 'Hawaiian League' was formed, consisting entirely of Americans, and the king was briefly warned never to interfere in politics in any way again, if he wished to retain his throne.

Polynesian independence was now a thing of the past. Expatriate American businessmen ruled in Hawaii, Eugen Brandeis governed Samoa for Bismarck and Johann Godeffroys of Hamburg; and even the supremely arrogant and pragmatic Tongans had escaped foreign commercial domination only to fall under a foreign theocracy: in 1887 four escaped prisoners attempted to assassinate Shirley Baker, on whose decree they had been jailed in the first place. Their performance was not equal to their intentions: missing Baker, they only succeeded in wounding the two Baker children who were travelling with him. Baker immediately took advantage of the situation to introduce a reign of terror against all who might have challenged his authority. The four would-be assassins were shot. Baker then opened a crusade against the Wesleyan Church itself, in order to secure his own supremacy as head of an independent State Church in Tonga. When the Tongans failed to abandon their former religious affiliations with sufficient enthusiasm, Baker showed his readiness to transform the crusade into a civil war, raising Ha'apai and Vava'u against Tongatapu. Conversion was carried out with the usual accompaniments of assault, outrage and murder; the authority of the Wesleyan Conference in Australia was rejected; and those who felt strongly enough about Baker's new position fled to Fiji, while Baker proceeded to entrench his position by rewriting the Tongan

Constitution for the fourth time, to make absolutely certain of its being fully comprehensible to nobody but himself.[18]

Meanwhile, the twilight of the Polynesians deepened. White and Maori New Zealanders alike protested about the fate of the Samoans – with differing motives but precisely similar results. The *New Zealand Herald* protested on the economic grounds that it was the destiny of New Zealand to become the emporium of the South Pacific, and no European intrusions should be allowed to get in the way. A Maori member of the New Zealand Parliament objected to the German domination on the grounds that Maoris and the Samoans were one people, and should not be politically separated. Twenty-one Maori chiefs sent a letter of consolation to Laupepa deploring German methods. All this, of course, made no difference whatsoever. In Samoa itself there was now total confusion. The Germans, having deported Laupepa, were attempting to rule through Tamasese. However, the British and Americans found Tamasese unacceptable as a German puppet, and favoured Mata'afa, who had become leader of the popular opposition since Laupepa's exile, and had in his absence acquired the Malietoa title. Tamasese in any case felt that he was dying, and was seeking to have the kingship held alternately by the rival candidates, as originally planned, so as to avoid bloodshed in Samoa for ever. In 1889 all three powers sent warships to Apia to impose order while they again tried to reach a solution. In a tremendous storm, which the Samoans did not hesitate to regard as symbolic of the consequences of Western rivalry for their country, six of the seven foreign warships were wrecked, with heavy loss of life. The main agreement reached was that Malietoa Laupepa should be brought back as king. This was made easier by the illness of Tamasese, who died in 1891. However, Laupepa himself now became identified by much of the population as an agent of foreign interests. Mata'afa declared himself a candidate for the kingship. The Germans as ever counselled direct action. Laupepa declared war on the rebels, who were forced to surrender by British and German warships; and Mata'afa in his turn went into exile. However, his place as pretender was immediately taken by the son of Tamasese, who in his turn raised a revolt and was suppressed by the British and Germans.

Samoa was by now as shattered by internal strife and foreign intervention as Fiji had been during the contest between Cakobau and Ma'afu. Villages had been sacked, institutions discredited and tribes impoverished by indemnities imposed as penalties for rebellion. Then in 1892 there was added to the depopulation already caused by the wars the devastation of a smallpox epidemic which killed off some 10,000 people, or about a quarter of the population. It was really little more than a case of the Westerners picking up the pieces.

Meanwhile, the Hawaiian farce had been played out at last. In 1888 an attempt to re-establish a genuine indigenous monarchy was quixotically launched by Robert W. Wilcox, a young American who had gone to Italy to study the explosive combination of engineering and military science. He marched on the palace of King Kalakaua with 150 followers, in an attempt to inspire the deflated monarch to try once more to restore Hawaiian greatness. But, after an ineffectual scuffle, Wilcox and his monarchists were defeated by the American palace guards, acting under the orders of the American Reform Cabinet. Kalakaua was still incapable of reading the signs. Presumably inspired by Wilcox's fiasco, he announced his intention of appealing to the Hawaiian race, now less than a third of the population of the Group, to assist him in restoring the powers possessed by the monarchy under the 1864 Constitution. However, Kalakaua thereupon fell seriously ill, sailed to San Francisco for treatment, and died there in 1891. His death coincided with the greatest blow yet to American prosperity in Hawaii. Foreign wealth in Hawaii had been based on the sugar trade with the United States. Export prices of Hawaiian sugar had increased tenfold in the past fifteen years. In 1891, however, domestic producers prevailed upon Congress to pay them a subsidy which would have the effect of an almost prohibitive tariff upon imported sugar. The only way the Hawaiian planters could cope with this situation was by arranging for the Group to be annexed by the United States, so that they would become domestic producers themselves. A Committee of Public Safety was formed in Hawaii on Kalakaua's death, dominated by members of the Annexation Club, long-standing advocates of cession to the United States. The Committee seized the palace, abrogated the monarchy and declared a republic. The natives rebelled, but order was restored by United States Marines landed from the cruiser *Boston*, which providentially happened to be in harbour at the time, having on board the United States Minister Stevens, a devoted protagonist of annexation.[19]

The government in Washington was nonetheless not quite ready to act. War was brewing with Spain over that country's failure to suppress rebellion in Cuba, and the Americans felt that it behoved them to walk warily until their supremacy at sea had been assured. There was also the problem of the heir to the Hawaiian throne, Queen Liliukalani, who still refused to accept the Republic. And there was still Samoa, where

Laupepa and Mata'afa were at war, and where British and German interests were involved as well as American. Considering the number of times in the past that Hawaii had almost become British, to say nothing of the number of times that it had almost become French, and considering that it had stayed independent so long only because one great power had been prepared to let it alone on condition that another great power did the same, it was appropriate for the United States not to seem too impatient.

This was, however, hardly appropriate where United States interests in Hawaii itself were concerned. The Republicans held on to power and waited for annexation. Their position was helped substantially by the quixotic Wilcox, who staged another nationalist and monarchist insurrection in 1895, on behalf of the non-reigning Queen Liliukalani. Wilcox was put down again by the Republicans, and Queen Liliukalani formally abdicated. The experiment of the Hawaiian Kingdom had come to an end. In 1898, after their victories over Spain had established them more convincingly as a Pacific power, the Americans finally annexed Hawaii.

The Samoan experiment was clearly almost at an end, too. The final eruption came with the death of Malietoa Laupepa in 1898, just as the Hawaiian monarchy had effectively ended with the death of Kalakaua seven years before. Civil strife at once broke out between the supporters of Mata'afa, now returned from exile, and those of Laupepa's young son, Malietoa Tanumafili. The Chief Justice ruled in favour of Tanumafili. Mata'afa and his allies rejected the decision and formed a provisional government. This in turn was dismissed by the British and Americans, who returned Tanumafili to office. Mata'afa promptly turned him out again. In April 1899 the British, Germans and Americans moved in for the last time. Mata'afa and Tanumafili were compelled to stop fighting. Tanumafili was restored once more, and thereupon ordered to resign to make way for an international settlement. The Triple Commission moved swiftly. Germany was to have Samoa west of longitude 171° West, in return for German concessions to British interests elsewhere in the Pacific and in Africa. The Americans got Tutuila and Manua. There was perhaps a certain lack of legal clarity about the German position : the government in Berlin contented itself with declaring a protectorate over Western Samoa, without a formal treaty of cession, on the grounds that there had been no effective Samoan Government in office at the time of the partition with whom to conclude a treaty. This gave the ever-hopeful New Zealanders a last specious chance to intervene in a matter which none of the powers considered to be any of their business.

Incredibly Prime Minister Seddon offered to send New Zealand troops and police to Samoa to maintain order while the new regimes sorted themselves out.

The offer was naturally declined, but this only moved the New Zealanders to greater efforts. Tiny Rarotonga had already passed under New Zealand protection in 1891, when a New Zealand agent had been appointed there at the request of the Queen to forestall any possible move by the French. Seddon had then made an offer to extend New Zealand protection over Samoa. This of course had been refused. With Samoa lost to the Germans and Americans, Seddon now proposed that New Zealand should annex Tonga, and gained the support of the small white population of the kingdom for such a move. But the Tongans had characteristically managed to find a way to preserve their independence substantially unimpaired. Baker had so effectively concentrated all the machinery of government in his own hands that his removal was liable to lead to anarchy, and anarchy was very liable to lead to annexation, especially with the New Zealanders clamouring for empire in the south. No direct move was therefore made against Baker. The people simply stopped paying taxes. Government in Tonga thus came peacefully to an end. The British authorities in Fiji were already wholly unsympathetic to Baker, partly because of the expense of maintaining the Wesleyan exiles who had fled to Fiji to escape his persecution. The British High Commissioner in Fiji accordingly decided that the most practical solution to the problem was to remove Baker. This was done in 1890. Baker was prohibited from remaining in Tonga and deported to New Zealand, leaving behind him a storeroom filled with champagne bottles, imported for the use of the Tongan Government so as to evade custom duties, as well as the vacant portfolios of Prime Minister, Minister of Foreign Affairs, President of the Court of Appeal, Auditor-General, Minister of Lands, Judge of the Land Court, Minister of Education, Agent-General and Medical Attendant to the King, all of which functions he had performed or at least reserved to himself.[20] The immediate problem was thus to re-establish a governmental system which had been largely kept out of Tongan hands for the past thirteen years. None of the king's potential advisers knew even where to find any records of the departments which Baker had perforce abandoned to them. There was at the same time no doubt that George Tupou and his chiefs were anxious above all to avoid anything that might lead to a recurrence of civil war. The British Government accordingly agreed to leave Basil Thomson to act in the capacity of Prime Minister, on the understanding that this was not to involve Britain in any direct responsibilities in Tonga.

A virtual protectorate had thus been achieved, which probably approximated more closely to an ideal arrangement from the point of view of the islanders themselves than any relationship achieved with foreigners by any other island people. The reasons for Tongan good fortune were simple : the Tongans were an orderly, disciplined people with an intense sense of national identity, who had got over their period of civil strife before Europeans had become interested in them; they were attractive and efficient, so that Europeans found it easy to meet them as virtual equals; and they were superior and condescending, so that Europeans found it disagreeable to live among them. Most important, they did not produce anything that Europeans were interested in farming for profit. Tonga produced enough to support its own inhabitants, only because of the efficiency with which its limited soil was already cultivated : there was thus no opportunity for plantation farming, and therefore no possibility of important foreign commercial interests developing. New Zealand merchants had certainly acquired some claims on Tonga, thanks largely to Baker's habit of raising loans in Auckland on the strength of shipments of copra yet to be taken off the trees; but all of New Zealand's trade with all of the Pacific islands amounted to only $2\frac{1}{2}$ per cent of the colony's total exports and imports. The emporium of the South Pacific did business with everybody in the world except the islands which it wished to occupy.

But New Zealand expansionism, like that of the French, had always been impelled by motives which were not purely economic. There was simple national self-esteem; there was the kind of reasoning which argued that it was only fitting that the relations of the Maoris should suffer the same fate at the hands of the same people as the Maoris themselves; there was the sheer boredom of New Zealand life, from which dreams of foreign adventures gave a certain welcome relief;[21] there was, probably most important of all, a deep anxiety about what might happen to New Zealand if foreign powers were allowed to establish bases within striking distance of the colony's shores; and there was the continuing tendency to identify New Zealand with Great Britain, and to forecast an imperial destiny for New Zealand because such a destiny had befallen Britain. This particular delusion was greatly strengthened by technological changes which before the end of the nineteenth century completely altered the balance of the New Zealand economy. New Zealand had, as has been said, perforce developed as a manufacturing country, simply because the original settlers had largely been compelled to make for themselves whatever they needed in the way of clothing and equipment. An extraordinary variety of industries had developed, which had become internationally competitive, either because they were based on the exploitation of natural resources such as timber, coal, gold, flax, kauri gum, sealskins and whale oil, or because they were produced under mid-Victorian conditions of sweated labour, unrelieved at first by any but the most elementary factory legislation. By the 1880s New Zealand was exporting 'woollen cloth to Scotland, England, India and Australia . . . disc harrows and ploughs to South Africa; refrigerating machinery and agricultural equipment . . . to Australia; gold dredges to Australia, Brazil, China, East and West Africa, India and Russia'.[22] This growth, however, was checked in the 1890s by the exhaustion of some of the natural resources being exported, and by the effect of social welfare legislation, which increased production costs. But now the development of refrigeration made it possible for New Zealand to begin exporting dairy products to the British market on a massive scale, thus making New Zealand almost totally dependent on trade with Great Britain in a limited range of items, and providing the most convincing material reason for associating the two countries in a common destiny. It also led to a concentration of political power in the hands of conservative farmers, unsympathetic to the problems of the cities.

The depressed social and economic conditions which accompanied the decline of New Zealand manufacturing helped more than anything else to stave off the extinction of the Maoris. About three-quarters of Maori land in the North Island had been alienated after the Maori Wars. The Maori was literally dying without land. But purchase of land naturally slowed down as depressed economic conditions continued. The Maori had been granted a breathing-space. The result was quite decisive. The Maori population, which had fallen to about 30,000, began to increase in 1896, for the first time since the Europeans had established themselves in New Zealand. This upturn fortunately passed unnoticed by the authorities, who continued to display towards the Maoris 'a mixture of ignorance, apathy and, occasionally, sympathy for a people who would soon cease to exist. . . .'[23] There was also, of course, a more positive reason for a policy of mild benevolence: a nation which had pretensions to annex all unappropriated islands in the South Pacific really required to show that it knew how to look after the welfare of the island race already under its control. In 1900 the Seddon government introduced a Maori Councils Act, under which elected Maori councillors had the power to

pass by-laws affecting health and sanitation, as well as taking responsibility for the remaining Maori lands. Young Maui Pomare, a graduate
of Te Aute College, who had received a medical degree in the United
States, was appointed first Maori Health Officer. Pomare had expected
to be opposed by Maori traditionalists. He found instead that the way
had been made easier for him by the Te Aute College students, who
had formed an Association for the Amelioration of the Maori Race in
1890, in an attempt to secure the advantages of education for their
people. Progressive chiefs also welcomed him. There was no question
that he was needed. One of the reasons for the population decline was
perfectly apparent : half of all Maori children born died before the age
of four, usually from tuberculosis or typhoid. This at least was a practical problem, for which the solutions were obvious : vaccinations were
provided by the thousand, unhealthy dwellings destroyed, new houses
built and sanitation improved. The Maoris themselves responded immediately, inspired by two other Te Aute College graduates of genius,
Te Rangihiroa (Peter Buck), a doctor like Pomare, and Apirana Ngata,
a law graduate from Canterbury University College, who became
Organizing Inspector, Maori Councils in 1902. For the first time since
the wars, the Maoris were taking command of their own destiny in the
most fundamental way.

Their success was, of course, limited. The Maori Councils in sheer
enthusiasm frequently exceeded their legal powers; Ngata and Pomare
found themselves hopelessly handicapped by lack of finance, authority
and even office space; and increasingly conservative New Zealand governments became more and more unwilling to divert finance to carry out
any of the urgent health measures Pomare recommended. It was in any
case congenial as well as easy to imagine that no measures were necessary, because the fate of the Maori was sealed anyway : as late as 1908,
after the Maori population had been rising for twelve years, the New
Zealand Institute proclaimed that the race was fast dying out. This
view was apparently held by the Government as well : in the following
year they disbanded the Maori sanitary inspectors, and refused to appoint
anyone to take the places of Pomare and Rangihiroa, although the
Maori Nursing Service was allowed to remain in operation.

New Zealand imperialism had by now ground to a dissatisfied halt.
Seddon made a last bid for glory in 1902, when he proposed to the
British Government that the boundaries of New Zealand should be
extended so as to include the Cooks, which were already a British protectorate administered from New Zealand; Fiji, which was a British

Crown Colony; Tahiti, which was French; and Tonga, which was also about to become a British protectorate. He went in fact so far as to intrigue actively with Shirley Baker, now in exile in New Zealand, to annex Tonga and appoint Baker as New Zealand Resident with all his old powers restored. The Tongan project had at least this much sense: the New Zealanders, although keen to federate with peoples they hoped to dominate, had decided not to federate with the Australians, for fear of being dominated themselves. They were now faced with the danger of being excluded to a serious degree from the Australian market, since the high tariffs of the other colonies were soon to be extended to New South Wales. Tonga, as part of New Zealand territory, would be forced to trade with New Zealand rather than Australia, while Fiji would be a doubly satisfying prize : at present it sold most of its exports to New Zealand, but bought most of its imports from Australia.

Seddon set out on a personal tour of Tonga, Fiji and Rarotonga in May 1900, a voyage which, in the words of Dr Fieldhouse, had much of 'the character of an inspection of properties about to be acquired. It was as though Louis XIV had made a Progress through the Rhineland territories before submitting his claims to annex them to the Chambres de réunion.'[24] He was greatly heartened by the discovery that there was a body of planter opinion in Fiji anxious to secure self-government in order to proceed with the exploitation of the country uninhibited by Colonial Office paternalism, and prepared to consider federation with New Zealand as a means of acquiring this goal.

Seddon accordingly proposed that Fiji should be federated with New Zealand at the Imperial Conference in London in May 1902. It was not a popular notion. The Australians in particular had no wish to sacrifice their own dominant economic position in the islands to New Zealand's Pacific ambitions. The British for their part had no reason to believe that the New Zealanders could do a better job in Fiji than they were doing themselves. Nor did the Governor of New Zealand, who secretly sent a message to the Colonial Secretary advising him against letting the New Zealanders take over Fiji, as they had so far displayed nothing but incompetence in their administration of the Cook Islands. New Zealand was simply not up to the imperial responsibilities which it was so anxious to take over from the Mother Country. There was also the embarrassing fact that no convincing economic interest could be proven : New Zealand trade with the islands was decreasing rather than increasing : by 1900 it had fallen to a minuscule two per cent of total New Zealand external trade. Undoubtedly, it might well get bigger if New Zealand were to take over the islands, but the prospect was hardly one for the British and Australians to get excited about. The general consensus was that the New Zealanders would have to put up a more impressive performance in the Cooks than they were doing already, before anybody would be justified in letting them loose on Tonga or Fiji, or anywhere else : indeed, Sir George O'Brien, the Governor of Fiji, warned the natives that if they did not behave themselves, they might find themselves handed over to the New Zealanders, who would take all their land, as they had already taken that of the Maoris : 'If any of you were to give trouble, that would only make it easy for New Zealand to get your country, and for you to lose your lands.'[25]

There was in any case rather a shortage of islands for even the most deserving colonial imperialists to annex. The New Hebrides were perhaps the most obvious group not yet appropriated. The New Zealanders duly put in a claim for these islands on strategic grounds in 1902, warning that they should not be allowed to fall away as Samoa had fallen away, simply because 'the British Government had not grasped the importance of the Group strategically considered'.[26] All that the British Government had grasped was the desirability of reaching an *entente* with the French. The situation was almost taken out of their hands in the same year when the Victorian Government abandoned only at the last moment a plan to follow the example of Queensland in New Guinea, and send units of its defence forces to the New Hebrides 'in a swift steamer with orders to hoist the British Flag and keep it flying'.[27] A further suggestion by Australian Prime Minister Barton that Britain should buy the New Hebrides outright for £250,000 drew a counter-proposal from Colonial Secretary Joseph Chamberlain that Australia might like to foot the bill.

The matter was taken out of the grasp of the Australians and New Zealanders, when London and Paris resolved in April 1904 to administer the Group jointly. It was certainly difficult to see how New Zealand at least, with a population of only three-quarters of a million and no experience at all in dealing with Melanesians, could hope to find the administrative talent to govern territories with a native population of at least 80,000, as well as 401 French and 278 British citizens. On the other hand, the Condominium set up by the British and French in 1906 hardly demonstrated high administrative skill either. Each of the two administering powers appointed its own High Commissioner, its own Resident Commissioner and its own body of Police. Public works and finance were however to be administered in common. No native was to

be allowed to become either a British or a French subject. A Joint Court
was instituted to deal with cases concerning more than one state. It was
to have a Spanish judge and Dutch officials to ensure impartiality, but
its proceedings were to be conducted in either French or English, or both.
Issues involving nationals of only one state could thus fall within the competence of a French tribunal, a British tribunal, a Joint Naval Tribunal,
or any combination of these. It would have been difficult to imagine a
more elaborate deterrent to litigation.[28]

Such a system was scarcely likely to contribute much to the advantage
of the people subject to it. It was not meant to. Its fundamental purpose was to ensure that the Anglo-French *entente* would not be disturbed
by any struggle for primacy between the partners.[29] The British had
simply felt obliged to reach the earliest possible understanding with the
French at a reasonable cost to the welfare of the inhabitants of the
New Hebrides, in order to avoid any danger of becoming entangled with
France, as an ally of Russia, in the conflict which had just broken out
between that country and Britain's new ally, Japan. The Japanese had
indeed managed to disturb the status quo totally in the thirty-six years
since the Meiji Restoration. They had seized Formosa from China in
1874; they had imposed a Treaty of Friendship on Korea in 1875,
similar to the one imposed on themselves by the Americans in 1854;
they had declared the Great Japanese Empire to be the style of the new
authoritarian regime in 1889; they had defeated China in 1894; and by
1897 the Japanese battle force outnumbered the capital ships of the
British China, Australia and Pacific stations by five to three. Japanese
defence expenditure had increased 500 per cent in three years, from
21 million yen in 1893 to 110 million yen in 1897. The Americans were
not slow to recognize the challenge which they had themselves called
into being. General Arthur MacArthur in the Philippines had pro-
phesied a war with Japan as early as 1903, and Senator Beveridge of
Indiana called on his people in 1898 to 'build a navy to the measure of
our greatness'.[30] but it may well have seemed at first that such alarmists
were misinterpreting the direction of the Japanese thrust. Japan was,
after all, apparently only moving into Asia, although its progress there
might well have disturbing repercussions for the interests of the Pacific
powers. In any event, Japan still had only eight battleships by 1904,
and its immediate rival Russia had twenty-two. But the situation was
altered completely by the incredible incompetence of the Russians, which
virtually guaranteed that every engagement at sea resulted in victory for
the Japanese. Observing the consistent inability of the Russians to do

anything right, or to take advantage of the frequent errors and mishaps of the Japanese, President Theodore Roosevelt admitted that he had 'never anticipated in the least such a rise as that of Japan . . . if they win out it may possibly mean a struggle between them and us'.[31] He consoled himself at first by reflecting that 'the Japs have played our game because they have played the game of civilized mankind . . . the descendants of Mongols are serving under the banners of Russia'.[32] Indeed, Roosevelt wondered at times if it might be desirable to use the United States Atlantic Squadron to bottle the Russians up in Vladivostock, to make things a little easier for the Japanese.

This assistance was quite unnecessary, as it proved. The knowledge that it was even being considered by the American President would have appalled the Australians, who were trying to make the Admiralty aware of the fact that it was 6,000 miles from Southampton to Cape Town, but only 4,600 miles from Tokyo to Sydney. Meanwhile, the indefatigable versifier Henry Lawson ground out a lament for the power which in the 1870s had been seen as the greatest of all threats to the British Empire in the Pacific and the Far East :

> While the crippled cruisers stagger where the blind horizon
> dips,
> And the ocean ooze is rising round the sunken battleships,
> While the battered wrecks, unnoticed, with their mangled crews
> drift past –
> Let me fire one gun for Russia, though that gun should be the
> last . . .
> Hold them, IVAN! staggering bravely underneath your gloomy
> sky;
> Hold them, IVAN! we shall want you pretty badly bye-and-
> bye! . . .
> It means all to young Australia – it means life or death to us,
> For the vanguard of the White Man is the vanguard of the
> Russ.[33]

Even Lawson's awful verses could not obscure a certain reality : Japan was in fact beginning to move east and south into the Pacific, as well as west into Asia, and certain Japanese publicists and politicians were beginning to be seized by the same chauvinistic dreams of empire as their fellows in every other great power past and present. In 1907 the influential writer Togu Minoru proclaimed :

From the ice-bound northern Siberian plains to the continental expanses of China, Korea, and East Asia; farther south, to the Philippines, the Australian continent and other South Sea islands; then eastward to the western coasts of North and South America, washed by the waves of the Pacific Ocean – there is none in these regions which cannot be an object of our nation's expansion. If our people succeed in constructing new Japans everywhere in these areas and engage in vigorous activities throughout the Pacific, then our country's predominance over the Pacific will have been ensured.[34]

The vision of the Yellow Peril could have received no more comprehensive expression. Admittedly, the actual Japanese movement across the Pacific was still minuscule. What was disconcerting was its rate of increase. In 1907 232,000 Japanese were living outside the Empire itself; 65,000 of these were in Hawaii, over half the number having arrived in 1906 alone; and there were almost as many in the United States. As a result of racial troubles in San Francisco during 1906–7 agreements between the United States and Japan in 1907 and 1908 provided for the regulation of further Japanese immigration into continental America.

The fact was that the Japanese were anxious, at least for the time being; to avoid open conflict with the United States. Japanese expansion was to continue, but it was to be accomplished peacefully, not by the military means which had hitherto proved so rewarding in Asia. Lieutenant-Colonel Tanaka Giichi of the General Staff warned in a memorandum of 1907 that neither Japan nor the United States had sufficient numbers of troops to be able to invade each other successfully. He did admittedly see some promise in attacking the Philippines, although this proposal was removed when his memorandum was referred to the Emperor. Tanaka's superiors continued to believe that the most desirable targets for future Japanese expansion were obviously Siberia, Manchuria and Mongolia. However, they accepted as a category of second desirability the Philippines, the Dutch East Indies and the South Sea Islands, which could include Australia and even New Zealand. Japanese policy was nothing if not flexible; and it was based on a global vision.

The Japanese Navy in particular remained consistently opposed to any conflict with the United States. Its views were strengthened by the world cruise of the United States Fleet in 1907–9, during which Yokohama was treated to a visit in October 1908. This was perhaps unnecessary as a gesture to convince the Japanese that a war with the United

States would be utterly hazardous. The Japanese knew that already. They did not contemplate other than peaceful expansion in the Americas. But the fact that aggression across the Pacific was ruled out only made the attractions of Asia and the South Seas more compelling.

Thus the eclipse of Russia did not seriously diminish European power in the Pacific. The reverberations of Japanese conquest did not disturb the torpor of French Polynesia. In terms of the proportion of public servants to population, Tahiti was now one of the most-governed places on earth : slightly more than 10,000 people received the attentions of 510 permanent officials, who generally managed to live in a state of modest luxury and total idleness. There were scarcely any Heads of Department or other high officials to be found, however, because no bureaucrat with sufficient ability to qualify for such a rank in the first place would have wished to waste his professional time in a place like Tahiti. Not that this shortage of senior officials made any significant difference, for the continuing rapid turnover of governors ensured that nobody was in office long enough to prepare any comprehensive policy anyway, even if he had the officials available to carry it out.[35]

This Upas-tree of administrative incompetence and negligence had withered life in the Marquesas even more comprehensively than in Tahiti. New Caledonia was a rather different picture, however. There the French experimented tirelessly with almost every possible variety of forced or induced settlement. The policy as regards the natives was undeniably simple : they were denied any rights at all to the territory of the island or its dependencies, driven by military force off any area designated for European development, and briskly shot down when they rose in protest. It was indeed essentially the same technique as that applied by the British in Australia, and, with considerably more legal obfuscation, by the Americans in dealing with their Indians. Policy on European settlement was much more complex and flexible. The original notion was simply to send out ordinary criminals who would otherwise be confined to jails or prison hulks. Those serving sentences of less than eight years were to remain in the colony after release for a period equal to their original sentence. Those sentenced for more than eight years would stay in the colony for ever. Promising convicts would be allowed small portions of land in the prison reserves to work for themselves, or they might be allowed to labour for hire for free colonists. These were the ordinary criminals. About 22,000 of them were sent out in all, though there were never more than seven or eight thousand actually in New Caledonia at any one time. A second category was provided by political prisoners. These were not subject to forced labour, were allowed to bring their families with them, and essentially could be regarded as the same as free colonists, except that they were not free to go anywhere else. About 4,000 of these were sent out, mainly from France itself but including assorted Arabs and Asiatic rebels against French authority. Thirdly, there were the exiles, *relégués*, who were transported not for single offences but because they had accumulated a sufficient number of convictions for minor misdemeanours over a ten-year period to be considered a burden to society. They were indeed a privileged lot : they wore a blue outfit to distinguish them from the grey-clad convicts, and were free to work in any capacity they liked as free settlers. In all 2,800 were transported. They proved to be by far the least promising human material of the settlement : the serious offenders were certain to be men of energy, and possibly of enterprise; the political deportees might well possess moral and mental qualities of the highest order; the *relégués* were merely incorrigible petty criminals, too inept to keep out of the hands of the police and physically or mentally unsuited for serious crime.

The French convict experiment was virtually a total failure. The New Caledonian climate was eminently unlikely to encourage a naturally irresponsible person to any useful effort, and the human material of most of the French convict settlements was uniquely unlikely to respond to even the most favourable conditions. The fact that a person could be judged to be of no living use to France was in itself a fair indication that he was unlikely to be of any great value anywhere else. Convict labour was utterly unproductive and unreliable. French mine owners found it more profitable to employ free Balkan peasants at seven francs a day than French convicts at one. The cost of surveillance was also severe: at the peak of the transportation experiment, 4,000 soldiers were guarding 22,000 convicts. The French effectively gave up in 1897, decreeing that no new convicts were to be sent out, although those already transported would have to serve their time on the islands. Fortunately, there was little problem in disposing of the last convicts. Over 7,000 had died already, and 4,684 had escaped. Epidemics then killed off 6,000 of the remainder, leaving only 3,855 survivors. The French authorities had something to thank the New Caledonian climate for.

It had been apparent from the start that transportation was not going to be the whole answer to the problem of populating New Caledonia with productive French citizens. The French Government had originally hope to inveigle 600 Irish families into settling there, but this scheme had been abandoned when the decision was taken to introduce transportation. Some settlers did however arrive on their own account, frequently from Australia. Unrestricted leasehold encouraged other enterprising spirits to set themselves up as great cattle barons on vast holdings; but the beef market became over-supplied, and the barons found themselves unable to pay for the acres they had confidently intended to buy. Free settlement was then disastrously impeded by a decree of 1884 reserving all the best land for convict settlers, and alienation of land was stopped almost entirely by a further law of 1892. Meanwhile, the discovery had been made that New Caledonia was extraordinarily rich in certain minerals, particularly nickel. Indeed, until the Canadian mines were developed, New Caledonia supplies virtually controlled the world market in nickel. This lasted for about sixteen years until 1892, when two-thirds of the mines closed under the impact of Canadian competition and New Caledonia relapsed into a state of crisis. Nevertheless, with the introduction of new techniques the mining industry began to recover again in 1911, by which time Governor Paul Feillet had been able to develop a scheme which did more than anything else to alleviate the population problem. This was indeed as bad as it could well be. The natives, dispossessed and confined to their reservations, were contributing nothing except periodical bloody revolts; the convicts, who did all the hard labour, did it as badly and lazily as possible; and the free settlers did no work at all as far as they could, in order to distinguish themselves from the convicts. It was really necessary to start again. Feillet launched a massive propaganda campaign in France, offering the inducement of freehold grants to settlers possessing capital of 5,000 francs or more. He managed to persuade 525 families to come out from France between 1895 and 1902. Only 300 actually stayed on, but their fecundity was such that their progeny outnumbered the convicts in a decade. The natives were dealt with by being finally rounded up and left to die off in their reservations, and indentured Asian labourers were brought in to provide a labour force more productive than the remaining ex-convicts. A certain measure of constitutional government was created by forming a General Council, elected by the island's male citizens, and nine rural communes with councils similarly elected. However, the familiar characteristics of French administration in the Pacific soon reasserted themselves. Feillet was recalled; ten different governors were sent out to replace him in the twelve years between 1902 and 1914; and the councils were humiliated in various ways, most effectively by not being convened for long periods.[36]

Their record undoubtedly suggests that the French lacked the resolve and perhaps even the competence to apply any kind of coherent development policy to their Pacific colonies. The contrast with the enormous though depression-racked British colonies to the south was certainly striking. It was clearly not entirely the fault of the French : Australia had been founded as a penal colony in a manner no more enlightened and far less resourceful than the French experiment in New Caledonia; and Australian conduct towards the Aborigines matched in callousness and ferocity French treatment of the New Caledonia Melanesians. The Australian climate could be as exacting at times as almost any on earth; and both Australia and New Zealand had become depressingly familiar with the boom and-bust experience of extractive industries developed by rapacious private enterprise. But there were important differences. The most significant one was that both Australia and New Zealand possessed vast areas of land with sufficient fertility to permit immediately profitable medium- and large-scale farming. In terms of climate, most of New Zealand and a sufficiently large area of the Australian seaboard were virtually ideal for European settlement, more ideal perhaps than England itself might have seemed at times, and even a successful inhabitant of the British Isles could see solid practical reasons why he might expect to live better in New Zealand or New South Wales. It is hard to imagine the depths of failure a Frenchman would have had to reach before he could really believe that he would be better off in New Caledonia, or what chance so unsuccessful a Frenchman would have had of improving his condition anywhere.

Samoa was certainly more attractive to European settlement than New Caledonia, although scarcely more stimulating to productive effort; and nobody doubted that the Germans possessed ability, will and imagination. The first German governor, Dr Wilhelm Solf, was clearly far above the customary level of colonial officials. He accepted the constitutional structure at Mulin'u, set himself to encourage the development of plantation farming as the most profitable course for Samoa and German interests, and attempted to win the co-operation of Mata'afa. In the meantime, 2,000 Chinese indentured labourers were brought in to provide a work force for the European planters, roads were built, and the Samoans themselves were instructed on scientific principles what and how much to grow. Nothing like this had ever been seen in the Pacific. Solf was similarly rational and at the same time imaginative in his dealings with Mata'afa. His immediate problem was that the Samoans tended to regard Germany as a temporary protector rather than a permanent occupying power. Solf accordingly suggested that Mata'afa should accept the position of Ali'i Sili or paramount chief, under the German Emperor, who would be Tupu Sili or paramount king. The role of the Ali'i Sili would be to make known to the people the wishes of the Governor, acting on behalf of the Tupu Sili. It was very intelligently thought out. However, the Samoans were intelligent, too. The Ali'i Sili, the Ta'imu, and the Faipule all recognized that executive authority would rest entirely in the hands of the Governor. The problem as they saw it was therefore to persuade the Germans to go away. A Samoan trading company was duly formed at Mulin'u, which would be financed by a levy on all villages, and would buy up copra at a price higher than that being paid by the Europeans. Samoans promptly stopped cutting copra for the German companies, in expectation of the better prices they were going to get. Solf responded by banning the project and some prominent Samoans were arrested for their part in it. Their friends broke into the prison and released them. Solf then dismissed both the Ta'imu and the Faipule; abused the Ali'i Sili for being 'two-faced' and disloyal to the Kaiser; and appointed a new council, the Fono of Faipule, entirely subservient to his command and composed of leaders from villages which had accepted German control.[37]

Ironically, this completely paternalistic structure led to a far greater Samoan participation in local government, for Samoans became clerks, administrative officers and plantation inspectors under Solf's orders. But the position of the Ali'i Sili had become effectively a mockery. Mata'afa and Lauaki Namulau'ulu Mamoe, an outstanding orator, invited the former Ta'imu to join with them in protesting to the Governor about the undermining of traditional Samoan concepts of authority. The protest was to be delivered to Solf at a mass meeting at Mulin'u, held ostensibly to welcome him on his return from Germany with a new wife. The movement thus initiated was named the Mau (testimony) of Pule. It was however sabotaged by the leaders of other districts who distrusted Lauaki and Mata'afa, doubted their chances of success, or simply found it more profitable to work with the Germans. Lauaki and the Ali'i Sili were nonetheless able to greet Solf with an impressive show of force. The Governor temporized at first, then sent for warships to arrest Lauaki, with the agreement of the supine Faipule. War was barely averted when Lauaki was persuaded by missionaries to give himself up peacefully and submit to being deported, as had become almost a tradition with Samoan leaders since the arrival of the Europeans. Solf for his part showed a certain judiciousness by respecting the person of the Ali'i Sili. Mata'afa was about to die anyway; but he managed before his death to persuade Solf's successor, Dr Frich Schultz, to agree that the title of Ali'i Sili should be retained, and that it should be held in turn by members of the lineages of Tupua, Malietoa and Tuimaleali'ifano. He himself had intended to be succeeded by Malietoa Laupepa's son, Malietoa Tanumafili; but as Tanumafili was still too young, he proposed instead Tuimaleali'ifano Si'u.

The Germans, however, had other ideas. The title of Ali'i Sili was in fact allowed to lapse. Instead, Malietoa Tanumafili and Tupua Tamasese Lealofi were sworn in as Fautua or advisers to the Governor.

This was in 1913. The new system was thus not given a chance to show whether or not it would actually work. What could not be doubted was that Samoa had prospered brilliantly under German direction. The average annual export of copra had increased in volume from 6,000 tons in 1900 to over 10,000 tons in 1912. Its value in cash terms had almost trebled in the same period, rising from £63,500 to £173,400. The volume and value of exports of cocoa had both risen in the same period by a hundredfold. The colony had indeed become completely self-supporting by 1912.

One would hesitate to argue that the colonial experience was ever actually beneficial for the people being colonized. Nevertheless, there were obviously cases where the impact of foreign culture on a native community had created a situation where the only solutions were either the permanent one of getting rid of the foreigners or the temporary one of bringing in a foreign government to regulate the activities of its own subjects. The latter solution always had the drawbacks that a colonial regime would run the territory primarily in the interests of foreigners, not of natives, and that its mere presence would necessarily discredit the traditional institutions of the people being governed. A virtually self-sufficient and self-supporting native economy would, for example, be restructured to produce cash crops for sale in overseas markets to suit foreign tastes, in exchange for commodities which the local inhabitants had not found necessary for their existence before. A few generations of intensive Western-type cultivation to suit the economic interests of a planter oligarchy could effectively wreck the ecology as well as the social order of a small community. Any demographic balance or ethnic unity was also likely to be destroyed, because the planters would find it in their interests to bring in indentured labourers from other islands or even from Asia to do their work for them. It was, of course, argued that the economic development of the Pacific islands would have been impossible without the use of indentured labourers from Asia. But this had

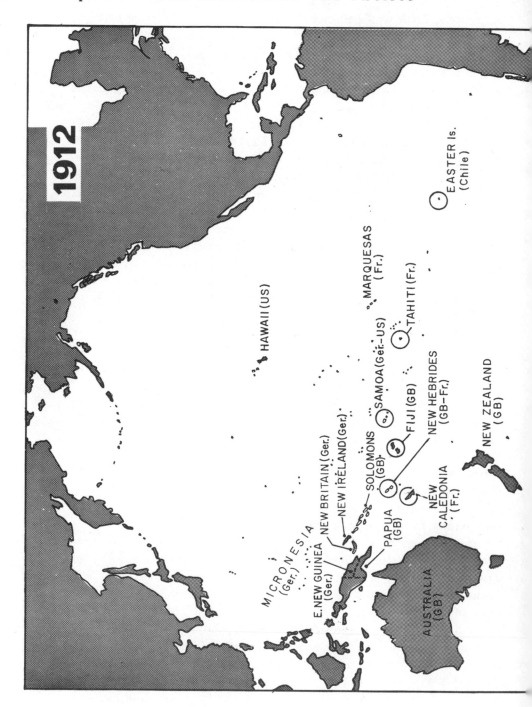

1912

HAWAII (US)

EASTER Is.
(Chile)

MARQUESAS
(Fr.)

TAHITI (Fr.)

SAMOA (Ger.–US)

FIJI (GB)

NEW HEBRIDES
(GB–Fr.)

NEW ZEALAND
(GB)

SOLOMONS
(GB)

NEW IRELAND (Ger.)

NEW BRITAIN (Ger.)

NEW
CALEDONIA
(Fr.)

MICRONESIA
(Ger.)

E. NEW GUINEA
(Ger.)

PAPUA
(GB)

AUSTRALIA
(GB)

never been true as long as the islands were being developed in the interests of the islanders themselves.

The Germans were no less guilty than anybody else in this regard. By 1912 2,184 Chinese and 877 Melanesians had been brought to Samoa to work for the settler economy. Nor had Solf, for all his scholarship and sheer intelligence, any intention of preserving Samoan institutions for their own sake. His concern had been unequivocally to translate German authority into forms acceptable in terms of Samoan traditions; but it was the authority that counted, not the forms. Solf indeed looked forward to the destruction of the traditional Samoan political institutions in the interests of efficiency, as soon as this could practicably be achieved. This approach was not likely to become any more appealing to the Samoans as time went by. There was also most convincing evidence that German economic efficiency itself was liable to pose problems for the German colonial administrators: some part at least of Samoan prosperity was finding its way into the hands of Samoans, or more frequently German-Samoans, who were naturally going to demand an increasingly free hand in the management of the island's affairs for their own profit.

The Germans never had the chance to show how they would have responded to these challenges. It is at least reasonable to assume that they would have responded no more ineffectually than anybody else. The contrast between the informed and imaginative enterprise of the Germans on the one hand, and the generally uninformed and undirected mindlessness of the British and the totally cynical negligence of the French on the other, is impressive enough. But empires do not survive according to their intellectual or humanitarian qualities. Empires are won and lost in wars. French colonial rule still lingers in the Pacific. The German experiment ended in 1914.

There was no doubt that the German experiment looked far better in Samoa than in New Guinea. The Melanesian possessions collectively named the Protectorate of German New Guinea consisted of two island groups. The 'Old Protectorate' comprised north-east New Guinea, New Britain, New Ireland, Buka and Bougainville. The 'Island Territory' was made up of the groups of the Pelews, the Marianas, the Carolines, the Marshalls and Nauru. The whole area was governed from Rabaul in New Britain. Rabaul itself had the natural advantages of a good harbour and proximity to the main trading routes across the Pacific. The Germans had set themselves diligently to work to create there an attractive and well-designed capital for their Pacific empire, something which no other colonial power except possibly Imperial Spain could so far be said to have achieved. But the problems of the Protectorate were utterly different from those of Samoa. In the first place, there was the simple ethnic factor. Europeans found Polynesian and particularly Samoan culture, life-styles and physical appearance sufficiently attractive by their own standards to make the task of working with the natives not too disconcerting. The Samoans especially impressed the foreigners as gentlemen. It might be mentioned in passing that the Samoans have not invariably struck other Polynesians in quite the same light : the limitless depths of Samoan self-satisfaction and desire for repose have, for example, not always endeared Samoan expatriates to New Zealand Maoris.[38] But the kind of culture shock produced by encounters with the Melanesians was something different again. Culture, appearance and society were alike completely alien to the Europeans, accordingly unattractive to them and readily adjudged inferior. 'Stone Age savage' was the most sympathetic expression likely to be applied to the inhabitants of New Guinea, with the very clear assumption that any change in their present ways of life could only be an improvement.

But culture shock was only one of the problems facing the Germans in the Protectorate. The inhabitants were not only incomprehensible and unappealing. They were also apparently extremely numerous. Nobody could be at all certain how populous these regions actually were, because they also happened to include some of the parts of the earth's surface most unapproachable for Europeans, so it was simply impossible to consider taking anything like an accurate census. Within obvious limits, the larger the guess the greater seemed to be the chance of its being right. Something like half a million all told seemed a reasonable estimate. Administering numbers like this was going to be rather different from dealing with buccaneers like Cakobau and Ma'afu, with their 30,000 or 40,000 subjects, or even the more numerous New Zealand Maoris, so adaptable and sophisticated that they could provide the main element in the economic development of an enormous colony for thirty years.

The vast numbers and alien and unacceptable nature of the Melanesians could of course work to their advantage in the long run, in terms of ethnic survival. The tragedy of the Polynesians lay indeed in the fact that they were all too adaptable to foreign ways and techniques, as became immensely skilled and cultured Asian adventurers, who were after all comparatively recent arrivals on the scene, historically speaking : the Danes probably reached Britain before the Marquesans had reached Hawaii. It was no doubt true, as Sutch eloquently says of the New Zealand Maoris, that

> All the aspects of Maori society ... were necessary to maintain the tribal economy in balance and self-regulating at a superior level : the land, the chief, the priest, the magic, the tapu, the specialist, the co-ordination of labour, the division of labour, the songs, the public gatherings, feats, public esteem or condemnation, the economy without money, war and prisoners of war, community decisions, the craft skills, the schools, the knowledge passed on by word of mouth, the discipline of the tribe.
>
> Alien to this remarkable civilization were money, private ownership of land, removal of the forest, steel tools, browsing animals, guns, alcohol, work without rhythm, working a fixed number of hours a day for an employer who wanted a profit from others' labour, neglect of the family or the group, majority rule instead of unanimity, discipline not based on the tribe or elders, a society without song, poetry or philosophy, or which taught varying religious beliefs, whether firmly held or not.[39]

But nothing was more impressive than the rapidity with which the Maoris and other Polynesians tended to adapt to such alien phenomena as guns, alcohol, the profit motive and varying religious beliefs, to say nothing of the despoiling of forests and every other natural resource that could be exploited for profit, including when appropriate their own people. The result was that by the turn of the century the Polynesians were everywhere expected to become extinct, even though the catastrophic decline in their numbers had in fact been arrested. The Melanesian was likely to last longer, simply because he was less eager to assimilate the more destructive features of the European way of life, assuming of course that he managed to survive the efforts of the Europeans to make him do so.

It is a characteristic of the Germans that they do their best, even when faced with a problem such as that represented by New Guinea, where it might well have seemed more reasonable to try to do nothing. German explorers pushed resolutely into the interior, and German punitive expeditions tracked down fugitives from justice. Excellent roads were built in New Britain and New Ireland at least, eight administrative centres set up within the Protectorate, and a most intelligent use made of what appeared to be the existing native system of political authority. The Germans had noted that in both New Guinea and New Britain tribal authority was vested in a chief or *luluai*, usually hereditary but apparently originally elected, who acted as a chief magistrate, assisted by executive officers or *tul-tul*. Wherever possible, the Germans sought the co-operation of the *luluai*; invested amenable ones with caps and batons as badges of office; and left them to continue their traditional functions, intervening only to depose an unsatisfactory *luluai* and appoint a more reliable collaborator when this seemed appropriate. Action of this kind was in fact kept to minimum, as it was observed that *luluai* appointed by governmental action without the approval of tribe were less trusted by the natives and had less *mana* than those who acquired the position in the traditional ways.[40]

Even the Australian Official Historian testified that German colonial authority in the protectorate was free from harshness, humane and beneficial – indeed far more akin to standard British colonial rule than to continental viciousness.[41] This, of course, was no more true of German civilian relations with the natives than it would have been true of Australia or Fiji. Floggings could be administered at the discretion of the civilian employer; and, more seriously, the shooting of natives for trespass or fancied threats to the peace was as liable to happen in the Protectorate as in British Fiji. The Germans indeed seem on occasion to have resorted to the Queensland or Tasmanian practice of hunting natives for sport, to take their minds off the climate and the incredibly uncomfortable life. The fact was as always that Europeans might be able to tolerate the existence of Polynesians, but they found it difficult to treat darker races as people : as late as 1907, a British member of the Governor's Council in Fiji proposed that the Fijians should not be allowed to live in Suva, as it was impossible to keep the town clean with natives around.

Economically, the German empire in the Pacific outside Samoa also faced considerable problems. Nauru was of very real commercial value, being literally covered with deposits of phosphate. But similar deposits had been found only 170 miles away on Ocean Island, which had been annexed by the British, who also supplied nearly half the white work force on Nauru. The Old Protectorate had originally been developed by Johann Godeffroys, and since 1885 by the Neu Guinea Kompagnie, which owned some 369,000 acres of the total 702,000 in the Protectorate. However, Burns Philp had established themselves as carriers for the region in 1896, and had been driven out by Nord Deutscher-Lloyd in 1900 only because the German authorities were prepared to support their own firm with massive subsidies. The economic pull of Australia to the south inevitably remained great : in 1912 Australian imports from the Protectorate were worth 5,970,000 marks, nearly all of which represented imports of phosphate from Nauru, while German imports were valued at 9,650,000 marks; but Australian exports to New Guinea, at 3,380,000 marks, exceeded German by 210,000 marks.[42]

The fact dominating and distorting the whole picture of the Pacific at the beginning of the new century was of course the colossal preponderance of British population in the south. Australia's population had reached 4,972,059 by 1914; New Zealand's, 1,128,160. The Australians, scarcely conscious of the existence of their own Aborigines, could hardly be called a Pacific people in any ethnic or cultural sense of the word; but their numbers meant that in the absence of great power intervention from outside the region the Pacific peoples were at their mercy in the event of war. New Zealand might be at the remotest end of the Pacific, but its 37,000 Maoris represented the largest surviving remnant of the Polynesian race. The Hawaiians had dwindled to 26,011, being out-numbered on their own islands not only by the Japanese at 79,663, but even by the Portuguese at 27,000, and almost matched by the 22,000 Chinese. The indigenous population of Samoa had now fallen to 33,639; the Marquesans had almost ceased to exist; the Tongans held grimly to a figure of 25,000; and the Tahitians numbered perhaps 11,000 at most. New Zealand might not be the hub of a Pacific empire, but it was likely to be the new centre of the Polynesian race.

Compared with the Australians and New Zealanders, the other European presences in the Pacific could only be termed insignificant. The total white population of the German Pacific Empire was not more than 1,750, of whom 1,391 lived in the Protectorate. The French numbered in all some 22,000 in New Caledonia and perhaps 1,000 in Tahiti. The Australians and New Zealanders could justifiably feel themselves isolated, and might choose to think of themselves as threatened by the endless succession of turnip-ghosts their imagination could conjure up; but the fact was that their shadow fell across every other European settlement in the ocean.

Militarily, the matter was one of simple arithmetic. The Australians and New Zealanders had the reserves of manpower to mobilize around half a million men for war purposes if they had a mind to. It was virtually certain that the Maoris would co-operate to some extent. On the other hand, any forces that the French could raise in New Caledonia would probably be engaged in keeping order among the natives. The

Germans might be able to enlist more support among their native peoples in the Protectorate, though they could hardly expect to do so in Samoa, which might well also need holding down; but Melanesian levies could be expected to perform adequately against European soldiers more accustomed to military methods and technology, only if they were well supported by European officers and NCOs; and there were exactly sixty-one of these in the Protectorate. There was no force in the Pacific capable of offering anything but token resistance against an attack from the British colonies.

Nor was there much likelihood of the balance being altered by forces from outside. Not less than ten divisions would have had to be sent out from Europe to the Pacific to neutralize the British colonies; no expeditionary force of that size could leave the Continent unless the British Fleet had first been destroyed; and there was no fleet in the world capable of destroying the Royal Navy in a straight confrontation. Logically, in any event, there would be no purpose in sending out an expeditionary force to occupy Australia and New Zealand once the British Fleet had been defeated, anyway: the war would be over, the Empire would be lost, and all that would be required would be a cable to Melbourne and Wellington apprising them of the fact.

This was the anomaly at the centre of the British colonies' pre-occupation with defence. Their enormous open spaces and isolation seemed to invite an invader; but no European invader could mount a force sufficient to overwhelm them unless Britain itself were defeated, and no such force would be necessary if Britain were in fact defeated. Admittedly this was a point of logic that would have seemed more apparent in the British Isles than in New South Wales. Yet these British colonists in the Pacific were among the least timorous and most aggressive peoples on earth. The Australians and New Zealanders were not paper tigers. Resolutely unalike in their martial traditions and united mainly by a refusal to give each other credit for anything, they had already shown more readiness to fight in British wars than the British themselves had bargained for. In 1885 750 volunteers had left New South Wales with ten field guns to march with Kitchener to Khartoum. Australia had sent 16,175 horsemen to fight in the Boer War, while New Zealand, with less than a quarter of the population of Australia, had sent 6,411; 518 Australians and 174 New Zealanders had died in Africa, and 882 Australians and 202 New Zealanders had been wounded in battle. The Australian and New Zealand dead admittedly amounted to only 3·4 per cent of the total number of British Empire troops killed in action or dying of disease, but their contribution had been made memorable by their extraordinary display of such military qualities as proficiency in riding and shooting, enterprise, dash, resolution under fire and sheer physical and moral toughness.[43] This last quality had indeed been shown in so uninhibited a fashion by the Australians especially that even Kitchener, himself a connoisseur of frightfulness in war, had found it appropriate to sentence four Australian officers to death, and actually to shoot two of them, for atrocities beyond the call of duty against the Boer civilian population. This action incidentally impelled the Australian Government to ensure that nothing of the kind would ever happen again, by passing legislation decreeing that no Australian soldier should ever be shot in future for anything more trivial than desertion or high treason.[44]

War was something that both Dominions were taking increasingly seriously in the new century. New Zealand actually introduced compulsory military training in its Defence Act of 1909. Every boy at school was compelled to receive military training in the cadets from the age of twelve, unless physically unfit; he then served in the Territorials until twenty-five, and the reserve until thirty, but remained liable to be called up under the terms of the Militia Act until fifty-five. The scheme was not entirely successful: the Federation of Labour denounced it as a plot to develop an officer caste to strengthen the power of the ruling class, and 10,245 persons were prosecuted for non-registration within two and a half years. At the same time, it was successful to the extent that by the middle of 1914 approximately 67,000 males were receiving some kind of military training, and of these the 29,447 in the Territorial Force could be regarded as tolerably ready for active service. They admittedly had no modern rifles, or indeed any rifles at all except for twenty-odd thousand outmoded ones earmarked for the secondary school cadets to practise with, but they were at least likely to know what to do with modern weapons when they were issued with them. This was certainly more than could be said for any native levies that potential enemies might be able to raise in the Pacific.

The Australian situation was rather more obscure. Defence Acts in 1903 and 1904 had made all male inhabitants between the ages of eighteen and sixty liable to serve in Australia for national defence in time of war. A further act in 1909 made military training compulsory in time of peace. Full compulsory military training was introduced in 1911. Physically fit males not otherwise exempt were required to train between the ages of twelve and twenty-six. In all, 89,138 Australians were undergoing military training in some form or another by 1914, of whom 45,645 were actually in the armed forces properly so called.

The naval sphere was the only possible area of danger. Australian naval strength in 1914 consisted of a battle-cruiser, the *Australia*, of 19,200 tons, armed with eight 12-inch guns; three cruisers of 5,400 tons displacement, with eight 6-inch guns; three destroyers; and two submarines. The ships were all new, and certainly comparable with their opposite numbers in foreign navies; indeed, they added up to the most impressive showing of naval strength in the South Pacific. The striking power of the German Pacific Squadron consisted of two smaller, older, less heavily-armed ships, the *Scharnhorst* and the *Gneisenau*, of 1,500 tons each and with eight 8-inch guns, which could not have been a match for the *Australia*, either singly or in combination. French naval power was represented by the quaint old *Montcalm*, of 9,000 tons and with two 7·6 guns, resting peacefully in Noumea. The balance of power in the South Pacific was all one way. No European power could possibly challenge the British in the Pacific until the United Kingdom itself had been decisively beaten in Europe. The only possible threat to the British Eastern Empire lay in an attack by an Asian great power, possessing its own bases in the Pacific Ocean and able to deploy from them forces which the British could not match if they were at the same time to preserve their own security at home. There would certainly be something totally appropriate in the spectacle of a new wave of Asian adventurers sweeping across the archipelagoes and out into the waters of the Pacific, following in the path of their epic predecessors 4,000 years or so before. This was, of course, the ultimate nightmare for the Australians and the New Zealanders. It was a nightmare which the British themselves were busily conjuring into reality. Asia was indeed breaking out into the Pacific again, at the urgent invitation of the greatest of Western colonial powers.

V

Under a Rising Sun

The United States Navy had been preparing for a Pacific war since the beginning of the century. The General Board proposed in 1909 that a separate battle fleet should be established in the Pacific to confront Japan. In 1910 their Plans Division drew up an Orange Plan for a war with Japan, in the event of aggression by the Japanese against American island territories in the Pacific. The British in fact had rather more concrete reasons for apprehensions about their new ally. The Anglo–Japanese system was virtually falling apart by 1913: the British had refused to assist Japan in a projected war with the United States; the Japanese had reached a secret understanding with Russia over Mongolia, and were fomenting revolution in China, in direct contravention of the terms of the Anglo-Japanese Alliance; British and Russian interests were colliding openly in the Balkans and Persia; and the British involvement with France had effectively hamstrung any possibility of a rapprochement with Germany. Meanwhile, Japanese naval power had outstripped that of any other nation in the Pacific and Indian Oceans. A situation had developed at last in which the European empires might find themselves at the mercy of Asian sea power. The Japanese admittedly still lacked bases in the Pacific, and could acquire them only by going to war with one of the other great powers, as there were no longer any independent island polities to snap up. However, opportunity to take this extreme step in virtual safety soon arose. The European powers went to war in August 1914, and the British invited Japan to stand by the alliance by neutralizing the German forces in the Far East.[1]

This proposal by London might well have seemed a little premature. The Germans were fully aware of their own military weakness in China and the Pacific, and had suggested that these areas should be excluded from the fighting zone by mutual agreement between themselves and the British. However, the British were also aware of German weakness in the Pacific at least, and were happy to take advantage of it. On the night of 6 August the Secretary of State for the Colonies cabled the Governors-General of Australia and New Zealand, informing them that if their Ministers desired and felt themselves able to seize the German wireless station at Samoa, in the case of New Zealand, and 'at Yap in the Marshall Islands, Nauru on Pleasant Island, and New Guinea' in the case of Australia, 'we should feel that this was a great and urgent Imperial service'. It was, however, pointed out to both the Dominions that 'any territory now occupied must be at the disposal of the Imperial Government for purposes of an ultimate settlement at conclusion of the war'.[2] At the same time, it was evident that the Imperial Government had decided to allow the Australians and New Zealanders to establish themselves by right of conquest in precisely those German-occupied areas of the Pacific of which they had been most anxious to gain possession. It was accordingly fair to assume that they would be allowed to keep what they were being invited to conquer.

There was certainly no reasonable doubt that the Australians and New Zealanders would conquer in any fighting that might occur : the forces of the huge British colonies could easily swamp any possible German resistance. It was true that nobody knew exactly what forces the Germans might have on Samoa : the New Zealand Government had asked London for information, and London had suggested that they try *Whitaker's Almanack*. In fact the Germans had no military forces on Samoa. Nor did they have any in the Marshalls or the Carolines. There was stationed around Rabaul an expeditionary force of 240 native soldiers and 61 Europeans. There were no fixed defences and no ammunition for the two saluting guns and one machine gun in Madang, in New Guinea. Resistance under these conditions would clearly have been futile.

There was nonetheless always the possibility that the German Pacific Squadron might try to intervene. It was therefore considered necessary to combine the Australian and New Zealand efforts in a single convoy, protected with all available naval strength. A New Zealand contingent of 1,413 men was organized by 11 August, with artillery and machine guns, and embarked on two troopships the following day. They were joined within a week by an escort of three light cruisers and set off for Noumea in New Caledonia to await the Australian ships. Both enterprises had their problems. The Australians, 1,023 infantrymen from New South Wales, plus six companies of the Royal Australian Naval Reserve, were embarked on the armed merchant cruiser *Berrima* from Sydney on 19 August. The object was to rendezvous at Port Moresby with the *Kanowna*, carrying 500 men from a citizen force battalion raised in North Queensland. The rendezvous was not a success. The firemen aboard the *Kanowna* mutinied rather than sail into any area of possible danger; the North Queenslanders were found to be unfit, untrained and ill-equipped; and the *Kanowna* was instructed to return to Townsville, leaving the *Berrima* to continue with the invasion.

In the meantime, the New Zealanders had narrowly missed running into the *Scharnhorst* and *Gneisenau* heading south. However, they reached Noumea safely, there to be greeted enthusiastically by the French population, and to receive the dubious support of the ancient *Montcalm*, while awaiting the arrival of the Australians. The fleet then put into Fiji for coaling, and at last left for Samoa on 27 August. On the way, they took the occasion to inform the King of Tonga that war had broken out, a development of which he had been unaware until then; and were informed in their turn that Tonga was neutral.

The New Zealanders went ashore at Apia on 29 August, carrying a piece of a tablecloth tacked to a broomstick as a flag of truce. The Germans politely surrendered; German-owned businesses were liquidated or placed in military receivership; and German officials were deported, their places being taken by New Zealand Army officers whose sole qualifications were that they happened to be around and available at the time.[3]

New Zealand had thus bloodlessly acquired a fragment of a Pacific empire, since the Kermadecs and the Cooks could hardly be seen in quite such a light. Meanwhile, the Australians were after bigger game. On 11 September the Australian convoy arrived off Rabaul in New Britain and demanded the surrender of the Protectorate. The German defenders, 150 in all, had already withdrawn. There was a brisk skirmish, in which the Australians demonstrated their extraordinary aptitude for jungle warfare, outflanking and encircling the Germans' native troops, who had simply not expected to find white men stalking them through the bush; and on 17 September the territories of the Protectorate passed under Australian military control. The Australians had lost six dead and four wounded, the Germans and their native troops about thirty-one dead and eleven wounded.

This still left the Carolines, Marshalls, Marianas and Pelews in the North Pacific in German hands. The wireless station at Yap had already been put out of action on 12 August by HMS *Hampshire* of the China Squadron. Nauru had been similarly taken care of by a landing party from the *Melbourne* on 9 September. However, it was clear that the islands would have to be occupied to ensure that the Germans did not start using them again. It had already been proposed that the Australians should take Yap. As the British did not know whether Yap was in the Marshalls or the Carolines, they presumably would not have minded which of the island groups the Australians occupied. However, the Japanese were invited to 'cruise in the Pacific around Marianne and Caroline Islands in order to hunt down a German squadron which is believed to be in these parts and which will prey upon British and Japanese shipping in the Pacific unless it is attacked'.[4] The paradox was that the Australians had wanted to unleash their navy to track down the Germans in the first place, but had been directed by the Admiralty to undertake the expeditions against the German colonies, which would have been helpless in any case once their ships had been destroyed. What happened now was that the Japanese despatched a powerful squadron which simply took strategic control of the Marianas, the Marshalls and the Carolines. The Australians went on preparing an expeditionary force to replace the Japanese, but there were now no ships available to transport them. Australian troops were needed elsewhere, in any case. The British accordingly decided that as the Japanese had already been in occupancy of the islands for more than a month, it would be 'discourteous and disadvantageous' to turn them out.[5] The Australians were therefore told that as the German islands north of the equator were 'at present in military occupation by the Japanese who are at our request engaged in policing waters in the Northern Pacific we consider it most convenient for strategic reasons to allow them to remain in occupation for the present leaving the whole question of future to be settled at end of war'.[6]

Superficially, this view made obvious sense. The Pacific was an area of minor strategic interest to the British. It was therefore appropriate to leave it to the Japanese, who had indeed nothing else to do, while all available resources were concentrated against the main enemy, Germany. Nor might it have seemed that the Japanese incursions constituted any real threat to white Australia: the total foreign population of the

1 *Top:* Carved door lintel from a Maori meeting house. The scene depicted is said to be Man being destroyed by the goddess Hiria as he tries to win immortality.

2 *Left:* Maori lintel showing a man holding a club: dating from the late eighteenth century.

3 *Right:* Vertical boards supporting the lintels of a Maori meeting house.

4 Feather cape from Hawaii.

5 An engraving by John Webber showing a native of the Sandwich Islands wearing a feather helmet.

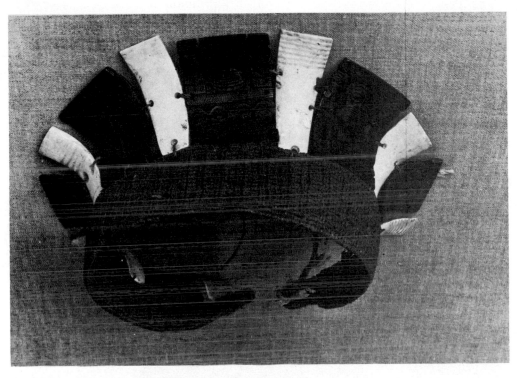

6 Diadem of tortoise shell from the Marquesas Islands.

7 Carved food bowl from the Marquesas Islands.

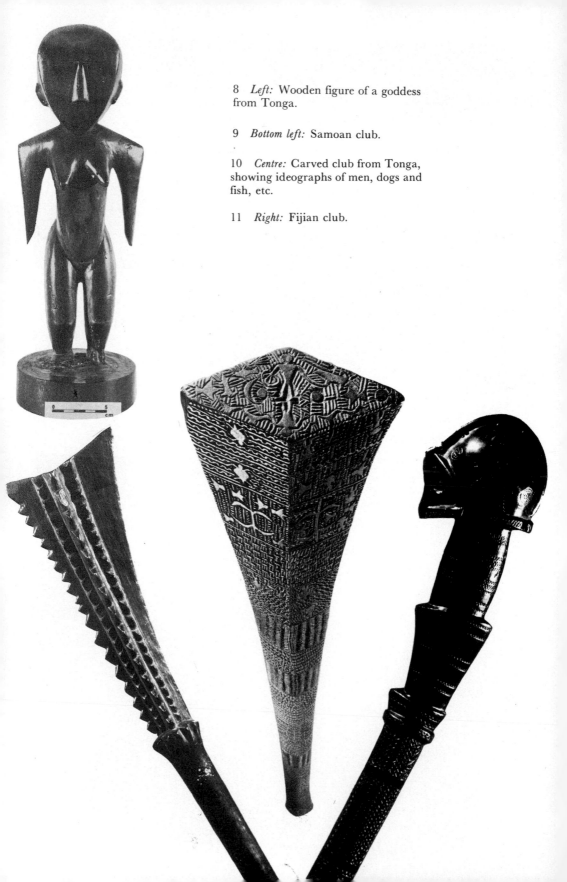

8 *Left:* Wooden figure of a goddess from Tonga.

9 *Bottom left:* Samoan club.

10 *Centre:* Carved club from Tonga, showing ideographs of men, dogs and fish, etc.

11 *Right:* Fijian club.

12 *Top:* Oil vessel from Fiji, carved in the form of a flying duck.

13 *Centre:* Pottery water-bottle in the form of a turtle, from Fiji.

14 *Opposite:* Serving platter or bowl from Fiji.

15 *Top left:* Lizard man from Easter Island.

16 *Above:* Wooden figure from Easter Island.

17 *Left:* Thor Heyerdahl standing by a stone figure from Easter Island.

18 Ferdinand Magellan, the Portuguese mariner.

19 Engraving of Abel Tasman's expedition to Fiji, 1643.

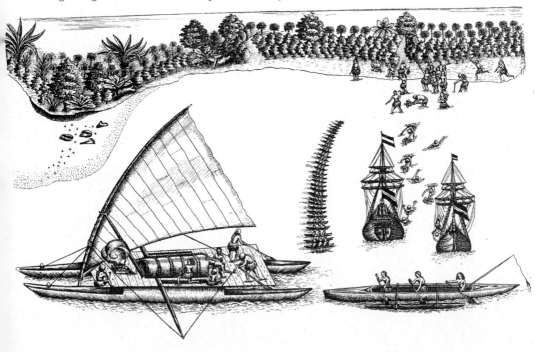

20 Interview between Captain Samuel Wallis and the Queen of Tahiti, 1767.

21 Captain Cook on the island of Tahiti, 1769.

22 The death of Captain Cook on Hawaii, 14 February 1779.

23 Encounter between Samoans and French sailors sent ashore by La Pérouse in 1787.

24, 25 and 26 Nineteenth-century paintings of Maori life.

27 and 28   Vicissitudes in missionary work in the Pacific in the nineteenth century.
Above: The baptism of Te Ngahue, a Maori chief at Te Ariki, 1851. *Below:* The death of
the Reverend Williams at Erromanca.

29   Anzac troops arriving in England in June 1940.

30   The destruction of the US battleship *Arizona* by Japanese bombers at Pearl Harbor, 7 December 1941.

US Navy plane bombing Woje in the Marshall Islands.

The crew of the US aircraft carrier *Lexington* swarming down from the deck after ship had been set on fire by Japanese bombers in the Battle of the Coral Sea, July 2.

33 General Douglas MacArthur with some of his commanders and troops during a tour of army installations in the Tanamerah Bay area of New Guinea, 1944.

34 Australian and native troops preparing to launch an attack against the Japanese in New Guinea.

35   Independence celebrations in Samoa in 1962. The Prime Minister of New
Zealand, Keith Holyoake, the joint heads of state, H.H. Malietoa Tanumafili and H.H.
Tupua Tamasese Meaole, and the Prime Minister of Samoa, Maka'afa Fiame
Faumuina, watching a march past of Samoan youth.

36   President de Gaulle with his ministers watching a French atom bomb exploding
over Mururoa atoll (37) near Tahiti, 13 September 1968.

38 and 39   The two faces of modern Papua, New Guinea: *Above:* A Baliem war chief with his hair pig greased and a string of cowry shells round his neck. *Below:* An oil strike at Puri by the Australasian Petroleum Company.

German islands in Japanese hands before occupation was barely 200, of whom only 80 or so were Japanese. The fact was, however, that the Australians were no more prepared than before to recognize any claim to the islands of the Pacific except their own : even the New Zealand expedition was regarded as trespassing somewhat on an Australian preserve, as the Governor-General of the Commonwealth noted : 'The occupation of Samoa rankles a little. It is felt that she got there thanks to the protection of the Australian fleet ... Australia regards the Pacific as her "duck-pond" and scarcely admits New Zealand's claim to a look-in.'[7]

It was thus not surprising that American observers in Australia should have formed the impression very early in the game that the halting of the Australian expedition to the Marshalls and the Carolines had caused 'bad blood' between the British colonials and the Japanese : 'the Japanese are thought over here to be on the make and they (British) hope that the US will stop them going too far'.[8] However, the Australians and New Zealanders gained little sympathy in London. The Foreign Office chose to believe that if Britain were to attempt to bar Japanese expansion in the Far East it would be to Japan's advantage to throw in her lot with Germany. The Australian Governor-General was assured that British fleets were so fully engaged in the north, the Atlantic, the Mediterranean and in convoy escort duties, that they could not have spared ships to deal with the Pacific, and had therefore to call in Japanese aid. However, the fact was that the Royal Australian Navy was more than adequate to defeat German naval power in the Pacific if it had been allowed to concentrate on that task instead of being diverted against the German colonies.

It was, of course, true that the Australians and New Zealanders had cried wolf too often in the past. But this time there really was a wolf. The other island possessions had been helpless before Australian and New Zealand military strength, so long as the British Navy could prevent them from being reinforced from Europe. But the British might well be unable to keep control of the Atlantic and the Pacific at the same time. This was indeed why they had been happy to leave the policing of the Pacific to a friendly great power which was there already, Japan. But this in itself was equivalent to admitting that the security of the British Empire in the Pacific and Indian Oceans depended on Japanese good-will, which on all past experience had been a diminishing asset long before 1914. The fact was, as the Australian Governor-General replied to London, that 'A first-class Pacific Power watches every move of the game in commercial and territorial expansion and is ready to pounce down upon a quarrelsome neighbour, a helpless prey and an empty continent.'⁹ There was no doubt as to the identity of the helpless prey and the empty continent to which he referred.

This was paradoxical in view of the astounding military contribution which Australia and New Zealand had made to the British war effort. Australia alone mobilized 416,809 men, or 8·34 per cent of its entire population of just under 5 million. Of these, 7,442 were in camp waiting to be sent to the front when the war ended; 79,780 had been discharged for various reasons, prior to embarkation; and 329,587 actually went overseas. Of these 59,258, or 14·2 per cent of those actually mobilized, were killed. New Zealand's contribution was equal to Australia's: out of a total population of about 1,130,000, 124,211 or 11 per cent were mobilized; 100,444 despatched overseas; and 16,302, or 7·6 per cent of the total mobilized, killed on service. Nor was their effort impressive solely by numerical standards: Australians provided 9·5 per cent of the British manpower on the Western Front in the last stages of the war, but captured 23 per cent of German guns and prisoners. Sober and experienced students of combat seriously described the Australians as the best infantry in the world; the Melbourne Jew, Monash, as the outstanding general of the war on either side; and the campaigns in which the Australian Imperial Force was involved as the most brilliant and intelligent in the war. The only people seriously contesting such claims were, of course, the New Zealanders, dour where the Australians were extrovert, relentless where the Australians were enterprising, bucolic where the Australians were brash; and in their own estimation more reliable, better behaved, nicer and in general superior in the more enduring military qualities.

Two things at any rate were not in doubt: the Australians and New Zealanders both fought with terrifying efficiency, endurance and consistency; and the Polynesian peoples under British authority could at the very least be counted on to support the Imperial cause. Some 2,050 Maoris, and approximately 918 Rarotongans, Gilbert Islanders and Fijians volunteered for service with the New Zealand Armed Forces, mainly overseas. The experience of French Oceania was rather more complex. One might think that actual contact with war would have aroused their enthusiasm: von Spee's ships had sailed to Apia after the New Zealand occupation, then sailed away again; bombarded Papeete, killing one native and one Chinese; and landed in the Marquesas, where they seized supplies of meat, which they paid for in money taken from the official treasury. The fact was that from a population of roughly 28,000 French Polynesia provided some 1,200 volunteers, who suffered in all 262 casualties in France and Salonika. New Caledonia was something else again. The 17,000 Europeans and 27,000 natives provided, respectively, 1,036 and 1,134 volunteers to the Pacific Battalion, a quite respectable 4 to 6 per cent of their populations. Casualties were heavy: 162 Europeans and 374 natives died, or over 25 per cent of the total strength of the battalion, even though 207 of the native deaths were due to disease. As the Governor of New Caledonia was to point out in 1943, forty Military Medals and Croix de Guerre were won by the Pacific Battalion at Verdun, in the Champagne and on the Somme. It was nonetheless not a contribution vital to the war effort of France itself, as the contributions of the Australians and New Zealanders had been to the British war effort, and against it had to be set the inconvenience of the revolt of 1917, provoked mainly by the damage being done to native lands by the cattle of the European ranchers, in which 11 Europeans and at least 200 natives had been killed, and it had been necessary to appeal to Australia for assistance. Indeed the Australians, viewing the instability of New Caledonia and the continuing decline of the native population, looked forward optimistically to the time when the big island would fall under their own economic and political control.

Meanwhile, the Australians and New Zealanders were faced with the task of digesting the territories which they had acquired already from the Germans, and which, as the British had always believed, they were totally unprepared to govern. Both the new empires got off to extremely unpromising starts. German New Guinea was governed by a succession of Australian military administrators, utterly unaware of the nature of the problems they were dealing with, subject to no effective control, and concerned only with the potential economic value of the territory and its inhabitants. They hoped to leave the German businessmen to run their enterprises until they could be taken over by Australians, and to work through the German administrative system until the Australian Government could devise something better. The trouble was that the *tululai* system was already running wild: the native magistrates exercised in general merely local and *ad hoc* authority, finding their greatest professional satisfaction in the application of corporal punishment. Flogging indeed seemed to be an essential part of the New Guinea scene, as if the territory had been handed over to a band of fifth-form bullies chosen from an inferior private school. In one incredible episode, a German doctor and four other Germans, assisted by a Belgian planter, had caned a British missionary because they thought he had been spying for the Australians. The Australian military administration dealt with the situation by having the Germans themselves flogged, despite the fact that corporal punishment of any kind was expressly forbidden by the British *Manual of Military Law*. Flogging of natives was officially abolished in 1919, despite the expressed belief of the Australian Prime Minister that this was the only way to stop natives from prowling around and molesting white women. The Australian Empire had got off to a rather sordid start.[10]

New Zealand's experience was far worse. The New Zealanders were no more interested in flogging Samoans than they were in flogging Maoris. Their catastrophes derived from simple human incompetence. The Samoans had indeed no reason not to welcome the New Zealand occupation. Many of them would have preferred to have had the New Zealanders or at least the British govern Samoa in the first place, and German power had not been established without a certain amount of rough handling. German rule had been strong, intelligent and productive, but it had also been in many ways humiliating, and had certainly held out some ominous prospects for the future. Now, under New Zealand rule, native Samoans or part-Samoans saw an opportunity to enhance their economic position at the expense of the deported Germans. However, within four years the New Zealanders had brought sheer disaster. The ship *Talune* left Auckland early in November 1918 for Apia, bearing passengers suffering from pneumonic influenza. The disease was not notifiable at the time of sailing, although its seriousness was appreciated by the authorities. It was indeed declared officially notifiable after the *Talune* left Auckland, but even then Apia was not informed that the disease was on board. The ship was quarantined in Fiji, where it called first, but the captain failed to tell the port health officer at Apia that this had been done. The chief steward did tell the port health officer, but the health officer took no notice. The disease began to spread, and it became increasingly hard to find any European in a position of responsibility who showed anything like the mental or moral qualities required to cope with the situation. The New Zealand authorities actually closed down a temporary hospital in Apia and the resident medical officer in Savaii stayed indoors throughout the epidemic on the grounds that nobody had ordered him to go and visit the sick. The American Governor of Eastern Samoa realized what was happening; imposed quarantine restrictions which proved totally effective; and unreservedly offered the services of his team of medical officers and trained assistants. The New Zealand military administrator ignored the American offer, and indeed shut down radio communication with American Samoa, apparently because he was annoyed at the fact that the Americans were quarantining mail from the rest of the island.

The total failure of the New Zealand authorities to cope with the situation resulted in a total loss of some 8,500 lives, or nearly a quarter of the population of Samoa. The United Nations Department of Social Affairs has described the epidemic as 'one of the most disastrous. . . recorded anywhere in the world during the present century, so far as the proportion of deaths to the population is concerned'.[11] It was hard to believe that human inadequacy had not been reinforced by malevolence to produce such a calamity. Samoans continued for decades to regard the epidemic as something 'done to' their country by New Zealand, as indeed in a sense it was. Although New Zealand's reputation for goodwill, if not exactly for administrative ability, was salvaged to some extent by a scrupulously fair commission of inquiry which made no attempt to find excuses for the appalling failures of all concerned, this naturally did not prevent many Samoans from petitioning to have their country taken over by the Americans, who at least knew what they were doing.

Apprehensions about the prospects of New Zealand rule deepened with further experience. Even the European community in Samoa was infuriated by a decree in early 1919 banning the importation of alcohol, as a precursor to full prohibition. More seriously, it also became apparent that the New Zealanders intended to introduce an essentially authoritarian system. Executive power would be vested in an Administrator, who would be advised by a legislative council with a majority of appointed members. Moreover, the members not officially appointed were to represent only the European community. The New Zealand Government itself reserved the right to legislate over a wide range of subjects. The Fono of Faipule remained in being, since the New Zealanders had concluded from the experience of Fiji that native customs should be left alone as far as practicable; but it was not to be given legal recognition.

Authoritarianism is scarcely enjoyable even when efficient. It is scarcely tolerable when inefficient. The Germans had been undeniably tough; but the Germans had had vast resources, vision and enormous expertise and technical intelligence. Expertise and resources were exactly what the New Zealanders conspicuously lacked. The Military Administration had resolutely deported 200 German managers, 676 of the island's 877 Melanesian labourers and 1,400 of its 2,200 Chinese. This experiment in racial purification was followed by a disastrous recession, which it undoubtedly helped to make far worse. New Zealand then had to reverse its policy and arrange for the re-importation of some 1,579 Chinese as indentured labourers.

It was not surprising that the Samoans began to petition for self-government almost before the New Zealanders had taken over. Nevertheless it was hoped that the new Administrator, Brigadier George Richardson, who arrived in 1923, would be able to introduce a new era of New Zealand–Samoan co-operation. Richardson took the trouble to learn to speak Samoan; he had a firm belief in his responsibility to promote the welfare of the natives; and he began promisingly by expanding the powers and responsibilities of the Fono of Faipule. He also developed initially cordial relations with members of the economically powerful 'European' community, including the prosperous and influential part-Samoan Olaf Frederick Nelson. Unfortunately, Richardson was also intolerant, authoritarian and totally paternalistic. He was therefore the type of ruler most likely to alienate the European Samoans, who had already begun to emerge as a challenge to colonial authority in the later years of German rule. Richardson's authoritarianism also began to arouse opposition at the village council level. By 1926 Samoans were simply declining to co-operate with what was evidently an attempt to impose an alien system upon their traditional society. A petition of grievances was assembled by Nelson and others for presentation to the New Zealand Minister of External Affairs when he visited Samoa in June 1927. The visit was however postponed, and Nelson now proposed that the Minister should receive a delegation from Samoa in New Zealand. Richardson, over-reacting to any overt opposition, refused to issue passports to the Samoan delegation; denounced Nelson's activities as an attempt by the European community to meddle in native affairs, which Richardson had convinced himself should be kept separate; and appeared to support the view of his secretary that the whole affair was merely 'a kick by the half-caste at the white man'.[12]

But the main trouble was perhaps that the white man was also kicking the native Samoan. Richardson and the New Zealand Government certainly seem to have believed that they were in fact strengthening native institutions by formally recognizing the Fono of Faipule and providing that all laws should be brought before it. But the Fono had been developed by the Germans; the Faipule themselves were all chosen by the Administrator; and holders of traditional authority who had not been appointed by the Administrator were treated with total disrespect, as impediments in the way of Samoan progress. Richardson's treatment of the Fautua was almost incredibly disrespectful. Tupua Tamaese Lealofi III was banished from Samoa for failing to remove a hibiscus hedge from land that he believed to be his own. When he returned to find out how long he was supposed to stay away he was promptly arrested, deprived of his title, jailed, and banished again. The Minister's eventual visit to Samoa in 1927 only served to intensify apprehensions. Nelson and the part-Europeans were denounced for seeking to undermine the confidence of the Samoans in their own institutions, and all non-Samoans who meddled in native affairs were threatened with deportation without warning.

Official fury had been raised by the formation of a protest movement, the Samoan League or O le Mau, created 'to endeavour to procure by lawful means the alteration of any matter affecting the laws, government, or constitution of the territory which may be considered prejudicial to the welfare and best interests of the people'.[18] Participation in the Mau was now declared illegal; fifty persons were deported in a matter of months, and Nelson himself was banished for five years.

Nelson left Samoa for New Zealand voluntarily, to avoid any occasion for violence. However, members of the Mau marched through the streets of Apia on the day of his departure, and its strong-arm men picketed European-owned stores. More seriously, the Mau imposed a ban on the making of copra, in the hope of rendering the Government bankrupt. Richardson responded by calling on the New Zealand Government to send two cruisers and marines to Apia. But the arrest of 400 members of the Mau only multiplied Richardson's problems, as there was not sufficient space in the jail to accommodate the prisoners, let alone the hundreds of other Samoans who declared their solidarity with the Mau by asking to be arrested.

Richardson was replaced in April 1928 by yet another soldier, Colonel Steven Allen, unlike Richardson a man of high education and reserved manner. His hope appears to have been that the Mau would die away if some of the more immediate grievances were removed. Something was indeed done in this direction. Taxes were reduced; and an attempt was made to streamline the machinery of government by suspending the Fono, and reinstituting the Legislative Council with two European-elected and two Samoan-nominated members. However, both the Samoan appointees were firm supporters of the government, and one was a former Faipule; clearly more would have to be done to reconcile colonial and traditional authority. Nelson's deportation made it impossible for the Administration to pretend that the Mau was a simple matter of Europeans or half-castes meddling in native affairs. The principal spokesman of the Mau was Tupua Tamasese, the representative of traditional native authority. While Nelson cultivated the support of the Labour Party and other sympathizers in New Zealand, awaiting an opportunity to plead Samoa's case before the League of Nations, Tamasese prepared to return to his homeland from banishment. A mass celebration was held to welcome him. Further demonstrations were organized to hail the return of other deportees. On 28 December 1928 the Mau marched through Apia to greet A. G. Smyth, who had been exiled with Nelson. For some reason the police attempted to arrest the secretary of the Mau while the procession was halted to salute the Union Jack; a policeman was knocked down, and his colleagues opened fire on the procession with revolvers, supported by a machine gun firing from the police station. Eleven Samoans, all of the highest rank including Tamasese himself, were killed, and scores more wounded. One European policeman died in the affray.

Matters were again made worse by the behaviour of the New Zealand authorities after the event. There was no way in which the procession could have been called violent, or even disloyal in any colonial sense; virtually all the bloodshed had been on one side; and the members of the Mau had fled to the bush, to avoid open war with the authorities. The New Zealand Government nonetheless again despatched a cruiser to Apia, and landing parties of marines scoured the villages, breaking into houses, smashing furniture, terrifying the families of suspected members of the Mau and in general expressing all the racist sentiments which it was unpopular or inexpedient to express in New Zealand itself.

The Mau now reverted to passive resistance and economic boycotts, disastrous in a time of world depression. The Administration sought to challenge the appeal of the Mau by reinstating the Fono of Faipule with a membership nominated entirely by the local village councils. The Mau however refused to participate in the new Fono, so it was representative only of a minority and accordingly exposed to ridicule by the bulk of Samoans. The New Zealanders became increasingly unable to respond rationally to developments. When Nelson came back from exile to Apia in May 1933, he was promptly rearrested again and sentenced to eight months' imprisonment and a further ten years' banishment. He then went to New Zealand, where he was yet again arrested. But a change was coming. The New Zealand Labour Party, which attained office in 1935, knew no more about the Samoan situation than its predecessors, but at least it was ideologically opposed to colonialism.

Nelson's sentence of banishment was quashed, and a parliamentary good-will mission was sent to Samoa to investigate grievances and prepare the way for his next return. The tone of the situation seemed to have changed completely. The New Zealand Government repealed the legislation declaring the Mau a seditious movement; Nelson returned in triumph; and a new constitution was introduced, increasing the number of Samoan members of the legislative council from two to four and creating a new Fono of Faipule with the responsibility of nominating the Samoan members of the council. Moreover, the Mau were authorized to advise on the election of the Faipule, thirty-three of whose thirty-nine members were in consequence candidates of the Mau. On the other hand, nothing like a concrete proposal for self-government had emerged; New Zealand still retained its mandatory right to legislate for Samoa; and apparently incompetent or racist officials remained in power in both Apia and Wellington, despite the furious protests of the Samoans. One of the main factors which helped to keep opposition within peaceful limits was the open enmity of many of the European planters towards the Labour Government, especially after it had decided, on the advice of the Fono, to bring in no more indentured Chinese labourers. It was sufficiently clear to the Mau that their only hopes for the future lay with the New Zealand Labour Party for them not to want to make it too difficult for that party to stay in office.

The New Zealanders had obviously failed to reconcile the Samoans to New Zealand colonial rule as a permanent prospect. The most that could be said was that they had removed a certain number of more pressing grievances with sufficient evidence of goodwill to keep Samoan opposition non-violent for the time being. But all the signs were that they simply did not know what to do next. They were certainly not likely to be at all sure when and how to get out of Samoa, as they would certainly be required to do sometime. A stalemate had been reached by 1938, when the Fono asked the New Zealand Government to repeal a number of oppressive laws, relating mainly to such matters as the transfer of prisoners from Samoa to New Zealand and the provision for banishment. The Minister declined on the grounds that the laws were in fact not operative at the time. Neither the Fono nor the Mau took any action in response to this decision, but neither did they indicate that they were at all satisfied. The New Zealand Government concluded unprofitably that the Mau doubtless fulfilled a psychological need for the Samoans, but as a political element it neither co-operated with the New Zealand Admin-istration nor actively hindered it.

This stand-off could not be expected to last for ever. The simple fact was that the New Zealanders lacked the overall resources to cope with the responsibilities they had undertaken. They could conceive and implement pragmatic schemes to relieve obvious human needs with an impressive lack of fuss and freedom from inhibitions. But large-scale or long-term social and economic planning was hardly within the range of their expertise or their material capacity.

Unfortunately, the New Zealanders had right at home a problem which required vision, perception and material resources all at once. This was the problem of their own Maori race. The problem initially arose from the fact that the Maoris were not going to die out after all, as had been confidently expected up to 1914. The need for positive action to relieve a situation which was not going to go away was made all the more obvious by the influenza epidemic of 1918, in which 5,471 New Zealanders died, nearly a quarter of them Maoris. The Maori death-rate from the disease was indeed four times as high as that of the European sector of the population. The reason was not obscure : examination showed Maori living conditions to be simply appalling. At least part of the problem was the inadequacy of Maori incomes. The amount of land left in the hands of the Maoris would have been inadequate to support their rising population even if it had been cultivated efficiently according to European standards. The problem was multiform, as always : Maori productivity had to be raised; the Maori race had to be encouraged to recover self-confidence and a hope for the future which would engender a will to work; and the fruits of increased productivity would have to be directed towards improving standards of accommodation and health. The New Zealanders tackled the problem in a characteristically pragmatic, if necessarily piecemeal fashion. A Native Trustee Act for the first time made money available on concessional terms for mortgages to Maori farmers; Maori Arts and Crafts Boards sought to stimulate a revival of interest in traditional Maori culture; the Division of Maori Hygiene was abolished, and local Medical Officers of Health were made responsible for the health of Maoris as well as of Europeans in their districts, so that the same standards of hygiene would be sought in both communities. Meanwhile, the Maoris themselves produced a messianic movement : in 1927 a Maori farmer, Wiremu Tahupotiki Ratana, emerged as a widely respected faith-healer, whose following developed into a separate eclectic church, similar in many respects to Christian Science. The Ratana Movement gained enormous importance in both numbers and influence : within two years it had become the second largest Maori church, with at least 11,567 adherents, and by the end of the 1930s all Maori Members of Parliament were also members of the Ratana Movement.

The New Zealand Government continued in its determination to foster a healthy racial pride in the Maori people : cultural subjects were taught in the afternoon to children at Maori schools, and by 1934 seventy-four different undertakings were afoot to foster Maori economic welfare. The demoralizing impact of the depression both helped and hindered this process : on the one hand, it led for the first time since the war to expressions of overt racial hostility between unemployed European labourers and Maoris, who were regarded as unfair competitors, prepared to work for lower rates of pay because they were accustomed to a lower standard of living. On the other hand, it brought into office a Labour Government, committed for doctrinaire reasons to programmes of social welfare, whereas such programmes had hitherto reflected more the goodwill of individual ministers than the ideological convictions of the parties to which they belonged. A Native Housing Act was introduced; a Native Development Scheme put into practice; and grants made available from a very small special fund to Maoris who had no security on the basis of which they could apply for loans under the Housing Act. Some progress was undoubtedly being made. Nevertheless, a study in 1938 indicated that dreadful gulfs still existed between the two races, in the area of public health : New Zealand as a nation had at the time very nearly the lowest death rate in the world, but the New Zealand Maori had very nearly the highest; New Zealand as a nation had the lowest infant mortality rate in the world, but the Maori rate was the fourth highest; New Zealand as a nation had a very low death rate indeed from tuberculosis, but the Maori death rate from that disease was the highest on record in the world. There was a lot to be done.[13]

By this time the New Zealanders had at least been cured of their imperial ambitions. Race relations in New Zealand itself, although probably more relaxed than in any other multi-racial community, were producing difficulties which the government lacked the vision, expertise or resources to deal with in other than an *ad hoc* way, hoping for the best; Samoa remained a financial liablity, an intense embarrassment in the League of Nations, and yet another problem for which the New Zealanders had no long-term solution; Niue and the Cooks were the responsibility of half a dozen public servants. The only satisfaction that the New Zealanders could draw from the partial realization of their imperial dreams was that at least nobody else held the islands they unhappily administered.

Lamentably, the older, richer and more experienced colonial powers were demonstrating little more administrative brilliance in the handling of their own Pacific empires. The New Hebrides Condominium, for example, functioned chiefly as a device to ensure that nothing could be done effectively in the public interest. The administrative record of the British and French was only a catalogue of negatives: nothing at all was done to combat disease or check depopulation until the Rockefeller Foundation began a campaign against yaws and hookworm in 1929; there were twenty-six regulations relating to the employment of native labour, but virtually none of them was ever enforced; public money was expended almost entirely on building houses for officials, and not until 1929 was the sum of £6,900 actually spent on road-building. Even within the administration itself there was a language problem, since only a quarter of the fifty-odd British and French officials were bi-lingual; and delays were made worse by the fact that the officials were housed in separate buildings and had to communicate in writing, so weeks could easily be spent in coping with problems that could have been solved by a few minutes' conversation.

This situation was deliberately contrived by the French. By 1924, the French had 750 nationals on the islands, and the British only 274; the French controlled 80 per cent of the economy of the group, and they were resolved to do everything to prevent the British from extending their share. More than 5,000 indentured labourers had been brought over from Indo-China to work on the French plantations, although the British had abandoned this practice in their Pacific colonies since the 1880s. The only possible challenge to the French hegemony came from Australia, which provided a more efficient shipping service, and consequently the French were at loggerheads with the Australians too. None of this was conducive to disinterested or even efficient administration, and circumstances were not likely to improve. The implications of all this for the native population were summed up by Dr Stephen M. Lambert of the Rockefeller Foundation in 1941 :

> The New Hebrides, with no enforced quarantines, no concerted effort to look into the causes of epidemics, no programme for restoring the best and healthiest of the native customs, no educational system, and apparently no sincere wish to divorce the savage from liquor and firearms, were well on the road to racial extinction.[14]

The only hope for a solution seemed to be to hand the islands over to the French, in recognition of their overwhelming demographic and economic preponderance, despite the pleas of the Australians that strategic considerations demanded that the islands should remain at least partly under British control. Nor indeed did the achievements of the French elsewhere in the Pacific inspire much confidence in their good will or competence, even where they did not have to contend with the British. Tahiti in 1920 had no secretary-general and no staff of permanent administrative officials; no customs statistics had been collected for two years, and the population of 10,000 was burdened by no less than 510 public officials. Moreover, 20 per cent of the population had been killed off by the influenza epidemic. The survivors demonstrated furiously against taxes when their incomes were cut by a depression in 1921, and at least succeeded in achieving some cuts in the expenditure of the administration, which was absorbing nearly three-quarters of the colony's revenues. A further protest was made in 1929 by the Mayor of Papeete against the dictatorial nature of the administration, under which the Governor retained complete control over the island's magistrates. This again seemed to achieve some measure of success : a new body, the Délégations Économiques et Financières, consisting of seven elected officials and three nominated native notables, was set up to advise on the budget. However, the French Government refused to grant the Délégations more than advisory powers, or to remove the nominated officials from it, despite the fact that they became notoriously involved in financial scandals after 1933. The elected members accordingly withdrew, leaving total authority as before in the hands of the Governor, who assessed taxes and published decrees by arbitrary fiat, in total disregard of the views of his subjects. Political development in French Polynesia was if anything moving backwards during the inter-war period.

New Caledonia was something else again. It was, after all, literally the only French colony outside Algeria where anything like a significant number of French people had gone voluntarily to settle. It had accordingly attained fairly early a high level of political sophistication : Noumea had become a municipality in 1874, and a full commune in 1879, and twenty-four rural communes were created over the next nine years. A General Council was also created, with sixteen members elected by universal male suffrage, and with a certain amount of control over the budget. This faint step towards local autonomy was, of course, challenged fiercely by successive governors, one of whom succeeded in 1924 in reducing the numbers of the General Council and eliminating its financial powers. However, the governors themselves were not in a strong position, because of their generally brief tenure of office : New Caledonia endured the attentions of twelve chief executives in the inter-war period. Violent protests by the French community succeeded in getting financial powers restored to the General Council in 1935, and its membership was increased to almost the original figure. What still remained, however, was to secure for New Caledonia an effective voice in the French National Assembly in Paris such as Cochin-China had enjoyed since 1882, despite having only half the European population of New Caledonia.

The trouble here was that metropolitan French interest in Asia was enormously greater than in the Pacific. Only a few representatives of mining interests could speak for New Caledonia in Paris. The convincing loyalty of the white settlers who had volunteered to serve in the war had not helped in the slightest : the metropolitan French were too impressed by their own sacrifices to regard the New Caledonians as anything except irrelevant and uncouth ex-convicts, as certain elements in England might have been tempted to regard the Australians, if only there had been fewer of them. By 1939 New Caledonia, like Samoa, was waiting for the next move.

Political evolution was something which the British for their part had conscientiously wished to avoid in Fiji. It had been hoped to govern the group by indirect rule, operating through the traditional institutions of the chief system. This was not succeeding either, however, partly because the apparatus of British rule had been introduced precisely because of the anarchic state of the islands; and also because the chiefs could not retain the respect of their subjects, as their own status had been reduced to that of lions under the throne. It was simply another manifestation of the colonial dilemma, that traditional social forces can retain their prestige only if they operate in opposition to foreign rule. Here again the British had hoped that their difficulties might be solved by the disappearance of the Fijians, who had indeed diminished to 87,000 by the beginning of the First World War. To cope with this expected disappearance of one colonial people, the British had introduced another : in by far the largest experiment of this kind, indentured labourers had been brought to Fiji from India. Between 1881 and 1917 their numbers had increased from 588 to 61,150.

As a result the British were faced with a racial problem of quite extraordinary magnitude, for it gradually became obvious that the Fijians were not going to disappear. The Government of India itself had begun to have misgivings about the system, particularly in view of the intensely unsatisfactory living conditions which the Indians were being forced to accept in Fiji. They were, for instance, put on arrival into long lines of floorless huts. The system was accordingly terminated in 1917. Nevertheless a substantial Indian community remained in Fiji, many of whose members were determined to improve the conditions in which they found themselves. Indians and Fijians were alike excluded from the public schools, and only one small primary school had been provided by the British in fifty years; but the Indians, unlike the Fijians, continued to show a desperate determination to acquire any form of education available. They were also becoming active in every variety of commercial or professional activity open to them, and were becoming increasingly concerned to acquire political rights. Recognition of the Indians' demands was at last given in 1929, when provision was made to have three Indians elected as members of the Legislative Council. However, the Indians were already too politically sophisticated to begin to be satisfied with this gesture. They demanded that council members should be elected on a population basis, so that Europeans and non-Europeans would vote together rather than as separate communities. This, of course, would have guaranteed an Indian majority in the Council. The Government accordingly refused to accept the proposal, and the Indian members duly resigned. The Governor beseeched them to come back. They did so, presented their demands again, had them rejected again, and resigned again. In 1936 the Colonial Office came up with a new constitution, providing for a council of sixteen members, with three Europeans elected by literate British subjects possessing a small property qualification; three Indians, elected by literate Indian males over twenty-one; five Fijians, selected by the Governor from a list of names submitted by the Council of Native Chiefs; and two Europeans and three Indians nominated by the Governor.

This could only be a compromise of an essentially temporary nature: nobody was going to stay happy with a council which possessed only advisory functions, however its members might be chosen. Moreover, the fact that the Indian community was officially recognized as politically more advanced than the indigenous Fijians could only lead to trouble. Racial conflict was virtually inherent in the 1936 constitution.[15]

It nonetheless endured into the Second World War. In a sense, the imminence of a great Pacific war rendered all administrative arrangements in the region necessarily temporary. There was little incentive for long-term planning when the whole question of imperial control was liable to put to the test of war.

The British Dominions were, in fact, as resigned to war as the Japanese. In this climate of opinion, the extraordinary progress of the Japanese Mandated Territories only served as further cause for alarm. It was all too easy to expand what was happening in the Carolines, the Marshalls and the Marianas into a vision of an Asian tide spreading over the whole ocean. Nor was this wholly unreasonable : the Germans had governed their whole Pacific empire with about twenty-four officials; the Japanese had built up an administrative establishment of 944 in their Mandated Territories by 1935. Part of this increase was due to the fact that the Japanese rejected the notion that 'Barbarians should keep order among other barbarians' : whereas the British and Germans had tended to rely on native police and levies for simple law enforcement operations, the Japanese brought their own police with them.[16] But what was most impressive was the staggering growth in Japanese emigration across the Pacific : the total foreign population of the Mandated Territories in 1912 was about 195, of whom 105 were Germans, 17 other Europeans, and 73 Japanese. By 1920 the number of Japanese in the islands had risen to 3,671. By 1937, it stood at 58,980. This was indeed not accompanied by any decline in the native population itself : the number of indigenes had actually risen from 48,505 in 1919 to 50,741 in 1937. It was true, however, that the Japanese regarded the native population rather differently from earlier imperialists. The British, even the Spanish at times, and certainly the Germans, had viewed their native subjects as the most valuable natural resource in the region, even while they pursued every social, moral, economic and judicial measure likely to ensure the reduction of the native population. The Japanese had no reason to share this view. The fact that the islands had become economically self-supporting by 1932, and that their external trade doubled in the four years following, was due entirely to the efforts of the Japanese migrants. The indigenes were cared for, disciplined, taught Japanese manners and generally preserved from extinction; but they could not be regarded as important.

The presence of 60,000 Japanese in the Mandated Territories and 130,000 in Hawaii did not in itself prove that the Japanese were about to flood the Pacific with their surplus population. The fact was that the Territories were very obviously in the category of Asian offshore islands. Yokohama was only 1,285 miles away from Saipan in the Marianas,

Carolines. By contrast, Hawaii was 2,000 miles away from San Francisco; Wake Island twice as far; and Guam 5,000 miles. It was not the Japanese who had thrust their authority into regions unreasonably far from their own frontiers. Relatively speaking the Japanese were still in home waters.

The problem was how long they were going to stay there. No foreign power could ever be far enough away from the Pacific to reassure the Australians. And there was a great deal about the Japanese presence to cause even a less xenophobic people some alarm. Essentially, the rise of Japan as a great military and industrial power had simply altered the balance of power throughout the world : by the mid-1920s, Britain and the United States could not possibly go to war with each other, or with any other great power, and still keep enough naval strength in reserve to contain the Japanese in the Pacific. This was all the more serious in view of the intense imperial rivalry which had developed between the British and the Japanese in the years immediately prior to the First World War. The Japanese had secretly negotiated with the Russians, to the detriment of British interests in China; they were challenging British economic predominance throughout Eastern Asia; and they had even been dallying with the Indian nationalists, as a means of undermining British colonial rule in the sub-continent. British anxiety to enlist the help of the Japanese against the Germans in the First World War had indeed been inspired by a desire to curtail possible Japanese mischief rather than by any sense of real Japanese usefulness to the Allied war effort.

All this had been concealed from the Australians and New Zealanders, on the grounds that nothing could be kept secret for long in those countries. Australia and New Zealand were thus encouraged to believe that the Japanese intervention had halted German attacks on British merchant shipping in the Pacific and Indian Oceans, when in fact these had not begun until after the Japanese had entered the war; and that the Japanese had performed invaluable services by escorting Anzac and Indian troop convoys to France and the Middle East, when the British themselves had had ample battleships available for this purpose.

After the war the great naval powers had continued with massive shipbuilding programmes. The British were the first to try to cry off the naval arms race, because of the economic impossibility of their being able to surpass the United States. The Americans for their part were prepared to be content with an arrangement which would give them at least parity with the British Empire in naval terms. But Japan was less easy to win over. It was hoped at first that this could be achieved by renewing the Anglo–Japanese Alliance, which in theory would give the Japanese a sense of security and at the same time require them to co-ordinate their own policies with British interests. It was, however, all too clear that the Alliance had failed to achieve either of those objectives so far. The Americans were anxious to see the end of the Alliance anyway, because of their own sentiments of rivalry and suspicion towards Japan; they proposed instead that a Conference of Pacific Powers should be called, to settle outstanding problems in that area. The Canadians supported the Americans, taking the simple view that the most important thing in the world was 'the continuance and improvement of our relations with the American people'.[17]

Practically speaking, it was scarcely a matter for the Canadians to concern themselves about, as they had no security problems other than those presented by the United States, about which nothing could be done, and were not in any sense a Pacific power, although they might well become involved in imperial squabbles in the Pacific. However, their connivance with the Americans helped to cut the ground from under the people most directly concerned, the Australians and New Zealanders, at the Imperial Conference in June 1921. This indeed was not too difficult. The New Zealanders had nothing positive to offer and Australian thinking on the subject had become quite schizophrenic. The British Admiral Jellicoe had been sent on a world tour in 1919, partly by way of banishment for his unimpressive showing at Jutland. In Australia he had delivered an analysis of prospects in the Pacific which was both totally accurate and calculated to multiply Australian fears. Jellicoe expressed the view that a war in the Pacific was practically certain; that the Japanese would intend to invade Australia, but would first seize the Dutch East Indies as a base, probably accompanying such a move with diversionary or covering attacks against Hong Kong and Singapore; and that no substantial British naval help could be reasonably expected. Jellicoe's pessimism found support in the writings of the American naval architect Hector C. Bywater, who had no difficulty in demonstrating the ability of the Japanese, given the present stage of naval design and construction, to make a bid for empire in the Pacific. The Japanese effort would ultimately fail, according to Bywater, because of the enormously greater resources available to the United States, but it would be a disagreeable experience while it lasted.[18]

The Australians were not reassured by the fact that the British authorities disassociated themselves from Jellicoe's views. Australian Prime Minister Hughes was almost equally worried by the difficulty of discovering what precisely the British Government did think about imperial defence. He went to the Imperial Conference in 1923 convinced that 'a great drama', indeed 'a struggle for existence', was going to be enacted in the Pacific, where Australia would play the role of 'the advance guard of the white population of the world, ringed about, at a distance much less remote than is the case in regard to any European nation'.[19] This was hardly specific, but there was no doubt about the real nature of the Australian concern. As one Australian senator argued : 'Australia is the hope of the white peoples of the world. It has the only truly cleanly bred white population in the world, even including Great Britain, and it is worth the expenditure of some thought and money – if necessary it is worth fighting for – to maintain it clean and white'.[20]

Again, these remarks, if true, would have raised some doubts as to the future of the white race in general, and of Australia in particular. But at least they made clear what the division within the ranks of the British Empire was all about. The Australians and to a lesser extent the New Zealanders were convinced that the Japanese wanted to export their teeming millions to the relatively sparsely populated territories of the big British Dominions. They also believed that the best way to ensure that this did not happen was to renew a treaty of friendship and mutual defence between Britain and these unclean but expansionary Asiatics. The New Zealanders also took the kindly but mistaken view that the Japanese had proved themselves to be good allies in the Great War, and that it behoved the British Empire to be grateful. They were thus a trifle surprised to discover that the British had already decided to scrap the Alliance and to replace it with a general Pacific Agreement along the lines desired by the Americans.

The Japanese were thus allowed to get away. The limitations on naval construction agreed under the terms of the Washington Conference in the following year only ensured that primacy in the Pacific would belong to the Japanese. It was not merely that the Japanese Combined Fleet was far stronger than anything which the British could afford to divert to the Pacific. The Japanese were also developing a more technologically advanced naval force. By the end of the 1920s they would be able to deploy a larger Naval Air Service than the entire Royal Navy, at a time when neither the British Admirals nor the Air Force Marshals were in general convinced of the real utility of ship-borne aircraft. In any case, even if the British were in a position to defend their Dominions against Japanese aggression, there was nowhere in the Pacific or Indian Oceans for a huge British fleet to operate from. It was accordingly urged strongly at the 1923 Imperial Conference that a naval base should be constructed at Singapore from which a British Main Fleet could operate for imperial defence in the Pacific. The British Government demurred, on grounds of expense. This was perhaps a little unfeeling, as the New Zealanders had made an almost incredible demonstration of imperial loyalty at the time of the Chanak crisis in September 1922 when 12,279 of them volunteered for combat or nursing duties in the Dardanelles, within forty-eight hours of receiving an invitation to do so from the British Government. Apparently London only understood the language of money. The New Zealand Prime Minister accordingly offered £100,000, presumably as a first instalment, towards the cost of a naval base at Singapore.

Domestic events in Britain itself proved the decisive factor, as always. MacDonald went out; Baldwin came in; and work commenced on the base. Meanwhile, the Australians followed up a two-pronged security programme. On the one hand, the Dominions themselves should make greater individual efforts towards their own security; on the other, Dominion forces should be incorporated within an overall imperial force, for greater effectiveness. The New Zealanders agreed, arguing that the very existence of the British Empire depended on an imperial navy, which strictly speaking did not yet exist. But the Australians and New Zealanders were talking to themselves, even within the Commonwealth. Desperately disappointed, Australian Prime Minister Stanley Bruce precipitated the most serious clash between the Dominions to that date, by denouncing the lack of interest of the Canadians in particular in matters of defence, and offering to lend them a couple of RAN cruisers. But Australia was clearly going to need all its own ships for its own security. The depression came; MacDonald returned to office; work on the Singapore base slowed down again, despite the opinion of the Permanent Under-Secretary for Foreign Affairs that in existing circumstances Britain could not hope to hold the Far East in the event of war with Japan; and defence spending slumped anew throughout the Empire.

It was precisely at this moment that the spectre of Japanese aggression rose with an altogether new capacity to inspire terror. In 1931, the Japanese Kwantung Army assumed control over the north-eastern provinces of China. A confrontation with the United States seemed inevitable. Secretary of State Henry L. Stimson warned that if the Japanese aggression continued 'nobody would trust Japan again'.[21] He then announced that the United States would not recognize any changes brought about in relation to China by the Japanese moves. However, the British made it clear that they were not going to become involved in any military or economic action against Japan; nor would they support a policy of non-recognition, which they dismissed as a peculiarly American technique. Stimson's own President Hoover lectured him on the folly of becoming involved in a war with Japan over China. The Japanese press nonetheless proclaimed the irreconcilability of Japanese and American foreign policy objectives, while the Japanese Government responded to a request by a Committee of the League of Nations that they should evacuate Chinese territory, by simply leaving the League.

The British and even the Australians were in fact slightly relieved by the Japanese move into China, which at least was a move away from the British Empire in India or the Pacific. But in 1934 Japanese expansionists formed the Southward Movement Society to press for the abandonment of limitations on Japanese naval construction, to provide for a development of the territories of the South Seas. An intelligence organization was set up to collect data from Japanese commercial travellers and tourists about Malaya, the Philippines and the Dutch East Indies. The Japanese were keeping their options open for future advances.

Unfortunately, the development of the Asian crisis was accompanied by tensions on the European continent as well. In 1935 Hitler repudiated the Treaty of Versailles; Italy invaded Abyssinia; and Germany began to rearm on land, at sea and in the air. The Australians were becoming desperate. They could decide neither on what kind of threat they were most exposed to, nor on how it could be met. The British Government, however, insisted that Japan was no more likely to attack Australia and New Zealand than those countries were to attack Manchuria. Indeed, it was quite evident that the main thrust of Japanese advance continued to be into China, as was indicated by the way in which a clash with Chinese troops at the Marco Polo Bridge outside Peking was swiftly escalated into a full-scale war.

This immediately alarmed the Americans. Roosevelt began in July 1937 to consider the possibility of maintaining a line in the Pacific to contain any further Japanese expansion southward, if the British were prepared to co-operate. At that time Foreign Minister Anthony Eden would have welcomed joint action with the Americans against Japan, but Chamberlain was determined that Britain should avoid any entanglements in the Far East at a time when it was militarily unprepared to cope with entanglements in Europe. Moreover, an absurd dispute had arisen between the British and Americans themselves over the sovereignty of various uninhabited and microscopic atolls around the equator. Both countries were contemplating establishing flying-boat routes across the Pacific, and both were investigating locations for suitable bases. The Americans hoped to exploit a scientific expedition to Canton Island to observe an eclipse of the sun by claiming United States sovereignty over the atoll. The British attempted to beat them to it by sending HMS *Leith* from Suva to plant a Union Jack before the Americans could arrive. The Americans ignored the Union Jack and left in their turn a cement plinth with a stainless steel United States flag embedded in the island. The British asked them to come back and take it away, and even offered to arrange for its removal themselves, 'if the United States Government should find it inconvenient to send a ship for that special purpose'.[22]

The Americans tried to inject some rationality into the issue by proposing a form of joint sovereignty in such cases. Roosevelt, for his part, trusted that the British would appreciate that the survival of the Commonwealth itself was at stake unless they could bring themselves to co-operate with the United States. In October he expressed the fear that Japanese, unless checked, would proceed to mop up first the British Empire in the Far East, and then the Dutch.[23] The British Admiralty in fact was, unknown to him, considering the possibility of providing eight or nine battleships to participate with the United States Fleet in an overwhelming display of strength in the Pacific. At first Roosevelt hesitated, afraid of the strength of isolationist or pacifist feeling in his own country, but after the sinking by the Japanese of USS *Panay* in the Yangtse in December he sent a naval mission to London for secret talks with the British, and attempted to interest British Ambassador Lindsay in joint action in the Pacific against the Japanese. But this time Chamberlain was reluctant, partly because he was convinced that there was nothing to be got from the Americans except words, but mainly because he did not want a confrontation in the Pacific at a time when he was developing the possibilities of appeasement in Europe.[24]

Meanwhile, the British continued to insist on their unfettered sovereignty over assorted collections of coral reefs and bird-droppings in the Pacific, with perhaps a total area of 180 square miles and a population of 167. Roosevelt furiously threatened to sign an Executive Order placing under the jurisdiction of the United States all islands not permanently occupied in the area between Samoa and Hawaii unless the British appreciated that both they and the United States had a common interest in all the islands, in keeping out Japan.

At this stage the New Zealand Government intervened, asking for a conference of the governments of the United Kingdom, Australia and New Zealand to discuss Pacific island matters. The New Zealanders

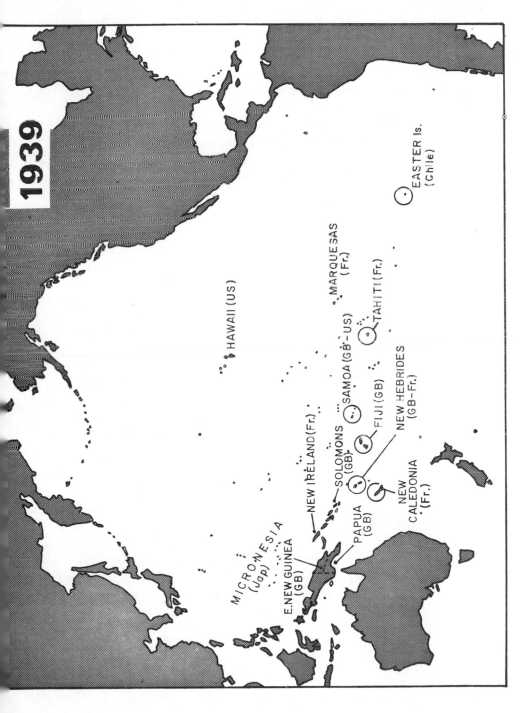

did not in fact wait for the conference : they immediately approached the British High Commissioner for the Western Pacific, explaining that the Fijian and Tongan groups were the key to New Zealand defence, and proposing to use Fiji as a focal point for four projected air routes to link the British islands in the Pacific for mutual support in time of war. The British still appeared more concerned with anticipating attempts by the United States to claim sovereignty over any more islands south of the equator than with helping the New Zealanders to defend themselves against a Japanese attack. Indeed, Defence Secretary Chatfield dismissed a proposal for a defence loan to New Zealand as late as April 1939, stating that he could not place very high priority on New Zealand defences.[25]

Some things at least could be agreed upon. Jellicoe had suggested twenty years earlier that Fiji was the key to the South Pacific, not because of the intrinsic value of the group, but because all trans-Pacific shipping lines converged on Suva. So most conspicuously did the vital Australia–New Zealand–United States shipping route. It also provided a link in the system of submarine telegraph cables. Finally, it was the obvious base for an attack against New Zealand, for anybody who might have so fruitless an exercise in mind. The New Zealanders accordingly accepted responsibility for Fiji as their immediate outpost in the Pacific. New Zealand would carry out air reconnaissance and defensive action along the line New Hebrides–Fiji–Tonga. Australia would do the same along the New Guinea–Solomons–New Hebrides front. For the first time in history, parts of the British Empire were undertaking to accept responsibility for the defence of other parts. The Dominions were guarding the Crown Colonies. Imperial unity was actually being achieved, in the particular context of Pacific defence at least.

A rather more relevant question was exactly what the Dominions were going to defend the colonies with. The Australians gloomily noted that the forces available for the defence of New Guinea itself were quite inadequate; that the Navy was not up to the standard necessary to cope even with what was termed a minor scale of attack, meaning raids against communications and the Australian coast, short of actual invasion; and coastal defences covering Sydney amounted to six new and thirteen old 6-inch guns, without adequate observation facilities. Nor was there even yet any agreement on what should best be done to make Australian and Pacific defence credible. General Blamey doubted whether ships were really vulnerable to aircraft, so presumably one could not rely on the RAAF to ward off attacks, even if its aircraft

were better than unbiased observers though they were. General Chauvel
suggested that as God had given the Australians an island, they should
make the most of their geographical advantages. Specifically, he suggested that the Government acquire two battleships. But the British
did not have two battleships to spare, and in any case two battleships
were not going to deter the Japanese Combined Fleet. The Prime Minister doubted whether the United States would be able to stay out if
Australia were invaded, presumably on the assumption that if the
Americans were prepared to defend Canada, they would also be prepared to defend far more remote parts of the British Empire, infinitely
less important to American security.[26] This, however, was anything but
certain. What was certain was that nobody else in the region was going
to be of any use. The Dutch had a large garrison in the East Indies,
and a fleet of four cruisers, six destroyers and fourteen submarines,
compared with the Australian strength of six cruisers and five destroyers;
but the Dutch Government was rigidly adhering to a policy of neutrality,
and was unwilling to enter into any military discussions with nations
which might become embroiled in war with Holland's European neighbour Germany, or Germany's anti-Comintern partner Japan. The
French were indeed allies, but the defence of French Polynesia or New
Caledonia was the last thing in which the Government in Paris or its
military advisers were likely to show the slightest interest. If there was
going to be war in the Pacific, the British Dominions might very well
have to face it on their own.

In fact, however, the decision for a southward advance against British
and American opposition was arrived at in Tokyo only by slow and pain-
ful stages. Initial Japanese approaches to Germany and Italy had been
inspired by fear of Russia rather than by any notion of seeking support for a policy of expansion in the South Seas. Throughout most of
1938, Japanese diplomats were primarily concerned with alienating
Britain from Russia, and subsequently drawing Britain and the United
States to their side. There were very practical reasons for this. In the
first place it was feared that Japan, without allies, might very easily be
overwhelmed by a sudden Russian attack. Besides, Finance Minister
Ikeda believed that Japan's financial and economic systems would not
be able to survive the strains of competition with a hostile Britain and
America. The Anti-Comintern Pact was therefore directed exclusively
against Russia, without any notion of estranging the British and
Americans. Even the most bellicose elements in the Japanese Navy were
still arguing at the end of 1938 that the alignment with Germany and

Italy was mainly valuable as a means of inducing the British and Americans to adopt a reasonable attitude towards Japan.[27]

The Australians and New Zealanders had no way of knowing this. In any case, Japanese policy was always liable to sudden changes, especially with the balance of power in Europe continuing to shift in favour of Germany. Some action had to be taken to secure the southern islands. The New Zealanders made the first move. A cable station had been established on Fanning Island, due north of the Cooks and three degrees above the equator. The island had no regular shipping or other service with the outside world, had an average rainfall of rather more than 100 inches a year, and was probably the last place in the Pacific on which any soldier would have wished to find himself. But Fanning had been attacked by a German raiding party in 1914, and New Zealand determined that its role as a communications link should not be endangered in this way again, without any effort to defend it. Accordingly, two unfortunate officers and thirty other ranks were assembled secretly and despatched from New Zealand to dig pits for the two machine guns with which they were to defend Fanning, fish and swim. Meanwhile, after some difficulties it was agreed that New Zealand should provide a force to defend vital Fiji, and at the same time meet any expenditure above the figure of £500,000 a year agreed by the British Government for the defence of Fiji.

The machinery for Pacific defence went into operation immediately on the outbreak of war with Germany in September 1939. New Zealand's key outpost Fiji was garrisoned by an almost unarmed territorial force, under the command of the Commissioner of Police. The Governor immediately appointed three other officers, while New Zealand hastened to supply the means for defence. Five hundred rifles were sent at once, and at the end of September a New Zealand cruiser landed two dummy guns for the protection of Suva. Presumably it was hoped that any enemy agents who had not seen the guns being carried ashore each by one sailor would mistake them for the real thing, and warn intending raiders to keep away. On 23 September another ship brought more rifles and two New Zealand instructors to arm and train the 100 men who had just been sworn into the Tongan Defence Force.

Meanwhile, the Australian and New Zealand divisions sailed away, as in 1914, to help defend the most obviously threatened areas of imperial security, in the Middle East and subsequently Britain itself. Both Dominion governments were understandably less happy about this strategy than they had been in the First World War : the New Zealanders had made clear as early as June 1939 their reluctance to undertake overseas commitments, but had found a genuine practical difficulty in the way of keeping their troops at home in wartime : as they explained to the Australians in November 1939, New Zealand just did not have the facilities to train more than one intake of soldiers at a time : those already trained would have to be sent overseas to make room for the next body enlisted. In any case, Winston Churchill hastened to assure all concerned that it was impossible that the Japanese, who were a prudent people, would embark on such a mad enterprise as an attack on Singapore. The British Chiefs of Staff concurred with this view, adding as a logical corollary that there was no danger to Australia and New Zealand from Japan.

This would scarcely have been a reasonable attitude, even if Britain had not been involved in a war with Germany at the time : Japan's Battle Force of ten modern or completely modernized capital ships would probably have been more than a match in a fleet action for even the full strength of the Royal Navy, especially when supported by the Japanese Naval Air Service, far superior in quality to the Fleet Air Arm, and at that time having almost four times as many shipborne aircraft.[28] The Japanese could practically be deterred only by their uncertainty as to the intentions of the United States, and by the possibility of an early Allied victory over Germany, unlikely though this already seemed.

The second element of uncertainty was effectively removed in May 1940. The fall of France the following month made the very survival of the British Empire thoroughly doubtful. It certainly ensured that the strategy of defending the Pacific empire by sending the Main Fleet to Singapore could not possibly be carried out. The fate of the French Eastern Empire was also very much in doubt. Vichyite authorities were well in control in Indo-China, and the area in any case was too easily subject to Japanese pressure. The prospect was made even more depressing for the British Dominions by the rumour that any peace settlement between the French and the victorious Germans would involve letting the Japanese have the New Hebrides and New Caledonia. The situation in the New Hebrides was not in fact serious : it would be possible for the British to continue to administer the islands under the terms of the Condominium even if the French officials there were disposed to collaborate with Vichy. As it happened, the French Resident

Commissioner in the New Hebrides, M. Sautot, declared for General de Gaulle on 26 June.

M. Sautot was thus at least a potential leader for New Caledonia as well, where the General Council had voted to continue the struggle against Germany. Unfortunately it had also voted for autonomous self-government at the same time, a resolution which was perhaps less acceptable to Governor Pelicier. In an attempt which could hardly have been other than genuinely conciliatory under the circumstances, the Australian Prime Minister sent Pelicier a message conveying the deep sympathy of Australia in the temporary defeat of France, his resolute determination to co-operate with French people all over the world, and his happiness if he could render Pelicier practical assistance. An Australian representative, Mr B. C. Ballard, was then despatched to New Caledonia to see what kind of Australian economic assistance might be appreciated. However, the Australians were not the only ones in the hunt. A similar bid for autonomy had taken place in Tahiti on the news of France's defeat, although this was not clearly linked as in New Caledonia with any desire to continue the war against Germany : few indeed of the islanders had heard of de Gaulle, though many had heard of Marshal Pétain, the hero of Verdun, who was now head of state in Vichy France. In any case, the French sloop *Dumont d'Urville* under Commander de Quivrecourt was in port at Papeete to suppress any movement towards autonomy or a declaration for de Gaulle. De Quivrecourt later sailed discreetly for Noumea, to perform the same function there. Meanwhile, de Gaulle himself had entered the scene, following an approach from a New Caledonian 'patriot' leader, Raymond Pognon. De Gaulle confirmed Sautot in his office in the New Hebrides, and asked the British to provide Sautot with a ship to take him to New Caledonia to rally that island to the Gaullist cause.

Toussaint de Quivrecourt was, however, there already with instructions from Vichy to replace the dithering Pelicier with the military commandant Colonel Denis; to reject demands for autonomy; to explain to those anxious to support de Gaulle that by doing so they would be guilty of treason against France; and to take any further action necessary to save New Caledonia from falling within the economic orbit of Australia. This was no doubt de Gaulle's concern as well. The Australian Minister of External Affairs desperately insisted that there there was no truth in the rumours that Australia desired to annex New Caledonia : the only wish of his government was to maintain the friendly relations which he inaccurately claimed had always existed between Australia and New Caledonia, and in particular to maintain normal trade and commercial ties.

This perhaps was not the whole truth. But it was obviously important at the time to avoid any impression that Australia might have designs on New Caledonia in more expedient circumstances, and particularly to avoid becoming involved in any conflict between Gaullist and Pétainist forces. Sautot sailed for Noumea in the Australian cruiser *Adelaide* on 30 August. Both the British and Australian Governments hoped that the arrival of a ship much more powerful than his own might induce de Quivrecourt to go away quietly. It was however insisted that there should under no circumstances be any use of force, if it could possibly be avoided, and the captain of the *Adelaide* was ordered to pretend that he had come to New Caledonia to look for a suspected German raider. Meanwhile the British High Commissioner for the Western Pacific, Sir Harry Luke, had also arrived in New Caledonia, and had formed the opinion that Sautot's position would be strengthened if he were given formal credentials by de Gaulle to act as Governor. De Gaulle agreed, at the same time instructing Pognon to form a Gaullist Committee in in Noumea to take control of the administration in preparation for Sautot's arrival.

The situation was escalating. A Committee for de Gaulle had already been formed in Tahiti, where 1,000 volunteers had rallied to the cause of Free France. On 18 September however the Pétainists staged a counter-coup. On the following day, Sautot arrived in Noumea harbour in the Norwegian tanker *Nordern*, with the *Adelaide* in company, allegedly as escort. De Quivrecourt was still there. Indeed, the *Adelaide* was warned that if it entered harbour it would be fired on by the defences. Sautot was accordingly sent on in the *Nordern*, to be welcomed enthusiastically by the Gaullist reception committee, led by Pognon. De Quivrecourt nonetheless refused to leave, and it was discovered on 20 September that another sloop, the *Amiral Charner*, had left Saigon to reinforce him. The gunboats were out again. Denis made his last play: the shore defences were ordered to fire on the *Adelaide* as she sailed closer to the *Nordern* to forestall any action by de Quivrecourt; the gunners refused; and honour was presumably satisfied. On 25 September, de Quivrecourt was persuaded to leave for Saigon, whither the *Amiral Charner* had already returned; and on 11 October the French steamer *Pierre Loti* left for Australia, of all places, with 230 Pétainists on board, including Colonel Denis, for onward passage to Indo-China. Another imperial showdown had been avoided.[29]

The Gaullists in Tahiti had also managed to outmanoeuvre their Pétainist rivals. On 3 November, de Gaulle appointed Dr Emile de Curton, Administrator of the Leeward Islands, as Governor. De Curton immediately began mass arrests of his personal as well as political opponents, impelling de Gaulle to send his Inspector-General M. Brunot to Tahiti to discover what de Curton was up to. Brunot however was no more conciliatory than de Curton : he appointed himself Governor and instituted another purge, arresting Gaullists as well as any Pétainists who had escaped the attentions of de Curton, and quarrelling with the British consul as well.

Meanwhile, another factor had intruded itself into the South Pacific chaos. The New Zealanders had been in contact with the Tahitian Gaullists as early as 6 September, to discuss the urgent problem of island defence. Tahiti itself was simply defenceless : the whole group could muster only two machine guns and five old, and probably in-effective, coast defence guns. New Caledonia itself was in a scarcely more formidable state : only one mountain gun was actually mobile, although it was found possible to enlarge this armoury to four 3-inch guns, two light quick-firers, four mortars and thirty-two machine guns. The Tahitians immediately asked New Zealand to send 300 men. This was declined, although Wellington did send money and twenty-four tommy guns to equip the Gaullist volunteers in the meantime. A Defence Conference among the British, Australians and New Zealanders in Singapore on 31 October discovered that their own defence position was scarcely more reassuring. It was agreed that Singapore was the key to Commonwealth defence in the Indian and Pacific Oceans, and that the presence of a British naval base at Singapore would be sufficient to rule out any possibility of a major expedition against Australia or New Zealand. At any rate it would simply have to do so, if the Dominions were to be able to continue to assist with the British war effort in Africa and the Middle East. What, however, could not be entirely disregarded was the fact that there was a base at Singapore, but inadequate strength to hold it : the minimum naval requirement for defence was considered to be one battleship, one aircraft carrier, five cruisers and five des-troyers, all of which were lacking. Indeed, it was not clear what they would have been able to do against the Japanese Combined Fleet even if they had been present. The situation could be redeemed only if the United States were to come to the rescue of the British Empire, as the British Empire had been pledged by Churchill to come to the rescue of the United States, if by some extraordinary miscalculation the Japanese moved against American territory first.

The New Zealanders had been urging throughout the second half of 1940 that the British Government should harmonize its policy towards Japan with that of the United States. To this end, the New Zealand Government itself unilaterally set aside all questions of sovereignty over the islands of the South Pacific, and attempted instead actively to encourage all signs of United States interest in the area. This policy received an immense boost when an Australian–New Zealand naval mission visited Washington secretly in November 1940 and discovered that the Americans had in fact already made plans for the support of British possessions in the Pacific and the reinforcement of Singapore from bases in Australia and New Guinea. The Americans indeed were openly anxious that Britain and Australia should send more reinforcements to Singapore, rather than to the Middle East, to provide a more effective deterrent against a southward move by Japan. Nothing could be done to influence British policy, but the New Zealanders at least did what they could by assuming responsibility for the defence of all British bases in the South-west Pacific. Fiji was naturally their first concern, being the place they still identified as the prime target for any Japanese aggression, as indeed it would have been if the Japanese had ever considered an invasion of New Zealand. The dummy guns outside Suva had already been replaced by two real 4·7-inch naval guns, and a territorial force of 42 European officers and 1,029 Fijian other ranks had been trained and more or less equipped. One machine gun had also been created with parts taken from a captured German First World War weapon. This was clearly not enough to deter the Japanese. In September the New Zealanders began training a brigade of 3,053 men to garrison Fiji. They arrived in the Group on 1 November. New Zealand had made history again: for the first time, the forces of a British Dominion had actually garrisoned the territory of a British Crown Colony. They unfortunately could not do anything about the air defences of Fiji, which consisted of exactly two DH89 aircraft, vintage immediately post-First World War. These could obviously do nothing at all against any invader. However, neither could any other British Empire air force in the Pacific: even in Malaya, the only British aircraft which were modern enough even to be termed obsolescent were thirty-five Bristol Blenheim bombers. Meanwhile, the only convincing deterrent against Japanese aggression in the region sailed away, as the United States pressed on with the reorganization of its Navy to meet the demands of the undeclared war against Germany in the Atlantic : from February 1941 onwards, American warships began to sail from Pacific bases to strengthen the newly created Atlantic Fleet. The Australians and New Zealanders protested bitterly; Churchill argued against them that the movement of American ships away from the Pacific would be a positive discouragement to the Japanese, because it indicated the mounting involvement of the United States in the war against Germany, and therefore suggested their readiness to take action against anybody who might enter the war on Germany's side. The Australians allowed themselves to be persuaded; but the New Zealanders continued to insist that the Japanese were not likely to take such a long view of things, and would be more inclined to take a risk to maintain the military advantage which had been presented to them by the withdrawal to the Atlantic of three American battleships, four cruisers, an aircraft carrier and nineteen destroyers. Another Australian–New Zealand mission went to Washington. The encouragement they received in May 1941 was certainly as emphatic as could have been hoped for : United States Chief of Naval Operations Admiral Harold R. Stark assured the Dominion representatives that the United States Pacific Fleet 'would . . . take such steps as would prevent the overseas occupation and the permanent support of such garrisons as the Axis Powers might seek to establish' in the British and French islands of the Pacific south of the equator.[30] All that was now lacking was a guarantee from the President and Congress that these promises would actually be kept. Roosevelt himself gave assurances at the beginning of December, but again without getting Congressional ratification.[31] In fact, it was unnecessary. The Americans did not have to make up their minds. The Japanese did it for them. On 7 December 1941, the Great Pacific War began, just as Bywater had forecast, with the Japanese risking the fate of their empire on a sneak attack on American naval power, while their ambassadors were negotiating in Washington for a peaceful settlement of the problems of the Pacific.

VI

The Great Pacific War

The Great Pacific War turned out in fact to be overwhelmingly more of a Great Asian War. Apart from Pearl Harbor itself, Japan's greatest victories took place on the Asian continent or around its offshore islands and archipelagoes; apart from the Solomons, so did its greatest defeats. There was no doubt in the minds of Japan's military planners where the major battles were to be fought : at its full strength, the Japanese Army had the equivalent of sixty divisions deployed to defend the home islands, thirty in China and Korea, twenty in the Philippines, nine in Burma, five in Okinawa, and only fourteen in the whole island chain on the south and south-eastern periphery of the Japanese defence line, from Sumatra to the Solomons.[1]

This was fully in accordance with fundamental Japanese policy. Japan's interests had always been primarily continental, not oceanic. The Greater East Asia Co-prosperity Sphere was really meant to be just that. The original plan, as outlined by the Japanese Foreign Office on 28 September 1940, proposed that : 'In the regions including French Indo-China, Dutch East Indies, the Straits Settlements, British Malaya, Thailand, the Philippines, British Borneo and Burma, with Japan, Manchukuo and China as centre, we should construct a sphere in which the politics, economy, and culture of those countries and regions are combined.'[2] This was not by any means wholly a plan for military conquest. It involved indeed as a primary objective the attainment of a truce with Chiang Kai-Shek, which might be followed by handing over to Chinese military occupation the northern area of French Indo-China.

Tokyo similarly hoped to conclude an agreement of mutual assistance with Thailand which might involve handing Cambodia over to Thai military control. The fate of the Philippines and the island of Guam would depend on the attitude of the United States Government. Even the British and Dutch colonies in Asia could be incorporated peacefully within the Co-prosperity Sphere, if the colonial authorities were agreeable, although it was considered that independence movements should be encouraged, in the hope that these regions would throw off colonial rule and enter the Sphere as independent states. Problems would, of course, arise if any of the colonial powers declined to let the various parts of their empires participate in the Sphere. It would then be necessary for Japan to seize the designated regions by force, if need be without waiting for a settlement with Chiang Kai-Shek or the emergence of effective independence movements within the colonies. It might also be necessary to strike at territories which could be used as bases from which the western powers might conduct operations against the Sphere, although there was no suggestion that these territories should be incorporated within the Sphere itself. In this category of potential hostile bases outside the Sphere were included Hawaii, Midway, Australia and New Zealand.

This was a Pacific war, indeed. The attack on Pearl Harbor in fact came some hours after the first Japanese assault on the Malayan coastline at Khota Bharu. It was, however, on so much greater a scale than the earlier thrust at the British Empire in Asia that it is appropriately remembered as the opening battle of the Japanese offensive. It was certainly one of the greatest and most complete victories in military history. Two waves of Japanese aircraft, 363 in all, sank 4 United States battleships, and 2 naval auxiliaries; crippled another battleship and 2 destroyers; destroyed 188 United States aircraft; and caused the deaths of 2,415 American military personnel. Japanese losses were 29 aircraft, 6 submarines and about 85 personnel, including one prisoner of war. Civilian casualties were comparatively light, amounting in all to 62 dead and about 335 injured. Some of these were due to low-level strafing by Japanese aircraft, but this occurred only in the vicinity of military installations. Virtually all the the damage to civilians and civilian property was caused by United States anti-aircraft fire, mainly from the Navy, according to United States Army officers.

It was natural to suppose that this disaster must have been due in part to treachery and sabotage. Navy Secretary Frank Knox said that Hawaii had been subjected to 'the most effective Fifth Column work that has come out of this war except in Norway'.[3] Every imaginable act of treason was attributed to the Japanese population. Japanese spies had murdered an American naval officer; newspaper advertisements carried veiled warnings and instructions to the Japanese population; Japanese bars and restaurants had been at unusual pains to get American servicemen drunk on the night of 6 December; guiding arrows or just Japanese characters had been cut or bulldozed in the canefields in the sugar plantations; a Japanese milk truck had fired with machine guns on the defenders; the water supply had been poisoned; signal lights had been flashed and cane fires lit as signals to the attackers. All these rumours were investigated and all proved to be unfounded. Every investigation came up with the same conclusion: no member of the Japanese population of Hawaii was ever found to have participated in any act of espionage, treachery or Fifth Column activity of any kind whatever.

Nor had the Japanese Government attempted to develop any espionage or Fifth Column system except through its own consular staff. The simple fact was that the Japanese had no intention at all of ever taking Hawaii over. By contrast, in Singapore, which was to be an intrinsic part of the Co-prosperity Sphere, and which the Japanese had decided that they would have to take by force of arms, they had formed one of the most effective Fifth Columns in history by virtually monopolizing sensitive service industries like photography, prostitution and catering. The Japanese had no interest in the Hawaiian group *per se* : their only concern was with the United States Pacific Fleet. They apparently went near the islands only once again, after the first ferocious blast, when one of their submarines fired a few shells at the island of Maui on 15 December 1941. Bombs indeed fell on a golf course near Honolulu on 4 March 1942, but they were probably jettisoned by a US Navy pilot, according to a US Army appraisal. The little island of Niihau was, however, subjected to a one-man invasion immediately after Pearl, when a Japanese pilot crash-landed and was disarmed by a native Hawaiian, who placed him under guard and took his papers. The Hawaiian unfortunately sent for the only two Japanese residents on the island to act as interpreters, while waiting for the weekly sampan to arrive from Kauai, so that the authorities could be informed of their prize. The pilot persuaded the interpreters to give him a gun and help him set up the machine guns from the wrecked aircraft to terrorize the population. This attempt at military occupation ended when some of the islanders stole the ammunition for the machine guns, and another, annoyed after being shot three times, picked up the pilot by the neck and leg and beat his brains out against a convenient wall.

After Pearl Harbor strong measures were taken to ensure internal security. The Governor of Hawaii, Joseph B. Poindexter, immediately declared a state of martial law. He then, in a decision ruled unconstitutional five years later by the United States Supreme Court, announced that all judicial functions would be transferred to the Commanding Officer of American forces on the island, General Walter C. Short, who immediately proclaimed himself 'military governor' of Hawaii.

This irregular situation did not last long. Major civilian courts were re-opened on orders from Washington on 16 December. General Short was sacked the following day. Poindexter himself was induced to quit in August 1942 by the Secretary of the Interior, Harold L. Ickes. This partial return to reason did not, however, do much to relieve the position of the enormous Japanese population of the Group. General Short had begun by arresting 370 Japanese, 98 Germans and 14 Italians on Oahu as enemy aliens. It was rather more difficult to see what could be done next about the remaining 100,000 or so Japanese in the islands, especially as no evidence was ever found to justify taking action against them. It was still an opportunity not to be ignored: a prominent businessman, John A. Balch, suggested as late as 16 January 1943 that at least 100,000 Japanese should be deported from Hawaii, to keep the islands safe for Caucasian exploitation. In the end, 1,875 Japanese, about 0·9 per cent of the Japanese population of the Group, were arrested and deported from Hawaii, either to prison camps or to relocation centres in Arkansas; and only 248 agreed to be repatriated to Japan, in exchange for American residents there. As against this, Japanese volunteers provided 49·9 per cent of the total number of Hawaiians serving in the American Armed Forces, compared with figures of 14·8 per cent for the Caucasians and 11·9 per cent for the native or part-native population, the remaining 23·4 per cent being supplied by the other ethnic minorities, mainly Chinese or Filipino.[4]

Hawaii never really had a security or an invasion problem, because it was never really a Japanese objective. Nor was New Zealand, but the New Zealanders could not be aware of this. Indeed, it seemed fully logical for them to undertake at first a bigger commitment to Pacific defence than the Australians were contemplating. The Australians had indeed four or five times the manpower reserves of New Zealand but they had thirty times the area to defend. General Sir Iven Mackay, appointed General Officer Commanding-in-Chief, Home Forces in

Australia on 5 August 1941, tried tactfully to explain to the Cabinet that any serious invasion of Australia would be directed most rationally at 'some compact, vulnerable area, the resources of which are necessary to the economic life of Australia'.[5] This was accordingly the area where it would be most rational to concentrate whatever defence capability Australia possessed at the time. General Mackay picked the Sydney–Newcastle–Port Kembla area of New South Wales as the prime target for a potential invader. It was, however, necessary also to reserve some forces for the security of other important areas and concentrations of population which could be attacked by minor enemy forces if left completely undefended. This meant extending some kind of umbrella over Brisbane, Adelaide, Fremantle, Albany and Melbourne as well. General Mackay pointed out that it would be difficult enough to defend even the vital south-east corner of the continent along a line 1,000 miles long drawn from Melbourne to Brisbane, with only two cavalry and five infantry divisions in all, with the fighting capacity of perhaps three fully manned and fully equipped divisions. However, he recognized that it would be necessary for reasons of morale to leave some units in the indefensible and necessarily expendable north and west of the country. His actual deployment on the eve of Pearl Harbor represented an attempt to reach some compromise between these conflicting and insoluble problems of defence: about 98,000 mobile and garrison troops were concentrated, if that is the word, in New South Wales, Victoria and South Australia; 4,380 were left in Tasmania; 10,000 kept watch in remote Western Australia; and 23,000 showed the flag in Queensland and the Northern Territory. It did not leave much for the Pacific islands which Australia had undertaken to protect.

Nor did the Australian Chiefs of Staff have any doubt that the islands were going to need protecting. They advised the War Cabinet on 8 December that the most likely Japanese moves after Pearl Harbor would take the form of attacks on Rabaul, Port Moresby and New Caledonia; a raid on Darwin, and possibly an attempt to occupy the town; and air and sea attacks on the vital areas of the Australian mainland. Australia had at the time 2,158 men in all stationed in Rabaul, New Caledonia and northern New Guinea, and a further 1,088 defending Port Moresby. Australia's island barrier was only a paper shield.

New Zealand's commitment to island defence was proportionately far more extensive, if still not exactly of an order to deter a major attacker. Major-General Cunningham's command in Fiji now amounted to 4,000 New Zealanders and 945 native Fijians, with six mobile

18-pounders and fixed coastal batteries consisting of four 6-inch and two 4·7-inch naval guns, all of First World War vintage, and unfortunately without any anti-aircraft guns at all; the Tongan defence forces had been brought to a strength of 462 native troops, led by nine New Zealand officers and warrant officers and equipped with two machine guns and two 18-pounders; in Samoa one New Zealand warrant officer had 150 natives armed with rifles under his command; 110 New Zealanders with one 6-inch gun held Fanning Island against anybody who might want to go there; in Rarotonga, perhaps the most unlikely target of the region, there were 100 native volunteers, one New Zealand officer, and two machine guns; and in Tahiti 300 men of very dubious fighting quality had been mobilized : as well as the usual two machine guns they had five ancient French cannon.[6]

The New Zealanders had certainly tried to make a gesture towards their obligations to defend the Pacific islands. Cunningham's men in Fiji were in fact the only Allied troops in the whole Pacific area who were actually standing to arms at the time of the Japanese attack on Pearl Harbor. This was of course coincidental, and did not make any difference to the course of events, except to suggest that the New Zealanders took their military responsibilities seriously. But the real question was whether anything that it was in New Zealand's power to do could make any difference to the speed and direction of the Japanese assault. The fact was that the Dominion's enthusiastic participation in the war against Germany in Europe had left it desperately short of everything necessary for its own defence. Only 13,250 men were actually in base camps in New Zealand; a further 4,600 fortress troops were divided roughly equally among Auckland, Wellington, Port Lyttleton and Port Chalmers; and there was a reserve of some 11,000 Territorials. Seaborne defence consisted of three cruisers. New Zealand's air power was made up of 36 Lockheed Hudsons, second-rate but still useful; and 29 Vickers Vincent biplane torpedo-bombers, virtually useless for modern warfare and far less formidable in every way than the 62 North American Harvards, 46 Hawker Hinds and 143 Avro Oxfords being used for training. There were exactly four 3·7-inch and four Bofors anti-aircraft guns in the whole Dominion.

The New Zealand Government nonetheless decided at once to send a further 3,500 men to Fiji, along with all the nation's anti-aircraft guns. By 10 January 1942 the number of men in camp had actually been trebled, and a Home Guard was being formed, equipped initially with 44 vintage machine guns of doubtful reliability. Slit trenches were dug in city parks; work was begun in Auckland on more elaborate shelter systems; and schoolchildren were drilled in the techniques of air raid precautions. It was still difficult enough to imagine any incentive for a Japanese invasion of New Zealand in the first place, let alone Tahiti or Rarotonga. However, it was all too easy to imagine a Japanese tide sweeping irresistibly over the whole Pacific Ocean. New Zealand anxieties were intensified in any case by the news that a Japanese submarine had actually shelled Samoa on 12 January.

Part of the strategic problem was that the Japanese themselves did not always know where they were going. A far greater part was that literally nothing seemed to be able to halt their progress. On 23 January 4,000 Japanese landed on Rabaul, to try to cut communications between Australia and the United States. They overwhelmed the Australian garrison of 1,400, only 400 of whom escaped. On 2 February the New Zealanders built up their forces in Fiji to 7,600. Port Moresby was bombed on the following day. Singapore surrendered on 15 February. The Dutch East Indies had gone already, with the exception of Java. Japanese aircraft bombed Darwin on 19 February, starting an exodus from the northernmost Australian capital. It was officially noted that one civilian at least did not stop retreating until he reached Melbourne. On 26 February the Australian and New Zealand General Staffs accepted the fact that their own countries would have to provide the only bases from which any counter-attack could possibly be launched against Japan in the South Pacific. But the position of the British Dominions themselves appeared even more precarious when on the very next day an Allied force of five Australian, British, Dutch and American cruisers and nine British, Dutch and American destroyers encountered two Japanese cruisers and fourteen destroyers under Admiral Takagi in the Java Straits. The Allies lost two cruisers and three destroyers, without sinking a single Japanese warship. The remaining Allied cruisers were sunk over the next two days, along with two more destroyers, still without any loss to the Japanese. And on 8 March Japanese troops landed in New Guinea, at the same time that General Sakurai's forces in Burma entered Rangoon, already abandoned by the retreating British.

Perhaps nothing was wholly clear at this stage, but some facts seemed evident on the surface. The most obvious was that the resources of the British Empire were simply inadequate to sustain a war against Germany in Europe and Africa and at the same time contain a determined attack by another major power in Asia and the Pacific. It was possible that the Japanese had already acquired as much of the British Empire as they wanted for the time being; but it was quite evident that they could take the rest whenever they wanted to, unless some other friendly great power were prepared to try to stop them.

There was no doubt who that would have to be. The Australians were already blaming the British, with complete justification, for the remarkable inadequacy of the defence of Malaya. It was also felt with equal justification that other battle fronts were regarded by the British War Cabinet as more important in the long run than the Pacific. In any case, with the best will in the world, the British lacked the capacity to send adequate reinforcements to safeguard their southern Dominions. It seemed as if the only hope was that the Americans might regard the Pacific front as being of greater urgency than the British apparently believed it was. Australian Prime Minister Curtin accordingly announced on 27 December that his Government regarded the Pacific struggle as primarily one in which the United States and Australia must have the fullest say in the direction of the fighting plan of the democracies. 'Without any inhibitions of any kind, I make it quite clear that Australia looks to America, free from any pangs as to our traditional links or kinship with the United Kingdom.'[7] In accordance with this view, he also expressed a preference for an American Commander-in-Chief in the Pacific, after the fall of Hong Kong.

This, of course, did not in the slightest degree represent any preference on the part of the Australian Government and people for an American rather than a British alignment. Even less was this the case in New Zealand, where the most influential of the Dominion's daily papers, the sober and internationally respected *New Zealand Herald*, had bitterly condemned the United States for the peril to which New Zealand was exposed, assigning primary responsibility to President Roosevelt himself for pursuing a policy which had effectively provoked the Japanese into starting a war which endangered the British Empire as well as the United States. The fact was that the Australians and New Zealanders could not count on British help arriving in time or in sufficient quantities. They had perforce to return to the only available source of aid. The Americans had to be made aware of their responsibilities.

Australian feelings were in addition exacerbated by a bitter disagreement between Churchill and Curtin regarding the return to Australia of the Australian components of the Eighth Army, at that time being thrown out of half of their Libyan conquests by a German counterattack. Roosevelt, on the other hand, seemed to give Curtin encouragement, assuring him that it would be easier for the United States to look after the reinforcement of the Allied 'right flank' in the Pacific. Some American troops had already arrived in Brisbane, having been diverted there from the Philippines after the Japanese had blockaded those islands. On 12 March 1942, other United States units replaced the hopelessly inadequate Australian garrison on New Caledonia. The Americans were undoubtedly coming. But they were not coming quite according to the Australian or New Zealand plan. Roosevelt as much as Churchill was committed to a strategy of beating Hitler first : the Pacific was going to have to make do with what could be spared from other more urgent and decisive theatres. Moreover, one of the basic assumptions of the Dominion governments had been that Australia and New Zealand would be united along with New Caledonia and Fiji in an 'Anzac Area'. Curtin had been allowed to get the impression that the Americans had agreed to this as well. Australian and New Zealand confidence was renewed when General Douglas MacArthur arrived in Australia on 18 March, fresh from his disastrous miscalculations in the Philippines, to become Supreme Commander of all Allied Forces in the South-west Pacific, or Commander-in-Chief, as he insisted on being called. On the same day, Roosevelt reaffirmed the United States' resolve to undertake the defence of Australia. However, on 24 March Curtin's Minister for External Affairs, Dr Evatt, reported that the Joint Chiefs of Staff had decided to divide the Pacific Front into a South-west Pacific Area, including Australia, under MacArthur, and a South Pacific Area, including New Zealand, under Admiral Ernest J. King. The New Zealanders also protested vigorously against this administrative separation from their fellow-Dominion. There was however nothing they could do to affect the American decision. They could only hope quite reasonably that in practice the distinction would become irrelevant.[8]

The American takeover was unavoidable in the circumstances. The war was going badly for the Allies on almost every front. The Russian counter-offensive was collapsing; the British had been thrown back in Africa; and units of the German Navy had dashed through the Channel from Brest, inflicting heavy casualties on British aircraft which attempted to stop them. Obviously the United States alone would be able to make a significant contribution to the defence of the Pacific. The British could not hold Burma, and might not be able to hold Africa or India. Australia and New Zealand were literally approaching the end of their man-power resources. By 18 March 1942, 67,264 men had been assembled in base camps in New Zealand, and the Home Guard had been increased to over 100,000. But this was about as far as the Dominion could go : 93·4 per cent of male New Zealanders between the ages of 14 and 64 were involved in the war effort in either defence or more or less essential industries, and 45·2 per cent of those between the ages of 18 and 40 were in the services.[9] The drain on Australian manpower was comparable : 40 per cent of Australian men between the ages of 18 and 45 were with the armed forces. The southern British Dominions had literally done everything humanly possible to assist Britain itself and at the same time look after their own defence. It is of course true that one does not need to defend oneself when one is not going to be attacked, and as indicated earlier the Japanese had no intention of attacking the Dominions. But the fact was that the British and Americans simply could not afford to leave an enormously enlarged and victorious Japanese Empire intact in their rear while they devoted themselves to the war against Germany and its European allies. Official Allied strategy might be 'Beat Hitler First', but Hitler could be beaten at all only if the Japanese could be held in check in the meantime. It was thus impossible for the British and Americans to leave the Japanese in peace to enjoy their conquests. It was therefore also impossible for the Japanese to leave the British and Americans in peace beyond the perimeter to develop their counter-attacks. Whatever the desired limits of the Co-prosperity Sphere might have been, the Japanese were in reality committed to nothing less than the total destruction of British and American striking power in the Pacific and Asia. They were committed to an Axis victory.

The Japanese never appreciated the necessity to reconcile the achievement of the Co-prosperity Sphere with their military priorities. They had gone hell-bent after an empire at a time when their primary objectives should have been all those elements of American sea and air power which had escaped destruction at Pearl Harbor. The result was that four months after Pearl, the Americans still had a carrier squadron; they still had their Pacific bases in Hawaii and Midway; and they could still send convoys across the ocean to Australia. The Japanese had not made the best use of their time.

They still looked unchallengeable on 6 May, when the last American forces in the Philippines surrendered. There is indeed no parallel in history to the Japanese march of conquest in the first five months of 1942. They had in that time killed, wounded or taken prisoner about 425,000 Allied soldiers; sunk 6 Allied battleships, an aircraft carrier, 7 cruisers, 6 destroyers and 15 other warships; and destroyed approximately 794 Allied aircraft. They had themselves lost 23,424 men; a minesweeper, a minelayer, 2 destroyers and 5 submarines; and about 1,000 Army and Navy aircraft from all causes. One would have thought that the only problem for the Japanese was to decide whom to defeat next.

This in fact was precisely where Japanese planning broke down. The Army, deployed in a fantastically wide arc touching India in the west and New Guinea in the south, would have preferred to fall back to a more practicable defence line for the protection of the Asian heartland. The Navy belatedly was insisting on the need to complete the destruction of United States striking power in the Pacific. Unfortunately, the Admirals themselves were undecided between the conflicting attractions of an invasion of Australia; an occupation of New Caledonia, Fiji and Samoa, to cut the supply route between the United States and the remaining British Dominions; and a search-and-destroy operation against the remaining United States Naval Forces in the Central Pacific, enlivened by a diversionary operation against the Aleutian Islands, of all places.

Two factors were causing the Japanese anxiety. One was the demonstrated ability of the Americans to strike at Tokyo itself, which was bombed by carrier-based aircraft on 18 April 1942. Far more important was the rapid development of Australia as an Allied base. Already 38,000 American troops had arrived, with some 300 aircraft, and Roosevelt had promised to send a further 190,000. The Australians themselves had organized massive defence forces consisting by the end of April of 104,000 men of the Australian Imperial Force and a further 265,000 in the militia, with about 5,000 machine guns and over 600 field guns of various calibres. Given that the Australians had already shown themselves to be among the most adaptable, physically tough, professionally competent and generally bloody-minded soldiers on earth, it would be reasonable to assume that the reduction of the continent as an American base would have required the use of rather more divisions than the Japanese had available at the time outside the Asian mainland. Churchill himself had pointed this out to Curtin, promising to send him a British armoured division if Australia were assaulted by ten or more Japanese divisions, the minimum force which the Japanese would need for a serious invasion.

In May 1942 the Japanese took the decision which could have enlarged the war for East Asia into a war for the Pacific itself. It had at last been appreciated that the Co-prosperity Sphere could be safe only if the Pacific were turned into a Japanese lake. On 3 May the Japanese

occupied Tulagi in the Southern Solomons. A seaplane base was established, to provide land-based air cover to offset the Allied bases in Port
Moresby and New Caledonia; another invasion fleet was assembled to
descend on Port Moresby itself; and a further striking force was deployed to catch the defenders in an enveloping movement in the Coral
Sea. Like most Japanese battle plans, it could be counted on to work
only if their opponents did everything wrong, which indeed they had
until now. But the slightest failure on the part of the Allies to perform
their designated role was likely to cause the whole extraordinarily complicated operation to fall apart: Admiral Inouye was trying to co-
ordinate the movements of five separate naval forces, as well as a land-
based Air Flotilla, and he was trying to do this from Rabaul, 600 miles
away from the actual scene of action. The Japanese certainly liked to
make things difficult for themselves.

Inouye and his Admirals were understandably not quite up to the
challenge. After a heavily fought but indecisive engagement, both fleets
withdrew to count their losses. The Allies had lost more heavily in ships,
the Japanese in the air. Japan could still easily have rallied overwhelming
naval power to cover any operation in the Pacific. The invasion fleet
bound for Port Moresby nonetheless turned back, for reasons which
the Japanese themselves must have known to be quite insufficient. But
the threat to the Pacific islands had not been diverted at all by the
engagement in the Coral Sea. Having bungled one excessively complicated operation, the Japanese hastened to press on with one far larger and
far more elaborate. On 18 May the decision was taken to capture Fiji,
New Caledonia and Samoa as well as New Guinea. Sea and air attacks
could then be launched from these bases to neutralize key points in
Australia and New Zealand. With the Germans and their allies now
triumphantly on the offensive in both Russia and Africa, the Dominions
knew only too well that they could not expect even an armoured division from Britain. They would have to do the best they could with what
they had got.

Meanwhile, the Japanese had landed some 10,000 troops in New
Guinea for the assault on Port Moresby. They were opposed by 13,000
Australians, accompanied rather than supported by 2,208 non-com-
batant Americans. The New Zealand garrison in Fiji had been built up
to 10,000 exhaustively trained fighting men, who had spent the swelter-
ing summer months furiously constructing entrenchments, barbed wire
entanglements, underground shelters and every kind of fortification. A
further 600 workmen from the New Zealand Department of Public Works

had been armed with American rifles and machine guns and trained for emergency operations. They had twenty-eight field guns for mobile defence, as well as the fixed coastal batteries, and a certain measure of air support provided by a squadron of elderly but rugged American Air-cobras. The New Zealanders had in addition begun to mobilize the superb if erratic fighting capacity of the Fijians themselves: three guerrilla units were formed, each composed of about 200 Fijians, led by 30 New Zealand non-commissioned officers. Plans were made to put into effect a scorched earth programme in the event of a successful Japanese land-ing. Tension rose when three Japanese midget submarines attacked Sydney harbour on the night of 31 May, and again when another two submarines shelled the eastern suburbs of the city on 8 June, causing a startling decline in land values in the most expensive real estate in Australia. But the tide was now manifestly turning: Australian and United States forces in New Guinea now heavily outnumbered their Japanese opponents, and on 6 August the first American landings took place on Guadalcanal in the Solomons.

The problem now was that the British Empire's presence in the Pacific would soon be dwarfed by that of the Americans. The number of United States service personnel stationed in Australia and New Zealand, for example, substantially outnumbered the forces available in both countries for overseas service by the end of 1942. Nor was there any particular reason to expect the attitude of the Americans towards British imperial interests in the region to be any different from their demonstrated attitudes towards the interests of other colonial powers. Japanese predominance might be replaced after victory by an even more comprehensive United States predominance, which would be im-possible to dislodge.

The experience of New Caledonia was a case in point. The Americans had accepted responsibility for the defence of the island, absolutely essen-tial to the maintenance of sea communications between the United States, Australia and New Zealand. Roosevelt had promised to send twenty-five pursuit aircraft and thirteen bombers to establish a striking force on the island.[10] He had, however, particularly requested the Austra-lian Government not to let the Gaullist authorities have any idea of the nature of the United States force until the aircraft were actually on their way. This attitude was explained by the actions of de Gaulle's High Commissioner in the Pacific, Thierry d'Argenlieu, an ex-Carmelite monk turned naval officer, who apparently saw the action of Free France in the Pacific as a species of crusade. D'Argenlieu had already succeeded in bringing the civilian population of New Caledonia almost to the point of rebellion by the end of 1941, through his authoritarianism and the un-monk-like manner in which he appropriated the best living conditions and automobiles available for the use of himself and his enormous entourage. In January 1942 he had flatly announced his determination to halt shipments of iron ore to the United States, unless he received the kind of military assistance he was demanding from both the Australian and United States governments. Washington attempted to conciliate d'Argenlieu by assuring him that French sovereignty over the island would continue to be recognized. This was at least good enough for Henri Sautot, who made a point of publicly welcoming the American contingents which began to arrive in March 1942. D'Argenlieu, however, reported to de Gaulle that Sautot was attempting to undermine his authority by currying favour with the local population as well as with the Americans, who had effectively taken complete control over the Group. De Gaulle ordered Sautot to report to him in London. Sautot appealed to the United States military commander, denouncing his critics as pitiable shipwrecks who allied themselves 'with everything that stands for disorder and opposition to the principles of authority'.[11] On 5 May Sautot was seized on D'Argenlieu's orders and placed aboard a French warship which carted him off to London. D'Argenlieu for his part requested that the United States commander use American troops to maintain order in a situation in which 90 per cent of the population were sympathetic to Sautot. The Americans prudently insisted on remaining neutral, but threatened to apply martial law in the event of political disturbances weakening the security of the island. The Noumeans thereupon rose in revolt against d'Argenlieu, who fled to the mountains of the interior, where he was effectively besieged by the supporters of Sautot.

De Gaulle himself recalled d'Argenlieu at the end of the month. In the meantime, some of the pressure had been taken off the Americans by the decision of the New Zealand Government to send troops to New Caledonia to replace the United States garrison, with the intention of freeing the Americans for offensive action against the Japanese elsewhere in the Pacific. D'Argenlieu however took time out to visit Australia in September 1942, to extract from the Australian Government a public statement to the effect that the governing body of Free France had earned the undying gratitude of the Australian people and of all those who were fighting for freedom; that Free France had rendered the greatest practical assistance to the United Nations; that, by its efforts and energy, Free France had firmly established its authority and prestige over all the territories, particularly the French Pacific possessions, which had renounced the Vichy Government; and that respect for the sovereignty of France and the French Empire and the eventual restoration of France as a world power would be mainly due to Free Frenchmen like de Gaulle and d'Argenlieu, who to everyone's surprise had suddenly been promoted to the rank of Rear-Admiral.[12]

This statement may have been expedient, but it hardly fitted the realities of the New Caledonia situation, where the local colonists, having got rid of d'Argenlieu, were enjoying unprecedented prosperity as a result of the American presence, and were about to enjoy as well the protection of 20,000 New Zealanders, who found themselves garrisoning an island which d'Argenlieu had literally left as defenceless as he had found it. This however was by no means the whole of the problem. D'Argenlieu had already communicated with the New Zealand Government, drawing from them also an assurance that their policy, like Australia's, was based on the maintenance of the integrity of France and the French Empire, and the eventual restoration and complete reconstitution of both. The New Zealand Government had also been required to recognize fully the efforts made by Free France in the furtherance of the common cause; and to state that they had an especial interest in the maintenance of the authority of the Gaullist governing body in all insular possessions and territories of France in the Pacific, including French Oceania, which territories were and should remain French. Indeed, a reawakening of the New Zealanders' old territorial ambitions in the Pacific was now unlikely. The same applied to the Australians; Evatt again went to the trouble of disclaiming any desire on the part of his government for aggrandizement in the Pacific at the expense of the French, the Dutch or even the Portuguese. He repeated that Australia envisaged the restoration of full French sovereignty over New Caledonia. The United States military commander had also explicitly recognized 'the status of New Caledonia as a Colony of Fighting France and under the control of the Fighting French authorities, the National Committee headed by General de Gaulle'.[13] There was however no allaying French suspicions. In December 1943 the new Gaullist Governor Christian Laigret condemned the failure of the American troops to recognize the French point of view; reminded the United States that the New Caledonians themselves had put the island into a highly mobilized state of defence; and hoped that American citizens would never forget that if their troops were in New Caledonia, it was only because a handful of French had permitted it. He considered this concession by the French authorities to be a historic event which had still more importance than Pearl Harbor.[14]

One could partly sympathize with French preoccupations with status in the Pacific. But Governor Laigret had overlooked many facts. Most serious was his exaggeration of the French contribution to the defence of the island. In fact, only 546 Frenchmen and natives had actually left the island to serve overseas, less than one-fifth of the number which had done so in the First World War.[15] Only 68 of those overseas were native New Caledonians. Another 971 natives were serving with the French armed forces in New Caledonia. However, the French authorities had actually discouraged natives from enlisting by using them as common labourers or domestic servants when they volunteered for combat duty.

American relations with the colonial authorities in Fiji were by contrast almost idyllic. The official United States Navy historian suggested that perhaps 'with no other Government in the Pacific Theatre have the associations and cooperation been greater than with the Government of Fiji'.[16] True, there were certain difficulties. The Fijian Council of Chiefs had expressed the desire in September 1942 that their warriors should serve overseas. This had been opposed and overruled at the time on racial grounds by the United States High Command. The New Zealanders nonetheless managed to organize a body called the South Sea Scouts, comprising some 77 New Zealanders, 223 Fijians, 50 Tongans and 200 Solomon Islanders, who fought in Bougainville, killing 418 Japanese at a loss to themselves of only 33 casualties in all, and earning the unstinted praise of the Americans. This was admittedly only a fraction of the 7,505 Fijians enrolled in the island's volunteer forces, and even a smaller percentage of the 2,224 Tongans similarly enlisted. It was still more ominous that the Fijian contribution to the war effort should have been virtually entirely native as distinct from Indian Fijian effort. An attempt to conscript an Indian Regiment in Fiji 'resulted, after two months of effort, in volunteering (under pressure) of about six Indians, one of whom had a withered arm, and another of whom was six feet tall and weighed 98 pounds'.[17]

Intervention in Tonga brought the Americans fully face to face with the complexities of the British system in the Pacific. It was difficult enough to comprehend that Tonga was an independent monarchy subject to a protectorate under which the British consul, who was also a deputy of the High Commissioner for the Western Pacific, advised the Queen and her government on all matters of importance, especially in connection with foreign policy. But this was only the tip of the iceberg. The Americans also discovered that it was

> customary in Tonga for any department of the Queen's Government to have as nominal head some distinguished Tongan native. He in turn is assisted by an European hired by the government with the approval (and generally on the recommendation of) the British consul. Thus the Minister of Police is a Tongan who knows very little about the job. The Captain of Police is a New Zealand former Army officer. The very important position of Secretary to the Government is, under this system, an able Oxford graduate and member of the British Colonial Service, who has been farmed out to Tonga after extensive service in the Solomon Islands. When his duties in Tonga are completed he will presumably return to the British Colonial Service and some other European will be sent out to replace him.[18]

It was no wonder that 'on at least three occasions naval personnel felt that: "Goddamn British were always sticking their nose in it" '[19] Working relations were made more tolerable by the tremendous admiration which the Americans felt for the Tongan monarch, Queen Salote, in their dealings with whom the United States Navy showed unfailing respect for protocol. For example, Navy officers attending royal receptions were required absolutely by Commander-in-Chief Pacific Fleet, to present themselves in dress whites and wearing gloves. In contrast, New Zealand troops provoked a walk-out by the Tongan Defence Force with their refusal to salute Tongan officers.

The most serious, and certainly least expected, tensions arose between the Americans and the peoples of the British Dominions. These revealed themselves in every aspect of the war effort. At first, the Australians and New Zealanders had been inclined to welcome the Americans as saviours and in some sense as relatives. The illusion of common ethnic and cultural ties was not entirely dissipated by experience with the members of the United States Navy and the United States Marine Corps, who were the first to arrive in the British Dominions. These were, by any standards, immensely well-trained and well-disciplined fighting men, a large proportion of whom were in fact of British or at least of western European origin. The United States Army was something else again, composed essentially of men who had failed to qualify for the Navy or the Marines and who were in large part of Central or East European or even African origin, with no sympathy at all for Anglo-Saxon traditions.

This might have been disillusioning, but was not necessarily serious : no two peoples had more in common than the Australians and New Zealanders, yet were more likely to start quarrelling with each other at the slightest opportunity. Far more ominous was the fact that the Americans were undoubtedly the best-paid fighting men in the world, with at least twice the purchasing power of their Australian or New Zealand counterparts; that the Marines and the officers of the other services were certainly among the best-dressed; and that Australian and New Zealand women appreciated the difference. Sexual rivalries were exacerbated by antipodean provincialism and American arrogance. Brawls between Anzac and American servicemen developed into riots in Wellington and Brisbane, made more serious still by the tendency of the Americans to use knives and guns to reply to the fists, boots and bottles of their allies. The most violent scenes occurred in the frontier town of Rockhampton in the north of Queensland, when a trainload of Australians leaving for the New Guinea battlefront drew in at a siding alongside a trainload of Americans returning for leave. The Americans assured the Australians that they would look after their women while they were away; the Australians drew their bayonets; the Americans produced carbines and automatics; and considerable loss of life took place on both sides before their officers and provosts managed to separate the two groups.

Antagonism, or at best alienation, could be found everywhere. Even the basic factor of food had a part to play. Americans grew to detest New Zealand mutton, which they strongly suspected of being goat. They found the New Zealanders themselves in general 'like the Australians on Bougainville . . . a rough and ready lot whose equipment, clothing, living quarters, food, and dental care are usually far below American standards'; while at the same time admitting that 'no one who has watched New Zealand troops in action can ignore the excellent quality of such men. . . . It is also true that the average American enlisted man (and many partially educated officers) did not like "bloody Limeys". There are probably few New Zealanders who served in close conjunction with American troops who were not at some time or another offended by American thoughtlessness and outspokenness.'[20] Anzac–United States co-operation was in any case made difficult by the fact that MacArthur and Blamey represented the opposite poles of the human personality in many important respects. Further, Australian and New Zealand soldiers, who had perhaps never known what it was to have sufficient military equipment for their needs, had a completely different approach to combat and especially logistics from that of the Americans, most of whom had never known what it was to be under-supplied. Even their common language sometimes proved a barrier as much as a bond, by encouraging confusion and misunderstanding. It was not simply a matter of different idioms, or of words used in different senses. American staff officers, articulate, enthusiastic, with an inexhaustible appetite for detail, were frankly baffled by the scanty and laconic reports they received from Australian and New Zealand officers in the field. National traits magnified the confusion; Australians would tend to describe a completely satisfactory defensive action, in which an enemy attack had been repelled with heavy casualties, in terms which would imply to Americans that the defenders had been routed. Australian staff officers were being anything but facetious when they suggested that what the Anzacs and the Americans needed most urgently was a corps of interpreters.[21]

Some of this tension was apparently in the highest echelons of command by the end of 1943. The Australian Government had continued doggedly to support MacArthur, despite his tendency to give the impression that the Pacific War was being fought entirely by the United States, neglecting to give the Australians credit even for actions in which they had in reality done most of the fighting. However, throughout the second half of 1943 the Australians also attempted to convince the British of the importance of maintaining a Commonwealth presence in the Pacific, proposing as one means of achieving this that the Solomon Islands should be placed under Australian control and Fiji under that of New Zealand. As victory in Europe became more imminent, Australian Prime Minister Curtin began to press for a British Commonwealth Command in the Pacific. Their concern became all the greater when spokesmen for the Roosevelt administration and Congressional leaders began to speak of the possibility of former colonial powers being required to hand over bases and even whole colonies to the United States in the Pacific after the war, in payment for lend-lease assistance. Neither Wellington nor Canberra were consulted when the British, Americans and Chinese resolved in December 1943 to annex all Japanese territories acquired since 1895. At an urgent conference held in Canberra in January 1944, the Dominion Governments agreed on the terms of what came to be known as the Anzac Pact, affirming the existence of a common Australasian point of view; resolving to continue applying the trading system of Commonwealth preferences, to which the United States had always been totally opposed; rejecting any notion of a condominion with the United States in the Solomons, New Caledonia or the New Hebrides, let alone the Cooks or Samoa; insisting that there should be no change of sovereignty over any of the island territories to which they had not themselves agreed beforehand; and suggesting that Australia and New Zealand should participate in the policing of the Pacific region south of the equator, leaving the Americans to do the same in the north.[22] The message of this Australian–New Zealand Agreement was quite unmistakable : the Dominions had been ready to turn to the United States for help when Britain had been unable to come to their aid effectively, but they were determined to maintain British authority in the South Pacific virtually undiminished by anything that might have happened since the Japanese attack.

Nor was this all. The Australian and New Zealand Governments had already in October 1943 stressed the idea that policing the South Pacific should be the responsibility of the British Commonwealth. They now proposed that at the earliest possible date there should be established 'a regional organization with advisory powers, which could be called the South Pacific Commission, and on which, in addition to representatives of Australia and New Zealand, there might be accredited representatives of the United Kingdom and the United States of America, and of the French Committee of National Liberation'. Further, one of the particular functions of the Commission should be to 'recommend arrangements for the participation of natives in administration in increasing measure with a view to promoting the ultimate attainment of self-government in the form most suited to the circumstances of the native people concerned'.[23]

This proposal had some surprising features. Australia could scarcely have been described hitherto as a Pacific polity in any sensible meaning of the term. Its position for the previous fifty years had been wholly insular, modified by obsessions about European and more acutely Asian hostility. Neither Australia nor New Zealand had ever formerly associated themselves with a viewpoint which could remotely be termed anticolonialist. However, the two Dominions now appeared to be placing themselves in the forefront of what might very well prove to be a movement towards independence on the part of the island peoples. The explanation was obvious. The Australians and New Zealanders still saw themselves essentially as they had seen themselves throughout their history : as the guarantors of a British imperial presence, the bastions of the white or at least Anglo-Saxon race, the wave of the future. Sheer weight of numbers and resources ensured that the South Pacific had to become increasingly an area of Australian–New Zealand predominance, unless the balance were amended by intervention from an outside great power. The great power there already was the United States, and it was liable to be there for all time unless a convincing counter-claim could be asserted while the situation was still unresolved. The only alternative to an American ocean after victory was for British Commonwealth authority to be confirmed and extended wherever possible before victory had been decided. Balance of power had always been the name of the game in the Pacific. Once again, the Australians and New Zealanders were trying to force the pace, while the British Government hesitated to become involved too vehemently in a remote region with powers which it wished to conciliate for reasons of its own. The difference was that the Australians and New Zealanders were now freer legally as well as practically to take independent action of their own. To bring the British in was, after all, only one of the means by which their objective could be achieved, the objective being simply to keep the Americans out.

It was not a viewpoint with which the Americans could naturally be expected to have much sympathy. They had not fought to keep the South Pacific safe for the British race. Nor had they any intention of detracting from the glory of their own armed forces by inviting Commonwealth forces to participate in a victory campaign which could obviously be won almost as quickly by American arms alone. State Department professed to be able to understand why the Australians and New Zealanders might want to reach agreement on post-war problems among themselves, but claimed to be frankly disturbed at the thought of any conference of powers with territorial interests, such as the Anzac Pact envisaged. The United States did not really wish to associate itself in any way with the problems of the anachronistic colonial empires in the Pacific. Still less did it intend to allow any international body to interfere with its own colonial rule in Eastern Samoa, which provided the only naval base in the South Pacific actually in United States territory. Moreover, it was difficult to reconcile so exclusive a regional agreement as the Anzac Pact with the principles of the United Nations, with its emphasis on global concepts and internationalism.

A meeting of Dominion Prime Ministers in London in May 1944 revealed the existence of still further clashes of interests between the United States and the British peoples in the Pacific. One of the pre-occupations of the Australians and New Zealanders had been to ensure that air communications in the Pacific should not fall entirely into the hands of the Americans. They had accordingly proposed that air facilities in the Pacific should be 'internationalized' by being made freely available to all airlines servicing the area. This meant essentially that non-American lines should be able to enjoy equal loading rights to Honolulu. Failing 'internationalization' of air services, British Commonwealth air routes should be established across the Pacific after the war. However, the Americans refused to accept either the concept of internationalization or any other suggestion for the international control of air services. Nor indeed were the British particularly concerned to press the Australian–New Zealand view in the face of American opposition. The Australians for their part protested that any Dominion was entitled to British support in any affair which was the regional responsibility of that Dominion. Prime Minister Curtin further took occasion to warn the United States that Australia for its part would not be abandoning the Imperial Preference trading system for any utopian schemes of which the Americans might become enamoured.[24]

The most obvious way of confirming British authority in the Pacific was, of course, to establish a British Commonwealth military presence alongside the victorious Americans, whether the Americans wanted it there or not. Curtin pointed out that he had indeed no objection to seeing United States influence extended in the region, so long as it was extended at the expense of territory that had been formerly Japanese, and not British. He accordingly welcomed the prospect of a British force being based in Australia, and proposed that two different regional commands be created for the war against Japan: a South-east Asia Command, in which the British could participate from their bases in India and Ceylon; and an Australian–New Zealand Command, in which Australia would provide the main British Commonwealth effort, along with British forces operating from Australian bases. The New Zealanders, already disgruntled at the fact that the Americans had not been able to find any duties for the RNZAF except to act as a garrison, agreed with the proposal; the Third Division of the New Zealand Expeditionary Force was withdrawn from Italy in preparation for service in the Pacific; a massive British naval task force moved into the Indian Ocean; and the Australians waited in readiness for the last drive to Japan. It all added up to a not unimpressive contribution: by the beginning of 1945, there were six Australian and one New Zealand division acting in support of the twenty-three United States divisions in the Pacific, as well as thirteen British Empire divisions in Burma. The trouble was that the Americans either did not want them or were unwilling to admit that they did. It was agreed that the Australians should be allowed to accept the surrender of Ocean and Niue Islands. However, Admiral King decided not to use an Anzac force in the Marshalls and Carolines; MacArthur found no role for the Australians in Balikpapan; and the war ended before the New Zealanders had finished training for the invasion of Japan. The Great Pacific War was over. The struggle for the Pacific continued.

VII

The Survivors

British and French fears of an American takeover in the Pacific after the defeat of Japan proved, in fact, to be unfounded. The United States had not gone to war to preserve the authority of the colonial empires. However, neither had it fought to extend its own authority through the medium of traditional colonialism. United States' influence had nonetheless certainly helped to undermine the prestige of colonial empires, which United States' victories had rescued from total destruction by the Japanese. And it was true that United States military personnel normally sided with the natives in any disputes that arose between them and their colonial overlords.[1] But probably more significant was the simple economic impact of American affluence, although this was often criticizised most severely by people who were themselves considered by the local population to be enjoying 'an extravagant and reckless manner of living', like de Gaulle's representatives in New Caledonia.[2] The fact remained that anybody who had witnessed American resources being deployed apparently without regard for expense was likely to become dissatisfied with the material limitations of life in the Pacific islands. To their own amazement, the first colonial overlords to receive a coherent statement of dissatisfaction, even before the war had ended, were the New Zealanders. Sir Cyril Newell, probably the most reluctant Governor-General of New Zealand, paid an official visit to Samoa in 1944. He was greeted with a flat statement that:

The terms of the Mandate have imposed on New Zealand the

solemn duty of educating the Samoans to self-government and the terms of the Atlantic Charter express the same aim for the small nations of the world. Thirty years have passed since New Zealand took over Western Samoa and we are appreciably no nearer this goal . . . we have lost confidence in the trusteeship of New Zealand which has shown a lack of interest in the territory and treated its people as stepchildren . . . we respectfully submit . . . our wish that the Samoans be granted a larger measure of self-government as has been given to the Tongans and to the Fijians.[3]

The shock could hardly have been greater or the timing better : nothing could have been more embarrassing for one of the signatories to the Anzac Pact than to have had its own colonial rule denounced by one of the politically more experienced Pacific peoples. After the initial alarms over the Mau, the New Zealanders had undoubtedly become complacent about the Samoan situation. For one thing, Samoa had in itself seemed a matter of only minor concern : the Chiefs of Staff had decided in 1939 that :

The Islands are of negligible importance in time of peace . . . Western Samoa is considered to be of small importance either as a base or as a source of supply in time of war. The Administration of Western Samoa has been no more free of difficulties under New Zealand control than it has been in its previous history under German and prior administrations, but the position is much easier at the moment. . . . A few odd natives have been attracted into the orbit of the Nazi Party, largely it is believed in the hope of obtaining monetary or social benefit for themselves . . . [but]. . . the great majority of the natives are quite unaffected by this propaganda and are believed to be opposed to [it].

Proof of this was found in the fact that during the Munich crisis 'the members of the Fono of Faipule . . . voluntarily offered the full support of 9,000 Samoans for the defence of the Territory and general purposes'.[4] The fact was, however, that it was found impossible to raise a Samoan militia for defence purposes during the Pacific war, although some Samoans did serve with the New Zealand forces, 'and not even a labour battalion for limited non-military service could be conscripted'.[5]

The New Zealanders had at least the saving grace of pragmatism. They were prepared to recognize their limitations as imperialists. Prime Minister Fraser hastened over to Samoa, conveyed his genuine sense of the situation, and appointed a vigorous and pragmatic administrator, Colonel Voelcker, to carry out as many practical reforms as possible while awaiting the next step. However, Fraser was not prepared to grant self-government immediately; and Voelcker's highly beneficial efforts in the areas of administrative reform and public works came dangerously close to alienating both mainstreams of Samoan political feeling : he was too pragmatic for the conservatives, and too paternalistic for the progressives. A Fono of all Samoa was summoned in November 1946 to consider the situation. Open conflict was averted mainly thanks to a lingering trust in New Zealand as one of the most progressive welfare states in the world, and particularly as a small power whose rule had never been too efficiently oppressive. None the less, nine-tenths of the Fono were in favour of an American takeover, until convinced by Malietoa and Tamasese that it might be safer to stick with New Zealand. A petition was accordingly submitted to the United Nations, beseeching that Samoa be granted self-government, but also praying that 'New Zealand will see fit to act as Protector and Adviser to Samoa in the same capacity as England is to Tonga'.[6]

The New Zealanders hastened to respond to this request. A visiting mission was organize to report back to the Trusteeship Council of the United Nations on the actual situation in Samoa. Another Fono was held, without Voelcker's permission but also without his interference, to assure the mission that the *matai* (heads of families) unanimously supported the petition for self-government. Voelcker, who realized as well as any colonial administrator has ever done what he was really there for, warned the New Zealand Government against rejecting the petition, and called in the services of expert and academically trained people to act as yet another fact-finding expedition. Wellington again was prompt to act on advice. The Samoa Amendment Act was introduced in August 1947, even before the mission had reported back to the United Nations. A genuine Samoan Government was to be set up, comprising a New Zealand High Commissioner as principal executive officer, who would form a Council of State along with the three Fautua; and a Legislative Assembly, with eleven Samoan members, not more than five European elected members, and not more than six official members. A Samoan Public Service would be established under the control of a local, independent authority, and the practice of grants to Samoa from the Reparation Estates would be continued. The Assembly would be free to legislate on virtually all aspects of policy except those affecting external affairs, defence or the Crown title to land.

This was a little less than full self-rule, although the Samoans now had their own government, their own flag and their own national anthem. It was at least convincing evidence that New Zealand was unlikely to temporize or equivocate over the granting of full self-government, as soon as there was reason to believe that the Samoans had either developed new political institutions or modified their traditional ones in a way which could cope with the problems of running a nation-state in the twentieth century. Meanwhile, the Cook Islands, with a population of about 14,088, were also agitating for local self-government, if not exactly for nationhood, with the support of the New Zealand Federation of Labour; and a Legislative Council was duly set up in 1946, composed half of official members, and half of delegates from the local island councils. Attempts were also made to give some effective recognition to the war effort of the Maori population of New Zealand, 5,300 of whom had been accepted for service overseas; 3,543 of whom had actually embarked in the Maori Battalion, exclusive of these who served with non-Maori units; and no less than 2,595 of whom had become casualties, including 618 dead and 1,710 wounded.[7] A Maori Member of Parliament, Sir Eruera Tirikatene, had the word 'native' replaced by 'Maori' in all official documents, thereby removing at least legally any implication of inferiority on the part of the original occupying race, as compared with those by whom they had been colonized. Theoretically, they were all New Zealanders, Maori New Zealanders or Pakeha New Zealanders, as the case might be. Practical measures to improve Maori living conditions and boost Maori self-confidence included the settlement of long-standing financial claims by various tribes against the New Zealand Government, the establishment of a Maori Rehabilitation Finance Committee, the appointment of a permanent Maori Education and Employment Committee, a massive development scheme for Maori-owned lands, and an enormous increase in the construction of meeting houses to foster the traditional community sense of the Maoris. New Zealand's problems, domestic as well as external, certainly did not appear overwhelming, and at least New Zealand policy was likely to prevent them from getting any bigger.

Meanwhile, the brainchild of the Anzac Pact, the romantically-named Conference of the South Seas, had assembled. Representatives met in the Australian federal capital, Canberra, on 28 January 1947. Representatives came from New Zealand, the United Kingdom, the United States, France and the Netherlands, as well as from the host country Australia. It was evident from the start that the organization would perforce have to tread carefully. The first problem was to agree on a name for the proposed Commission. It was decided to change the title from 'South Seas' to 'South Pacific', as being rather less extensive in implication, and to provide some justification for the demand of the Dutch that only Western New Guinea, out of all the colonies in the region that they were still struggling to maintain, should be regarded as coming within the scope of the Commission. The frontiers of the Commission area were finally delimited as incorporating the Marshalls and Marianas, but not Hawaii, to the north; the Carolines, to the west; Norfolk Island, but not Australia, New Zealand or Tonga, to the south; and Pitcairn Island, but not Easter Island, to the east. It was perhaps reasonable to exclude what were recognized as independent nation-states. However, it very soon became clear that the British, the Americans and the French, to say nothing of the Dutch, were simply not going to admit the right of the Commission to have any authority over the administration of the colonies and dependencies within its area. The French representative indeed ominously congratulated the Commissioners on the 'wisely restricted scope of our activities', which 'shall not include political and ideological problems which France for her part has in any case resolved in setting up the French Union'. It was finally agreed that the Commission 'shall be a consultative and advisory body to the participating Governments in matters affecting the economic and social development of the non-self-governing territories within the scope of the Commission and the welfare and advancement of their peoples'.[8] It was further agreed that each of the six participating governments should appoint two Commissioners; that a permanent site should be established to house the Commission, somewhere 'within the territorial scope of the Commission', thereby heading off claims by the Australians and New Zealanders that it should be in one of their cities; and costs should be apportioned in the order of 30 per cent for Australia, 15 per cent each for New Zealand, the United Kingdom, and the Netherlands, and $12\frac{1}{2}$ per cent each for the United States and France.

The site finally chosen was Noumea, where the Commission held its first meeting in 1948. The choice was perhaps unpropitious, but then the possibilities were rather limited. The New Hebrides were clearly out of the question. So were the Solomons, now in a state of general revolt after the American occupation, with British warships meeting the challenge of the Marching Rule Movement, under whose banners thousands of natives moved about the islands regardless of official restraints, hundreds of them winding up in British jails. Suva would have been an agreeable choice, but lacked the kind of accommodation and office space which the Commission hopefully considered that it might need. Australian and New Zealand cities had all the facilities, but were rejected by the French. According to the familiar post-war pattern in international conferences, the French solution was finally accepted because it was the only solution which the French would accept themselves.

There was indeed a considerable familiarity about the whole New Caledonian scene. The island had enjoyed a most agreeable prosperity during the American occupation, despite the furious denunciations of American attitudes by the Gaullist officials. The Paris Government took immediate action to deal with this situation. All the island's export production of coffee and copra had to be sold to France, whether the French market could absorb it or not. At the same time, earnings of foreign exchange from the sale of New Caledonian minerals to Australia or the United States were annexed to augment France's own reserves of convertible currency. In return, the New Caledonians were allowed minimal allocations of exchange to purchase manufactured goods from the Americans and Australians, even though French industry could not yet itself supply their needs. On the political side, the Gaullists promised to grant autonomy to New Caledonia, but reneged on their promise in 1946, leaving the island subject to government by decree as before, although the New Caledonians at least had the consolation of being allowed to elect deputies to the French National Assembly, Senators to the French Council of State, and representatives to the Assembly of the French Union.

It was obvious from the start what the new pattern of relationships in the South Pacific was going to be. Only extraordinary reversals of policy could avert a confrontation between a French colonial enclave and a mass of British-speaking and generally British-aligned territories becoming more vocal as they moved into self-government. Nor could it be pretended that there was anything like sufficient goodwill on either side to play down the differences. The Australian press perhaps fired the first shot in 1950, claiming that Noumea had been chosen as a site for the Commission only because the French authorities hoped thereby to boost the attractions of New Caledonia as a tourist resort by giving it a measure of international fame. This was in fact not the case; but worse was to follow. It was suggested in Melbourne that serious consideration was being given among the Pacific peoples to an arrangement whereby New Caledonia as well as other islands might be 'attached' to Australia or New Zealand. The highly responsible *Sydney Morning Herald* took up the same theme, suggesting further that the inhabitants of the French Pacific islands did not seem to like the French colonial system.[9] It was at least fairly certain that some of the other islands had little regard for the civilizing mission of France. Tonga was acquiring a new cause for self-satisfaction through quite startlingly rapid improvements in public health. The kingdom had joined the South Pacific Health Service in 1947, and Queen Salote had given impressive leadership to a campaign to clean up Tonga's depressingly inadequate systems of sanitation and water supply. The extraordinary success of her campaign was witnessed by the fact that within a few years infant mortality had dropped in Tonga from a shamefully high level to the lowest in the Pacific. From this pinnacle of sanitary excellence, Crown Prince Tugi now condemned the failure of the French to do anything equally impressive in New Caledonia, in particular recommending that the Melanesians should be taught the techniques and benefits of birth control.

Something very close to a breakdown in relations between the French- and British-speaking peoples of the Pacific was obviously in train. The New Zealanders, attempting to solve by typically small-scale and *ad hoc* measures their difficult relations with the Cook Islanders, found their position rendered considerably more difficult and embarrassing by French attempts to induce Cook Islanders to work in Tahiti. Australian racist opinion was antagonized by French measures giving the vote to the native population of New Caledonia; by the opening of an Indonesian consulate in Noumea; and particularly by the extremely tardy manner in which the French were implementing their policy of Asian repatriation. They, indeed, appeared to have reversed any policy they might ever have had in that direction, for they were now actually proposing to recruit a further 2,000 Japanese workers. Violent Australian objections did in fact persuade the French Government to abandon its negotiations with Tokyo on this score. However, Franco–Australian relations were given no chance to improve: in February 1951 the publisher of the *Pacific Islands Monthly* suggested again that French Oceania might within a decade or two have 'weakened its ties with France and sought closer relations with its Anglo-American neighbours'.[10]

There was no evidence that the New Caledonians favoured such a course, however dissatisfied they might be with their treatment by France. On the other hand, the growing economic power of Australia was something the French were now forced to take into account. General de Gaulle himself in the course of a private visit to Noumea in 1956 made statements which at least appeared to imply a warning to the New Caledonians to beware of Anglo-Saxon predators in the South Seas. Early attempts by Governor Hoffherr to adopt a more outgoing policy in the external relations of the island were hastily brought to an end after the Governor had invited Australian schoolchildren to visit New Caledonia to correct any misapprehensions they might have gained about the place from their own government. Nor was Paris prepared to relinquish its control over finance, the civil service, telecommunications or mining, or even to make the newly-conceded Government Council in Noumea responsible to the legislature.

By contrast, the Anglo-Saxons were making impressive moves towards total decolonization in the South Pacific. Relations between the Cook Islands and New Zealand had passed through a particularly uncomfortable period, due to the most basic financial considerations: the Cook Islands Producers' Co-operative Society, the main political movement in the Group, had sought to gain control over trade with New Zealand by buying the little steamer *La Reta* in 1949. However, the CIPCS had been unable to raise the finance necessary to refit and run the ship, and *La Reta* had had to be sold. They then sought relief by complaining about the application of ferocious New Zealand tax laws to the Group, and in 1955 the New Zealand Cabinet ordered an economic survey to be made of the islands, to find out exactly what the inhabitants were concerned about. The report was admirably responsible and perceptive: it agreed that the islanders were worried about taxes; it also pointed out that they were worried about their future; and it particularly brought to the notice of the New Zealand Government the fact that the Cook Islanders were in a genuinely different position from their fellow-Maoris in New Zealand. Total integration with New Zealand was therefore not likely to be the real answer, although it was also evident that independent nationhood was neither feasible nor actually desired. The real need at the moment, which New Zealand was in fact able to satisfy, was for substantial subsidies to improve facilities for transport and marketing in the islands.[11]

New Zealand colonialism was looking particularly enlightened and benevolent by 1957. The newly-constructed legislative assembly for Western Samoa met in Apia for the first time. Only eleven of its forty-six members had had any previous parliamentary experience, but at least their economic problems were reduced by the decision of the New Zealand Government to hand over the lucrative Reparation Estates to the Western Samoa Trust Estates. In the meantime, the Cook Islanders also received their first Legislative Assembly under the terms of the

Cook Islands Amendment Bill, which provided for an assembly comprising five official members and fourteen elected ones, seven of the latter to be chosen by the various island councils. Hope for the economic future was also provided by the development of trade by the giant New Zealand processed foods company of James Wattie, while the belated but energetic public health services introduced by the New Zealand Government had managed to cut the rate of infant mortality from 269·29 per 1,000 in 1948 to less than 40 per 1,000.

The honeymoon continued. In 1959 the New Zealand Government agreed that the Samoans could have full independence whenever they chose to proclaim it. The Samoans for their part decided to modify their previous idea that New Zealand should adopt towards them the same relationship that the United Kingdom had adopted towards Tonga. The tendency to assume that whatever was right for Tonga was right for everybody else in the Pacific was difficult for Samoans to resist, but it had become sufficiently evident that Samoa was not Tonga and New Zealand was not the United Kingdom. In any case, it was perfectly probable that the British–Tongan relationship would be liable to change in the near future, with the impending withdrawal of the British presence from the region. It seemed more rational from every point of view for New Zealand and Samoa to develop their own relationship, whatever that might be.

It appeared at least that it would be a friendly one. Samoa became fully independent in 1962, after enormously prolonged and exhaustive discussions among the Samoans themselves on every aspect of the proposed constitution. Two things were proved beyond any reasonable doubt: the Samoans, as they repeatedly pointed out, were a conservative people, on whose traditional concepts of authority New Zealand rule had made no significant impression at all; and the New Zealand Government was prepared to let them be exactly what they wanted. The result was immensely cordial: a plebiscite was held in a manner which the head of the UN mission, Dr Rifai of the United Arab Republic, no doubt drawing on his experience of orderly democratic political processes amongst his own people, described as a model of order, strict impartiality and perfect freedom; and Samoa became an independent state of a rather unusual kind. The franchise was to be held by the *matai*, or heads of families; and rivalry among the great families was to be controlled by appointing the present Fautua as joint heads of state for life; their successors would be chosen by the legislative assembly for a term of five years each, thus observing the great Samoan principle of turn and turn about as a means of averting conflict. A Treaty of Friendship was also contracted with New Zealand, under which the New Zealand Government agreed 'for as long as the Government of Western Samoa wishes, and in such manner as will in no way impair the right of the Government of Western Samoa to formulate its own foreign policies, [to] afford assistance to the Government of Western Samoa in the conduct of its international relations'.[12] What this meant in very simple terms was that New Zealand would undertake to perform consular services for the Samoans free of charge, and represent their interests in international forums, thereby saving the Samoans the trouble and expense of having to send their own missions. The international organizations which the Samoans chose to join and at which they chose to represent themselves were the practical and profitable ones like the World Health Organization, the United Nations Economic Commission for Asia and the Far East, the South Pacific Commission and certain other technical agencies. It was a typically sensible and sophisticated decision by the Samoans, and carried no possible implication of neo-colonialist plotting on the part of New Zealand.

The New Zealanders were indeed going through one of their periods of forward-looking enterprise abroad, at a time when they were reverting to somewhat conservative and even reactionary policies at home. The Assembly of the Cook Islands was given full authority to control all expenditure within the Gorup, whose constitutional status it was also asked by the New Zealand Government to decide. The Cook Islanders replied quite emphatically that full independence on Samoan lines was not in fact their goal. A similar reply to a similar question was received from the Legislative Assembly of Niue Island. The New Zealand Government invited the Niueans to consider whether they wanted full independence, integration with New Zealand, participation in some as yet unborn Polynesian Federation, or merely internal self-government. The Assembly was still perhaps uncertain what might actually be involved in the fourth prospect, but it had no hesitation in rejecting the first three.

The Cook Islanders got what they apparently wanted in 1964: internal self-government, but association with New Zealand under the Queen as head of state for both, and common citizenship with New Zealand; full cabinet government followed in 1965. Meanwhile, the Commissioner's Executive Committee in Niue was reconstituted as a responsible cabinet, and limitations on its authority to revoke or amend New Zealand legislation began to be removed. In 1965 the barriers against independence in formerly British South Pacific territories finally fell away. The Cooks attained effective self-government, with a Cabinet of four members responsible to a Legislative Assembly of twenty-two, with full power to repeal or amend New Zealand legislation; the position of New Zealand Resident Commissioner was amended to that of a powerless High Commissioner, acting solely as representative of the New Zealand undertook to provide a subsidy of £750,000 a year, £50,000 more than the current annual figure for Cook Islands exports, virtually all of which went to New Zealand anyway. Once again the head of the United Nations mission invited by New Zealand to observe the transfer of power, Dr Adeel of that other model democracy, the Sudan, gave a glowing report, informing the world that his appreciation of New Zealand's work in the Cooks was boundless; that no words could express the honour felt by the members of his mission when invited by the New Zealanders to be present; and that the United Nations had agreed with pride to be associated with so historic an experiment in self-determination.[13] New Zealand was clearly on the side of the angels.

It was a very opportune time for a Pacific government to find itself in such a position. The confrontation between British and French Polynesia was blazing up again. Back in 1950 Sir Brian Freestone had attempted to put a traditionally paternalistic stopper on such developments by warning the South Pacific Commission that they might be a sort of parliament of the South Pacific peoples, but politics were no concern of theirs, and he was not going to allow any of the representatives to waste the Commission's time by talking about such things. But the time for paternalistic control was over. In 1961 the New Zealand representative, getting in on the wave of the future again, had asked for more regionalism in the Commission, proposing that more responsibility should be given to the island peoples themselves. His proposal had been rejected. But changes were on the way. The Netherlands withdrew from the Commission in 1962, following the loss of Dutch New Guinea to Indonesia. The allocation of expenses was changed in 1963 by a decision that Australia should now pay 32 per cent of the costs of the Commission, the United Kingdom and New Zealand 17 per cent each, and France 14 per cent. Newly independent states joining the Commission should pay 1 per cent each. Samoa became the first state to join under the new provision in 1964. Its representative immediately denounced the Commission for not providing sufficient scope for national participation. Even stronger words came from Fiji, not yet independent or a member, where Ratu Kamisese Mara described the Commission categorically as obsolete and exclusive. He also informed the other representatives that his own people, the Fijians, were the most politically advanced nation in the South Pacific. Times were clearly about to change for the Commission.

Ratu Kamisese Mara's claim might indeed have been disputed by the Tongans, although no one could deny the cultural and numerical significance of Fiji. However, it was the oldest stable monarchy in the South Pacific which took a new step forward in 1965. Queen Salote had died in Auckland in the previous year. She was succeeded by her son Prince Tugi, who came to the throne as King Taufa'ahau Tupou IV, combining as his mother had done the offices of Tui Tonga and Tui Kanokupolu. His previous office of Prime Minister was then inherited by his brother Tu'ipelehake. One of the first actions of the new regime was to amend the Treaty of Friendship with the United Kingdom, leaving only Foreign Affairs subject to British direction, and that for only as long as the Tongan Government wished. The 'Tongan Relationship', in effect, no longer existed.

This gesture of independence and maturity did not of course imply any sudden disenchantment with Britain on the part of the Tongans. British colonial rule in all its forms was being phased out in the Pacific with incomparably fewer displays of tension and mutual ill-will than anywhere else in the world. Even the Australians, traditionally perhaps the most uncompromising of colonialists, ushered their only Polynesian possession, Nauru, into independence in a mood of complete cordiality. The island had indeed fallen under their full responsibility only in 1947, when Australia assumed direct administration of the territory. The position of the Nauruans had then been desperate enough. Their land had been seized by the Japanese during the war and 1,200 of the 1,800 inhabitants deported to Truk in the Carolines. Only 737 survived to be repatriated. About half those left on Nauru had also died from neglect, deprivation or maltreatment. It looked as if a unique island group, a blend of Micronesian, Melanesian and Polynesian, with wholly individual traditions and language, was about to disappear. In any event, even if the people survived, their only source of livelihood was doomed: the phosphate reserves which provided Nauru's main source of revenue would be exhausted by the end of the century, and it was not clear that any other viable economic system could be established on the island. The Australian Government suggested that the Nauruans might like to emigrate to an island off the Queensland coast. However, the islanders declined the offer, on the grounds that accepting Australian citizenship would imperil their national identity as a separate and independent people. The Australians did not argue. On 24 October 1967 they agreed to grant Nauru full and sovereign independence. The first Legislative Assembly of Nauru was elected on 29 January 1968. On 31 January, twenty-two years after the survivors returned from Truk, the Republic of Nauru came into being with the superbly-named Hammer de Roburt as its first President. Numerically at least, the prospects for survival have certainly improved : Nauru now had a total population of 6,048, of whom some 3,000 were native Nauruans, with approximately 1,500 Gilbert and Ellice Islanders, 1,200 Chinese and 400 Europeans. It was also clear, as de Roburt noted later in New Zealand, that Nauru could count on friendship and help from its big brothers : Australia and New Zealand agreed that the new Republic should be accepted as a full member of the South Pacific Commission, even though Nauru like Samoa did not propose to join the United Nations, and that it should be accorded 'special membership' of the Commonwealth, which meant in effect that Nauruan representatives could participate in any Common-wealth conferences they liked, except only the Prime Ministers' Conference. A special legal relationship was also confirmed with Australia in 1976, under which the Australian Government authorized its High Commissioner in Nauru to sign a treaty covering procedures to allow appeals from the High Court of Nauru to the High Court of Australia.

There could be no doubt that the problems and practice of decoloni-zation in the Pacific differed radically from the pattern in Africa or Asia. In Oceania the colonial overlords in general needed little persuading to hand over authority to their former subjects. The subject peoples more-over seemed inclined to place far higher priority on maintaining the closest possible relations with the former colonial powers, than on pre-tending to an international role in the United Nations. The experience of Australia with Nauru was virtually duplicated in the transfer of power from New Zealand to Niue. Here the Islanders showed themselves most apprehensive when presented with a timetable for constitutional development which would have denied them the assistance of the New Zealand Resident Commissioner. The Island Assembly finally asked the New Zealand Government in 1970 to suggest various forms which their future constitutional progress might take. The New Zealand Government concluded that the people of Niue were at least sure of three things : they wanted 'to keep their New Zealand citizenship and right of access to New Zealand; be sure of continued financial and administrative support from New Zealand; and yet to achieve substantial control of the affairs of their own Island'. The first task for the New Zealand Government was therefore to 'reassure the people that there is no question of their being asked to give up any of their three main requirements . . . nor is there any question of their being forced to take decisions before they are ready'.[14] Accordingly, no changes were suggested other than a confirmation of the Executive Council of the Niuean Assembly in the possession of the powers which it already held by delegation from the Resident Commissioner. This policy was approved by a United Nations mission, which reported back in 1972 that the overwhelming majority of the population was in favour of full internal self-government combined with a continued close relationship with New Zealand. In other words they wanted the best of both available worlds. As there were after all only 4,600 of them, New Zealand could afford to let them have their way. It was accordingly agreed in early 1973 that the Niueans would complete their movement towards full internal self-government by the end of 1974; that they would remain New Zealand citizens; and that New Zealand would continue its financial assistance to the Island, currently at $1 million annually, and that New Zealand would represent the interests of Niue internationally, as it did those of Samoa, and as Australia did those of Nauru. As the Leader of Government in the island's Executive Council put it : 'Perpetually accepting someone else's generosity diminishes one's self-respect, but we believe that if we genuinely make an effort to run our own affairs, we can at least show that we have more than a charitable claim to New Zealand's continuing assistance . . .'[15] This notion of accepting the responsibilities of self-government as a means of earning the right to economic aid, was an interesting contribution to the ideology of decolonization.

But if the British-aligned island peoples were making giant strides in their various ways towards political independence, the French-aligned peoples were if anything moving backwards. A new autonomous party had been formed in Tahiti in 1965, under the traditional title of Te Ora. It asked the French Government to abandon formally nuclear testing in the Pacific. However, the Paris Government responded by strengthening its control over the administration of the Group by compelling native-born public servants, who numbered 1,720 out of Tahiti's 1,858 officials, to adhere to the Metropolitan Code, thereby exposing themselves more directly to professional pressures from Paris. The Tahitians were positively losing control over their own administrators.

It was perhaps only to be expected that the French would do everything possible to tighten their grip on Polynesia, as the time approached for the next series of tests for their nuclear *force de dissuasion*. The **autonomist** parties in Tahiti naturally asked the Gaullist regime to abandon the project, or at least perform the tests somewhere else. But there were limits to how emphatically they dared protest. One autonomist leader, Pouvaana Oopa, had already been jailed for eight years, under orders to be deported for a further fifteen, on the impressive charge of having tried to burn down Papeete. Some kind of leverage nonetheless seemed to have become available to the islanders in 1966, when the governing parties in the French National Assembly momentarily lost their overall majority because the deputy from Polynesia, Francis Sanford, had strategically resigned from the Gaullist-aligned Independent Republicans and joined the opposition Party of Progress and Democracy. In Tahiti itself, the autonomist leader Teariki suggested to the visiting President de Gaulle that the French should do in Tahiti exactly what de Gaulle had so eloquently told the Americans to do in France : clear out, with their aircraft, their troops and their bombs. Teariki assured de Gaulle that in those circumstances Tahiti would be happy to remain French. Naturally his words had no effect; and the same result was achieved by the Assembly in Papeete when it requested that France should send an independent mission of three French scientists and three foreigners to observe the tests and report objectively on their likely implications for human life in the region. Georges Pompidou commented imperturbably that he saw no reason to introduce any change in the relations between Tahiti and France, even when Sanford managed in 1969 to gain an autonomous majority in the Assembly in Papeete, winning ten seats against the Tahitian Gaullists' five, and persuaded the Assembly to vote seventeen to ten in favour of opening negotiations on outright self-rule for French Polynesia.

Nothing modified French determination. The students' revolt in Paris in 1968 indeed forced some changes in the development of Gaullist defence policy. Defence Minister Michel Debré told the Pacific islanders that there would be no tests in 1969. They were then however advised by the new Gaullist President Pompidou that tests would be resumed in 1970. When this decision was condemned in the South Pacific Commission, the French representatives simply walked out. The tests were duly held off Muroroa atoll; Governor Angeli deported a few protesters to demonstrate that France could neither be moved nor overcome; Michel Debré swam in the lagoon after the tests to prove their harmlessness to the human physique; and the world was informed that France would continue nuclear tests in the Pacific until 1975 at least.

If this was what the French wanted to do, there was nothing anybody in the world could do to stop them. There were however new forces becoming free to register more audible objections. Tonga finally renounced the Treaty of Friendship with Britain in 1970, assuming full responsibility for its own foreign policy and defence. Fiji became fully independent on 10 October of the same year, as the thirtieth member of the British Commonwealth, with a constitution which represented by far the most elaborate piece of political machinery in the region. There was to be a Senate of twenty-two members, comprising eight nominated by the Council of Chiefs, seven by the Prime Minister, six by the Opposition, and one by Routuma; and a Legislative Assembly with twelve Fijians and twelve Indian representatives chosen from the communal roll of electors, and ten of each chosen from the national roll, together with three representatives of the rest of the nation chosen from the communal roll and five from the national roll. It was a complex system of representation for a nation about 490,000 people, but at least its complexity allowed for consensus and conciliation.

The newly independent peoples met with the Australians and New Zealanders in Wellington in the South Pacific Forum, between 5 and 7 August 1971. Fiji, Samoa, Tonga, Nauru and the Cook Islands sent representatives, as well as the two white Pacific powers. Agreement was easily reached. The Forum resolved that officials of the five newly independent island states should meet every three months to discuss the development of trade; that they should investigate the possibility of setting up a regional shipping line; that the development of tourism and natural resources should be undertaken jointly; that the University of the South Pacific in Fiji should take account of traditional Polynesian values in its teaching and administration; that they reaffirmed their support for the South Pacific Commission, but hoped that its structure and objectives would be modified; that they would continue to hold meetings annually; and that the New Zealand Government should be requested to protest to Paris in the name of the Pacific peoples against the continuance of French nuclear tests in the region.

This last resolve was very likely to be a forlorn hope, as far as immediate results were concerned. The most that could be hoped for was that the French might be induced by public disapproval to conduct any future experiments underground. On past experience, one could only expect that they would carry out their scheduled series in 1973 exactly as planned. Defence Minister Pierre Messmer warned the Tahitians that the form of internal self-government sought by the local opponents of nuclear testing would hamper the economic development of the territory and would also lead to government by assembly, and the Gaullists considered that the experiences of France under the Fourth Republic had shown this to be harmful for democracy. Their opponents countered with the claim that nuclear tests had been shown to cause leukaemia. Surprisingly, this did not seem to concern unduly the voters of French Polynesia. In elections held in 1972, the autonomist parties actually lost five seats, leaving a virtual deadlock in the Assembly, with thirteen autonomists, thirteen Gaullists, two dissident autonomists and two independents. In New Caledonia, the four anti-autonomist parties combined to secure a bare majority of eighteen against the seventeen autonomists. The French were accordingly able to announce confidently that they would not be granting autonomy in the near future.

One obvious reason for French success in containing the opposition in Polynesia was, quite simply, cupidity. The development of a nuclear testing centre in Polynesia had enormously increased the prosperity of the islands. In 1965 the average income in Tahiti was only $617. In 1972 it had risen to $2,193, almost as high as that of New Zealand, and six times as high as that of any other Pacific country. It was understandable that the President of the Territorial Assembly, M. Gaston Flosse, should have commented : 'Our high standard of living, recognized even by biased observers, is due essentially to the installation of the [testing] centre. The only worry that we, the most interested parties, have is that the centre will end its activities.'[16]

This enormous growth in affluence reflected one of the most significant factors in the world scene in the 1970s, the phenomenal return of France to world power. French economic statistics had become oppressive. By the middle of 1973, France had become the most rapidly growing power in Europe, with approximately the fourth highest standard of living in the world, calculated on a basis of gross national product per head; it held the world's fourth strongest reserves of gold and foreign exchange; and enjoyed the position of the world's third trading nation, having edged out the Japanese, as the Japanese had formerly edged out the British. The French also occupied a genuinely unique bipolar position in world diplomacy : effectively the spokesmen for the great quasi-capitalist enterprise of the European Economic Community, they were also treated by the Russians with a consideration extended to no other Western-type nation except the United States itself, and were developing a relationship of unequalled cordiality and practicality with the Chinese, as fellow-giants of the second rank. The only pressure which could be applied against France would be that coming from the underprivileged, the uncommitted and the relatively powerless, and even this would be restricted by the dependence of too many of such countries upon France's massive programmes of foreign aid and the sale of weapons. The effect of such pressure on the French of all people was likely to be minimal. It is probable that very little would in fact have been attempted but for the electoral coincidence that put Labour governments in office in both Australia and New Zealand at the end of 1972. In an unprecedented gesture, the Australian Prime Minister Gough Whitlam crossed the Tasman to visit New Zealand in January 1973. He agreed with the New Zealand Prime Minister Kirk that an appeal should be made to France to refrain from nuclear testing in the atmosphere in the South Pacific. The two Prime Ministers also affirmed their belief in the value of the South Pacific Forum, noted with approval that Niue would soon become completely self-governing, and pledged their two countries to work together for the progress and advancement of the peoples of the Pacific, guided by the wishes and aspirations of the Pacific peoples themselves.

The South Pacific Forum duly convened at Apia, on 17 April. It was attended this time by Nauru, Fiji, Tonga and the Cook Islands as well as Australia and New Zealand, as full members; and by observers from Niue and Papua-New Guinea. It was resolved that the Government of Samoa this time should be authorized to appeal to France to head the call of the United Nations and cancel the scheduled tests. The appeal was naturally ignored. The New Zealand Government then resolved on 28 April to appeal to the International Court of Justice. So did the Australians. Senator Lionel Murphy and the New Zealand Deputy Prime Minister Hugh Watt visited Paris at the end of the month for talks with the Gaullist leaders. The French had meanwhile decided how to treat the protests from the Antipodes. M. Achille Fould, the Secretary of State for the Army, claimed that the campaign was inspired more by political considerations than by any concern for the environment. The considerations he was alluding to had already been made quite specific by Jacques Decornoy of Le Monde, who remarked that Prime Minister Whitlam had shown excessive political interest in the 'scattering [poussière] of island territories, small or very small, situated in the Pacific to the east of Australia; "We will have to become the natural leader of the South Pacific," he declared in an electoral address last November'. Decornoy went on to speculate on the prospect of the South Pacific soon becoming once again an arena for opposing spheres of influence, 'one holding to the colonial methods of the nineteenth century, the other using methods more modern and, legally at least, unobjectionable. It does not seem superfluous to pose this problem in the sense in which this affair of

French nuclear experiences would seem to constitute only one facet of a question vast in other respects as well'.[17]

This was almost a conditioned response for the French. Australian opposition to French settlement in New Caledonia in the past guaranteed than any suggestion of an extension of Australian influence in the South Pacific would be regarded in Paris as a deliberate bid to impose Australian neo-colonialism on formerly French territories. The Australian Government naturally denied any intention of taking part in a competition for spheres of influence in the region : Whitlam insisted on 1 May that Australia in no way sought to dominate in the South Pacific. This did not affect the French position in the slightest. Prime Minister Messmer referred sarcastically to the complacency with which the Australians and New Zealanders had allowed the British to carry out tests at Monte Bello, off Western Australia; ridiculed the idea that the Mururoa tests could involve any real danger to human welfare; and even spoke of the aesthetic beauties of nuclear explosions. Senator Murphy then suggested reasonably that the French should stage this particular cultural activity off Brest, to attract the tourists.[18]

The outcome was none the less not quite total failure. The International Court of Justice upheld the Australian–New Zealand case; the French denied the competence of the Court in any area of national security; and the tests went ahead, presumably as planned, with a series of small-scale explosions. Protesters who attempted to deter the French by sailing into the blast area were scooped up by the massively efficient French air and naval cordon, apparently roughed up mildly, and tossed into gaol until the show was over. Meanwhile, the Australians and New Zealanders staged a singular silent protest of their own. New Zealand's two General Purpose frigates, with Members of Parliament on board, took it in turns to join the French naval cordon outside the danger zone, moving out as required to draw stores from a Royal Australian Navy ship, still further removed from any possibility of danger. The gesture was doubtless sincere, despite the apparent inequality of risk, and it may even have had some effect : the French continued their present series of tests in the atmosphere and indeed assured the world that they would continue testing in 1975 at least, but also began massive excavations in the atolls, presumably with the idea of carrying out at least some of their future tests unobjectionably underground, This was perhaps the most that could have been expected.

It also served to indicate what in all likelihood will be the next stage in the development of the Pacific peoples. The decolonization process itself is virtually at an end. The Solomons are expected to achieve independence in 1977; the British appear anxious to leave the New Hebrides, but cannot do so because the French are determined to stay; a majority of the New Caledonian Assembly are still in favour of the continuation of the present association with France; and the American Samoans have repeatedly indicated their unwillingness to accept any change in their relationship with the United States, or even to elect their own Governor. But whether the remaining structure of traditional colonialism vanishes or endures, the economic dependence of the Pacific peoples upon the old colonial powers is likely to increase.

Rivalry between Australia, New Zealand and France may be expected to assist considerably in itself to assure the Pacific island peoples a moderate degree of affluence for the foreseeable future. They are also, of course, not without their own resources. New Caledonia is admittedly still the only island territory outside Australia and New Zealand which at the present time could be termed an important supplier of industrial raw materials on the world market. Papua-New Guinea will probably become another. Fiji has small desposits of gold, and traces of other exportable minerals have been found. Fiji and Tonga are both expected to benefit to some degree from the exploitation of offshore oil. But for most of the bigger islands, even including the New Hebrides, tourism is and is likely to remain their major source of income. The physical and geographical attractions which brought Europeans to the islands in the first place are now bringing them back as tourists. It is also likely that even in times of inflation and recession sufficient people will have the desire and the means to seek escapist holidays, and it is really difficult to imagine any other part of the world competing with the South Seas in this specific area of tourism. On the other hand, the tourist attractions of the smaller islands like Nauru, Niue and the Cooks can at best be termed limited. Here of course the real problems present themselves. For all practical purposes, Nauru's sole source of revenue is its phosphate resources, and these will be exhausted at present rates of utilization by the end of the century. Nauru and Australia have attempted to safeguard against this eventuality by investing a proportion of the revenue from exports of phosphate in a trust fund which, it is estimated, will amount to $400 million by the time the deposits have been exhausted. Dividends from the fund should then guarantee some kind of permanent income for the Nauruan people.

Obviously, the adequacy of the Nauruan solution will depend primarily upon factors like earning rates on invested capital in the twenty-first

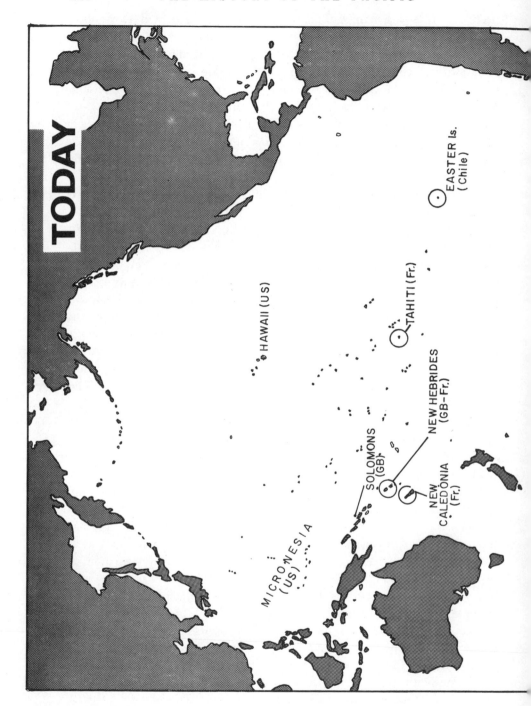

TODAY

EASTER Is.
(Chile)

TAHITI (Fr.)

HAWAII (US)

NEW HEBRIDES
(GB-Fr.)

SOLOMONS
(GB)

NEW
CALEDONIA
(Fr.)

MICRONESIA
(US)

century, and particularly trends in population movement. The more
Nauruans, the lower their individual welfare in this situation. The same
problem applies to the Tongans, who have been able to continue their
social tradition of providing each Tongan male with his *api* of eight and
a quarter acres only because many eligible Tongans have not bothered
to claim their share of the kingdom. In any case, attempts to forecast
the economic future of the island peoples are made uniquely difficult
by the inadequacy of statistics on their present level of welfare, the dis-
parities between those statistics which are available, and the difficulty of
assessing the actual relevance of national incomes figures in self-sustain-
ing subsistence economies. What is evident at least is that levels of affluence vary widely. The Tahitians for example enjoy an average income of
$2,193 a year, almost as high as that of the Norwegians or West Ger-
mans. However, this figure represents an increase of 200 per cent since
1965, and is due essentially to the French military presence in Polynesia.
If the French were to abandon their nuclear testing and withdraw their
establishments, the Tahitian income would probably drop by two-thirds.
Nauru claimed a similar figure of $1,800 in 1966, one of the highest
in the world at the time. By contrast, Fiji's figure of $390 or Papua-
New Guinea's $210 would rank among the lowest quarter of the nations
of the world. As against this, the peoples of the South Seas are not
exposed to famine, and Professor Maude has suggested that foreign aid
may have raised the real standard of living in Fiji to about that of Spain,
or approximately equivalent to an average income of $800 per year.[19]

The recovery in numbers among the Pacific peoples is perhaps the
most arresting and encouraging aspect of their present stage of development. The picture is of course not universally heartening. For example,
Hawaiians, the most numerous, culturally sophisticated and politically
advanced of the island peoples, have almost disappeared as an identifi-
able racial group in their own islands, after experiencing a population
decline from an estimated 400,000 to a recorded 20,000. The Marquesans similarly dwindled from one of the leading centres of Polynesian
civilization, with an estimated maximum population of 71,000, to a low
level of 1,000, in 1936 which has since recovered to just over 4,000. The
Easter Islanders suffered a less massive but culturally devastating depopulation from an estimated pre-European level of 7,000 to 434 in 1935,
before recovering to the present level of about 1,000. The demographic
situation of the other island groups is dramatically different, however.
The problem for most of them is now one of overpopulation, rather than
depopulation. In nearly all cases, the present recorded level of the native

population is substantially above the most respectable estimates of pre-European population, the majority of which may indeed have been considerably in excess of the actual population figures. For example, even the Condominion-ridden New Hebrideans, after declining from an estimated 70,000 to a recorded 40,000 in 1927, have now recovered to 72,237. The New Zealand Maoris, originally estimated at around 200,000, have increased from a low level of 37,000 at the end of the nineteenth century to some 214,000. But these are only the low achievers in the reproduction stakes. The Melanesian New Caledonians, not the happiest of colonial peoples, declined from 27,000 in 1860 to 16,500 in 1927, but have since increased to 48,000. The indigenous, non-Indian population of Fiji, originally estimated at around 200,000 and down to 84,475 in 1921, has now grown to 220,000. The Tahitians, fallen from 35,000 to 10,000 by 1860, have now grown to 61,519. The Samoan population fell from 60,000 to 31,600 by 1921, but has since risen to 140,000, possibly the greatest rate of natural increase of which human beings are capable. Even the indomitable Tongans, who alone seem to have escaped the depopulation effect, have now grown from a steady 27,000 throughout the nineteenth and early twentieth centuries to 76,121.

Population increase is, of course, unlikely to be regarded as an un-qualified success story in an age understandably obsessed with the prob-lems of ecology. It is however at least heartening to observe that the descendants of the Polynesian adventurers, apparently marked for extinc-tion at the turn of the century, are quite clearly not going to disappear in the foreseeable future. In any case, birth control measures are already being fostered in Fiji and other territories where the pressure of popula-tion growth does give rise to concern, and they appear to be having effect. Growth rates have certainly fallen already significantly below the African, Asian or Latin American norms. More important, at least in the short run, levels of prosperity in the Pacific territories are rising far more rapidly than population, and appear likely to continue to do so, except possibly in Papua-New Guinea. Finally, and most important, the actual order of the population increase is still manageable in terms of practical politics, while those of more populous underdeveloped countries may very well be unmanageable. The demographic problems of the South Pacific are of a completely different nature from those of India, Pakistan, Brazil or Indonesia, or even of many of the smaller Asian, African or Latin American countries. Foreign aid and developing natural resources can still make a perceptible impact on living standards in communities like

Fiji or Samoa, instead of being simply absorbed without trace in the general poverty of scores of millions. The Pacific peoples have the enormous advantages of being small, and of having rich friends who have their own reasons for wishing to pursue policies of something like mutual benefit. France needs the Pacific dependencies for their mineral resources, their investment opportunities, and as part of the general panoply of a nuclear and global power; Australia seeks a sphere of influence close to home for markets, for investments, and perhaps to provide outlying bastions for a Fortress Australia defence policy; New Zealand, with a rapidly growing and already substantial Polynesian minority at home, has domestic as well as economic reasons for wishing to cultivate the goodwill of its Polynesian neighbours to the north. All in all the prospect for the Pacific peoples is about as promising as one could reasonably hope for in an anxious world.

Notes and References

Chapter I: THE ADVENTURERS

1 A. Buhler, T. Bauer, C. P. Mountford, *Oceania and Australia* (London, 1962), 20.
2 E. Giles, 'Human Biology and Melanesian History', in *The History of Melanesia* (Port Moresby, 1968), 391–7.
3 J. Guiart, *The Arts of the South Pacific* (London, 1963), 24.
4 I. Goldman, *Ancient Polynesian Society* (Chicago, 1970), xxiv.
5 A. Sharp, *Ancient Voyages in the Pacific* (Auckland, 1963), 32.
6 Guiart, op. cit., 21.
7 D. P. Singhal, *India and World Civilization* (Michigan, 1968), II, 79.
8 S.R.Rao, 'Shipping in Ancient India,' in *India's Contribution to World Thought and Culture* (Madras, 1970), 83–107.
9 Singhal, op. cit., II, 75.
10 Sharp, op. cit., 97.
11 R. A. Derrick, *A History of Fiji* (Suva, 1946), I, 18–19.
12 Goldman, op. cit., 224.
13 Goldman, op. cit., 566.
14 Goldman, op. cit., 255–6.
15 Derrick, op. cit., 18–19.
16 Derrick, op. cit., 19.
17 Guiart, op. cit., 376.

Chapter II: THE IMPERIALISTS

1 Lallanji Gopal, 'Indian Shipping in Early Mediaeval Period'. *India's Contribution to World Thought and Culture* (Madras, 1970), 108–22.
2 W. J. Bassett-Lowke and G. Holland, *Ships and Men* (London, 1946), 42.
3 Ibid., 51.
4 J. Previte-Orton, *The Shorter Cambridge Mediaeval History* (Cambridge, 1962), 847.
5 J. H. Parry, *Europe and a Wider World, 1415–1715* (London, 1966), 19.
6 L. S. Stavrianos, *The Balkans Since 1453* (New York, 1958), 71.
7 Parry, op. cit., 24.
8 J. C. Beaglehole, *The Exploration of the Pacific* (London, 1947), 36.
9 Ibid., 43.

10 A. Sharp, *The Discovery of the Pacific Islands* (Oxford, 1960), 35.
11 P. Geyl, *The Netherlands in the Seventeenth Century, 1609–1648* (London, 1961), 160.
12 J. Hemming, *The Conquest of the Incas* (London, 1970), 113–16.
13 C. R. Boxer, *The Portuguese Seaborne Empire, 1415–1825* (New York, 1969), 57.
14 Beaglehole, op. cit., 81.
15 Ibid., 136.
16 Ibid., 161.
17 Ibid., 168.
18 Ibid., 173.
19 Sir Basil Thomson, *Diversions of a Prime Minister* (London, 1894), 311–12.
20 Derrick, *A History of Fiji*, I, 120.
21 Thomson, op. cit., 320.
22 J. C. Beaglehole (ed.), *The Journals of Captain James Cook, The Voyage of the Endeavour, 1768–1771*, lxxiii.
23 L. Jore, *L'Océan Pacifique au temps de la restauration et de la monarchie de juillet* (Paris, 1959), 41.
24 A. Moorehead, *The Fatal Impact* (London, 1956), 15.
25 Ibid., 35.
26 Beaglehole, *The Voyage of the Endeavour*, clxxxii.
27 Ibid., cclxxxii.
28 Ibid., 75.
29 Ibid., 78.
30 Ibid., 80, n. 2.
31 Ibid., 123–4.
32 Ibid., 127–8.
33 Ibid., 169, n. 2.
34 Ibid., 170, n. 3.
35 Ibid., 278–82.
36 A. H. Reed, *The Story of New Zealand* (Wellington, 1945), 62.
37 Beaglehole, *The Voyage of the Endeavour*, 397–9.
38 Jore, op. cit., 43.
39 J. C. Beaglehole (ed.), *The Journals of Captain James Cook, The Voyage of the Resolution and Adventure, 1772–1775* (Cambridge, 1961), 106.
40 Moorehead, *The Fatal Impact*, 57.
41 Beaglehole, *The Voyage of the Resolution and Adventure*, 252, 272.
42 Ibid., 257.
43 R. S. Kuykendall, *The Hawaiian Kingdom, 1778–1854* (Honolulu, 1947), 30.
44 J. C. Beaglehole, *The Journals of Captain James Cook, The Voyage of the Resolution and the Discovery, 1776–1780* (Cambridge, 1967), 512–13.
45 Ibid., 1208–13.
46 Ibid., 286.
47 Kuykendall, op cit., 34.
48 Moorehead, op. cit., 196.
49 *Historical Records of New South Wales* (Sydney, 1892), 1–5.
50 Moorehead, op. cit., 134.
51 H. E. Maude, *Of Islands and Men* (Melbourne, 1968), 183.
52 Kuykendall, op. cit., 41.
53 Hemming, *The Conquest of the Incas*, 113–16.
54 C. Hartley Grattan, *The Southwest Pacific to 1900* (Chicago, 1963), 197.
55 Moorehead, op. cit., 80.

Chapter III: THE CONQUERORS

1   H. E. Maude, *Of Islands and Men* (London, 1968), 185.
2   Ibid., 192.
3   Ibid., 205.
4   Jean Ingram Brookes, *International Rivalry in the Pacific Islands. 1800–1875* (Berkeley, 1941), 2–3.
5   Maude, op. cit., 188.
6   Kuykendall, *The Hawaiian Kingdom*, 56–9.
7   Thompson, *Diversion of a Prime Minister*, 338.
8   Ibid., 339.
9   Maude, op. cit., 159.
10   Harrison M. Wright, *New Zealand, 1769–1840* (Cambridge, Mass., 1959), 28.
11   Ibid., 26.
12   Derrick, *A History of Fiji*, 48–50.
13   R. J. Barton (ed.), *Earliest New Zealand, the Journals and Correspondence of the Rev. John Butler* (Masterton, N.Z., 1927), 79.
14   Wright, op. cit., 101.
15   Kuykendall, *The Hawaiian Kingdom*, 79.
16   Ibid., 79.
17   Ibid., 91.
18   Ibid., 157.
19   Ibid., 148.
20   Ibid., 152.
21   Ibid., 152.
22   J. Young (ed.), *Australia's Pacific Frontier* (Melbourne, 1967), 8–9.
23   Kuykendall, op. cit., 166.
24   Brookes, *International Rivalry in the Pacific Islands*, 97.
25   A. Ross, *New Zealand Aspirations in the Pacific in the Nineteenth Century* (Oxford, 1964), 13–14.
26   Kuykendall, op. cit., 190.
27   Ibid., 186.
28   Ibid., 197.
29   C. Haldane, *Tempest Over Tahiti* (London, 1963), 27–9.
30   Brookes, *International Rivalry in the Pacific Islands*, 107.
31   *Sydney Morning Herald*, 8 June 1844.
32   Ross, *New Zealand Aspirations*, 34.
33   Derrick, op. cit., 139.
34   Ibid., 140.
35   J. W. Davidson and D. Scarr (eds.), *Pacific Island Portraits* (Canberra, 1970), 150.
36   K. Sinclair, *A History of New Zealand* (London, 1959), 140.
37   George Alexander Lensen, *Russia's Japan Expedition of 1852 to 1855* (Gainesville, 1955), xiii.
38   Millard Fillmore, President of the United States of America, to His Imperial Majesty the Emperor of Japan, 13 November 1852, in W. G. Beasley (ed.), *Select Documents on Japanese Foreign Policy, 1853–1868* (London, 1955), 99.
39   Matthew C. Perry to His Imperial Majesty the Emperor of Japan, 7 July, 1853, in Beasley, *Select Documents*, 101–2.
40   Ii Naosuke to Bakafu, 1 October 1853, in Beasley, *Select Documents*, 117–19.
41   Lensen, op. cit., 134.

42 Ibid., 130.
43 Paul Akamatsu, *Meiji 1868* (New York, 1970), 235.

Chapter IV: COLONIAL OCEAN

1   E. Potter and Chester M. Nimitz, *Sea Power* (Englewood Cliffs, 1961), 237.
2   Davidson and Scarr, *Pacific Island Portraits*, 151.
3   Derrick, *History of Fiji*, chapter XX, *passim*.
4   Davidson, *Samoa Mo Samoa* (London, 1967), 44.
5   Ibid., 47.
6   Ross, *New Zealand Aspirations in the Pacific*, 112.
7   S. S. McKenzie, *The Official History of Australia in the War of 1914–1918: The Australians at Rabaul* (Sydney, 1938), 21.
8   Ross, op. cit., 129.
9   Davidson and Scarr, op. cit., 124.
10 Davidson and Scarr, ibid., 125.
11 Thomson, *Diversions of a Prime Minister*, 226.
12 Governor of Queensland to Chief Justice J. M. Gorrie, 4 June 1878, GOV/62, Queensland State Archives, H. C. Brown, 'Queensland's Annexationist Ambitions in New Guinea, 1859–1884', unpublished thesis, University of Queensland, 1972, 40–5.
13 Ross, op. cit., 185.
14 S. H. Roberts, *The History of French Colonial Policy, 1870–1925* (London, 1929), 539.
15 Agent-General to Colonial Secretary, 28 November 1884, COL/92, Queensland State Archives.
16 McKenzie, op. cit., 21.
17 R. S. Kuykendall and A. Grove Day, *Hawaii: a History* (New York, 1961), 168–89.
18 Thomson, op. cit., 227.
19 Kuykendall and Day, op. cit., 211.
20 Thomson, op. cit., 16.
21 Ross, op. cit., 293.
22 W. B. Sutch, *Poverty and Progress in New Zealand* (Wellington, 1969), 99–100.
23 R. A. Kelly, 'The Politics of Racial Equality', *New Zealand Journal of Public Administration*, March 1962, 25.
24 D. K. Fieldhouse, 'New Zealand, Fiji and the Colonial Office'. *Historical Studies: Australia and New Zealand*, May 1958, 116.
25 Fieldhouse, op. cit., 123.
26 Ross, op. cit., 285.
27 A. Deakin, *The Federal Story* (Melbourne, 1963), 22.
28 Roberts, op. cit., 535.
29 V. Thompson and R. Adloff, *The French Pacific Islands* (Berkeley, 1971), 246.
30 Outten J. Clinard, *Japan's Influence on American Naval Power, 1897–1917* (Berkeley, 1947), 19.
31 Theodore Roosevelt to Cecil Spring Rice, 13 June 1904, Elting G. Morison (ed.), *The Letters of Theodore Roosevelt* (Cambridge, Mass., 1951), 829–32.
32 Theodore Roosevelt to John Hay, 26 July 1904, Morison, op. cit., 865.
33 C. Roderick (ed.), *Henry Lawson, Collected Verse, 1901–1909* (Sydney, 1961), II, 135–6.

34 Akira Iriye, *Pacific Estrangement* (Cambridge, Mass., 1972), 132.
35 Roberts, op. cit., 512.
36 Thompson and Adloff, op. cit., 247.
37 Davidson, op. cit., 83.
38 Sutch, op. cit., 318.
39 Ibid., 21–2.
40 McKenzie, op. cit., 221.
41 Ibid., 224.
42 C. D. Rowley, *The Australians in German New Guinea, 1914–1921* (Melbourne, 1958), 61.
43 P. Firkins, *The Australians in Nine Wars* (Sydney, 1971), 8–14.
44 Ibid., 15.

Chapter V: UNDER A RISING SUN

1 G. Barclay, 'Strange Bedfellows', in J. M. Roberts (ed.), *Europe in the Twentieth Century* (London, 1970), 132–6.
2 H. T. B. Drew, *The War Effort of New Zealand* (Wellington, 1923), 23.
3 Davidson, *Samoa Mo Samoa*, 90.
4 A. W. Jose, *Official History of Australia in the War of 1914–1918, Vol. IX, Royal Australian Navy* (Sydney, 1937), 136.
5 Secretary of State for the Colonies to Governor-General of Australia, 23 November, 1914, in S. S. McKenzie, *Official History of Australia in the War of 1914–1918, The Australians at Rabaul* (Sydney, 1927), 157–8.
6 Secretary of State for the Colonies to Governor-General of Australia, 3 December 1914, in McKenzie, *The Australians at Rabaul*, 160.
7 Novar Papers, National Library of Australia, 4.
8 William R. Braistead, *The United States Navy in the Pacific, 1909–1923* (Austin, 1971), 163.
9 W. Roger Louis, 'Australia and the German Colonies in the Pacific' in *Journal of Modern History*, vol. 38, 1966, 407–21.
10 Rowley, *The Australians in New Guinea*, Part I, *passim*.
11 Davidson, *Samoa Mo Samoa*, 94.
12 Ibid., 117–18.
13 Ibid., 119.
14 L. A. Mander, *Some Dependent Peoples of the South Pacific* (New York, 1954), 478–9.
15 Ibid., 429.
16 T. Yanihara, *Pacific Islands Under Japanese Mandate* (London, 1940), 429.
17 W. Riddell (ed.), *Documents on Canadian Foreign Policy, 1917–1939* (Toronto, 1962), 63–4.
18 Hector C. Bywater, *Sea Power in the Pacific* (London, 1921), 300.
19 Australia, *Commonwealth Parliamentary Debates*, vol. 97, 11638; vol. 93, 4390.
20 *Commonwealth Parliamentary Debates*, vol. 103, 1066.
21 James B. Crowley, *Japan's Quest for Autonomy* (Princeton, 1966), chapter III, *passim*.
22 Lindsay to Hill, 16 July 1937, in *Foreign Relations of the United States, vol. II, The British Commonwealth, the Far East* (Washington, 1958), 126–7.
23 J. Harvey (ed.), *The Diplomatic Diaries of Oliver Harvey, 1937–40* (London, 1970), 69.

24 J. McVickar Haight, 'Franklin D. Roosevelt and a Naval Quarantine of Japan', in *Pacific Historical Review*, vol. XL, May 1971, 203–26.
25 Chatfield to Ismay, 23 April 1939, Public Records Office, CAB. 21/497/22.
26 Commonwealth Archives Office, AA1971/216, item 1/1939.
27 GHQ, United States Armed Forces, Pacific, Far East Command, Special Studies No. 161, Microfilm, *Saionji-Harada Memoirs*, 2019–511.
28 A Hezlet, *Aircraft and Seapower* (London, 1971), chapters V and VIII, *passim*.
29 C. Hermon Gill, *Australia in the War of 1939–1945: Navy: Australian Navy, 1939–1942* (Canberra, 1957), 263–6.
30 National Archives of New Zealand, *Files of the Governor*, G50 (9), C.O.S. 102.
31 Raymond A. Esthus, 'President Roosevelt's Commitments to Britain to Intervene in a Pacific War', in *Mississippi Valley Historical Review*, L, 1 June 1963, 28–38.

Chapter VI: THE GREAT PACIFIC WAR

1 A. D. Cooke, *Japan* (London, 1970), 34.
2 Gillespie, *Official History of New Zealand in the Second World War: The Pacific*, 17.
3 G. Allen, *Hawaii's War Years, 1941–1945* (Honolulu, 1949), 47.
4 Ibid., 264.
5 D. McCarthy, *Australia in the War of 1939–1945: Army: South-West Pacific Area, First Year, Kokoda to Wau* (Canberra, 1959), 246–8.
6 Gillespie, *The Pacific*, chapter 2 and 3, *passim*.
7 *Melbourne Herald*, 24 December 1941.
8 Commonwealth Archives Office, CRS A989, item 44/80/1/67/2.
9 F. L. W. Wood, *Official History of New Zealand in the Second World War: The New Zealand People at War* (Wellington, 1958), chapter 8, *passim*.
10 Commonwealth Archives Office, CRS A989, item 44/735/192 (1).
11 South Pacific Area and Forces, 'Report on Franco-American Relations in New Caledonia', OPNAVINST 5510.1c, MS., Microfilm Job No. E-48-A8-974, 2; also Thompson and Adloff, *The French Pacific Islands*, 274.
12 Gillespie, op. cit., 95.
13 'Report on Franco-American Relations,' 1.
14 Gillespie, op. cit., 102.
15 'Report on Franco-American Relations', G-2 Report dated 18 December 1943, 5.
16 South Pacific Area and Forces, Alfred B. Potts, 'Historical Narrative, Fiji Islands', MS., Microfilm Job No. F-108-AR-88-74, 1.
17 Tongatabu Advanced Naval Base, 'History of Tongatabu', MS., Microfilm Job N. F-108-AR-89-74, 69.
18 Ibid., 6–8.
19 Ibid., 6.
20 Ibid., 130–1.
21 McCarthy, *South-West Pacific Area*, 246.
22 Paul C. Hasluck, *Official of Australia in the War of 1939–1945: The Government and the People, 1942–1945* (Canberra, 1965), 482.
23 T. R. Smith, *The South Pacific Commission* (Wellington, 1972) 35–6.
24 Commonwealth Archives Office, CRS A989, item 44/80/1/67/2.

Chapter VII: The Survivors

1   'History of Tongatabu', 9.
2   'Report on Franco-American Relations in New Caledonia', 2.
3   A. Ross (ed.), *New Zealand's Record in the Pacific Islands in the Twentieth Century* (Wellington, 1969), 186.
4   National Archives of New Zealand, Files of the Governor, G48, D.C.5, *Possible Effects of German Demand for Return of Mandated Territories.*
5   'History of Tongatabu', 69.
6   Ross, op. cit., 191.
7   K. R. Hancock, *New Zealand at War* (Wellington, 1946), 10–11.
8   Smith, *The South Pacific Commission,* 47.
9   Thompson and Adloff, *The French Pacific Islands,* 343.
10   *Pacific Islands Monthly*, February 1951, 3.
11   Ross, *New Zealand's Record*, 101.
12   Davidson, *Samoa Mo Samoa*, 416.
13   Ross, op. cit., 112–13.
14   *New Zealand Foreign Affairs Review*, June 1971, 54–60.
15   Ibid., January 1973, 10.
16   C. Dyer, 'French Attitudes to Nuclear Experiments in the Pacific', *Australian Outlook*, August 1973, 172–8.
17   *Le Monde*, 23 March 1973.
18   Dyer, op. cit., 172–8.
19   H. E. Maude, 'South Pacific', *Round Table*, July 1971, 369–82.

Bibliography

A – Primary Sources *(unpublished)*

Commonwealth Archives Office (Australia)
CRS A816, item 11/301/213, Defence 11, Correspondence Files.
CRS A989, item 44/80/1/67/2, P.W.R. Far East and Pacific–American Discussions.
CRS A989, item 44/735/192 (1), P.W.R. Prime Ministers Conference May 1944. Documentation.
CRS AA1971/216, item 1/1935, Council of Defence II, Records of the Council of Defence, 1935–1939.
CRS AA1971/216, item 1/1939, Council of Defence II, Records of the Council of Defence, 1935–1939.

National Archives of New Zealand
G48, D.C.5, Possible Effects of German Demands for Return of Mandated Territories.
G48, D/6, Defence Committee, Wellington, April 1939.
G48, P/31, Notes on the Vulnerability of Australia and New Zealand.
G50 (9), Chiefs of Staff, 102, 1940.

National Library of Australia
Novar Papers.

Public Record Office, London
CAB. 21/497/22, Imperial Defence, General Annual Review.

United States Navy Department: Operational Archives, Naval History Division
GHQ, United States Armed Forces, Pacific, Far East Command, Military Intelligence Section, General Staff, Special Studies No. 161, Microfilm, *Saionji-Harada Memoirs*.
Samoan Defense Group, 'United States Naval History of Western Samoa', MS., Microfilm Job No. F-108-AR-87-14.
South Pacific Area and Forces, 'Report on Franco-American Relations in New Caledonia', OPNAVIST 5510.1C, MS., Microfilm Job No. E-48-A8-974.
South Pacific Area and Forces, Alfred B. Potts, 'Historical Narrative, Fiji Islands', MS., Microfilm Job No. F-108-AR-88-74.
Tongatabu Advanced Naval Base, 'History of Tongatabu', MS., Microfilm Job No. F-108-AR-89-74.

B – PRIMARY SOURCES *(published)*

Beaglehole, John C. (ed.), *The Journals of Captain James Cook, The Voyage of the Endeavour, 1768–1771* (Cambridge, 1957).
——, *The Journals of Captain James Cook, The Voyage of the Resolution and and Adventure, 1772–1775* (Cambridge, 1961).
——, *The Journals of Captain James Cook, The Voyage of the Resolution and the Discovery, 1776–1780* (Cambridge, 1967).
Beasley, William G. (ed.), *Select Documents on Japanese Foreign Policy 1853–1886* (London, 1955).
Harvey, J. (ed.), *The Diplomatic Diaries of Oliver Harvey, 1937–1940* (London, 1970).
Morison, Elting G. (ed.), *The Letters of Theodore Roosevelt* (Cambridge, Mass., 1951).
New South Wales Government Archives, *Historical Records of New South Wales* (Sydney, 1892).
Riddell, W. (ed.), *Documents on Canadian Foreign Policy, 1917–1939* (Toronto, 1947).
United States, Dept of State, *Foreign Relations of the United States, Diplomatic Papers, The British Commonwealth, the Far East, 1937* (Washington, 1958).

C – OFFICIAL HISTORIES

Drew, H. T. B., *The War Effort of New Zealand* (Wellington, 1923).
Gillespie, A. O., *Official History of New Zealand in the Second World War: The Pacific* (Wellington, 1952).
Hasluck, Paul C., *Australia in the War of 1939–1945: The Government and the People* (Canberra, 1965).
Jose, A. W., *Australia in the War of 1914–1918: Royal Australian Navy* (Sydney, 1937).
McCarthy, D., *Australia in the War of 1939–1945: Army: South-West Pacific Area, First Year, Kokoda to Wau* (Canberra, 1959).
Mackenzie, S. S., *Australia in the War of 1914–1918: The Australians at Rabaul* (Sydney, 1938).
Milner, S., *The United States Army in World War II: The War in the Pacific, Victory in Papua* (Washington, 1957).

D – SECONDARY SOURCES *(unpublished)*

Brown, H. C., 'Queensland's Annexationist Ambitions in New Guinea, 1859–1884', unpublished thesis, University of Queensland.
Saunders, Kay, 'Uncertain Bondage: An Analysis of Indentured Labour in Queensland to 1907', unpublished thesis, University of Queensland.

E – SECONDARY SOURCES *(published):* ARTICLES

Barclay, G. St. J., 'Strange Bedfellows', in J. M. Roberts (ed.), *Europe in the Twentieth Century* (London, 1970).

Dyer, C., 'French Attitudes to Nuclear Experiments in the Pacific', *Australian Outlook*, 27 (1973).

Esthus, Raymond A., 'President Roosevelt's Commitment to Britain to Intervene in a Pacific War', *Mississippi Valley Historical Review*, L (1963).

Fieldhouse, D. K., 'New Zealand, Fiji and the Colonial Office, 1900–1902', *Historical Studies, Australia and New Zealand* (1958).

Giles, E., 'Human Biology and Melanesian History', in *The History of Melanesia* (Port Moresby, 1968).

Gopal, L., 'Indian Shipping in Early Mediaeval Period', in *India's Contribution to World Thought and Culture* (Madras, 1970).

Haight, J. McVickar, 'Franklin D. Roosevelt and a Naval Quarantine of Japan', *Pacific Historical Review*, XL (1971).

Kelly, R. A., 'The Politics of Racial Equality', *New Zealand Journal of Public Administration* (1962).

Louis, W. Roger, 'Australia and the German Colonies in the Pacific', *Journal of Modern History*, 38 (1966).

Maude, H. F., 'South Pacific', *Round Table*, LXII (1972).

Rao, S. R., 'Shipping in Ancient India', in *India's Contribution to World Thought and Culture*.

Tate, Merze, 'Hawaii's Early Interest in Polynesia', *Australian Journal of Politics and History*, VII (1961).

F – Secondary Sources *(published):* Books

Akamatsu, P., *Meiji 1868* (New York, 1970).

Barclay, G. St. J., *The Empire Is Marching* (London, 1976).

Barton, R. J. (ed.), *Earliest New Zealand, the Journals and Correspondence of the Rev. John Butler* (Masterton, N.Z., 1927).

Bassett-Lowke, W. J., and Holland, G., *Ships and Men* (London, 1946).

Boxer, C. H., *The Portuguese Seaborne Empire, 1415–1825* (New York, 1969).

Bragamini, D., *Japan's Imperial Conspiracy* (New York, 1971).

Braisted, William R., *The United States Navy in the Pacific, 1909–1923* (Austin, 1971).

Brookes, Jean Ingram, *International Rivalry in the Pacific Islands, 1800–1875* (Berkeley, 1941).

Buhler, A., Bauer, T., Mountford, C. P., *Oceania and Australia* (London, 1962).

Bywater, Hector C., *Sea Power in the Pacific* (London, 1921).

Coulter, John W., *The Drama of Fiji* (Baltimore, 1967).

Crowley, John B., *Japan's Quest for Autonomy* (Princeton, 1966).

Dalton, B. J., *War and Politics in New Zealand* (Sydney, 1967).

Davidson, J. W., and Scarr, D., *Pacific Island Portraits* (Canberra, 1970).

Davidson, J. W., *Samoa Mo Samoa* (Melbourne, 1972).

Derrick, R. A., *A History of Fiji* (Suva, 1946).

Doumenge, F., *L'Homme dans le Pacifique Sud* (Paris, 1966).

Firkins, P., *The Australians in Nine Wars* (Sydney, 1971).

Geyl, P., *The Netherlands in the Seventeenth Century, 1609–1648* (London, 1961).

Gilson, J. (ed.), *Polynesian Navigation* (Wellington, 1962).

Goldman, I., *Ancient Polynesian Society* (Chicago, 1970).

Gopal, L. et al., *India's Contribution to World Thought and Culture* (Madras, 1970).

Grattan, C. Hartley, *The Southwest Pacific to 1900* (Chicago, 1963).

Guiart, J., *The Arts of the South Pacific* (London, 1963).
Haldane, Charlotte, *Tempest Over Tahiti* (London, 1963).
Hemming, John, *The Conquest of the Incas* (London, 1970).
Heyerdahl, Thor, *American Indians in the Pacific* (London, 1952).
Hezlet, A., *Aircraft and Seapower* (London, 1970).
Howells, W., *The Pacific Islanders* (London, 1973).
Jore, L., *L'Océan Pacifique au temps de la restauration et de le monarchie dé
    juillet* (Paris, 1959).
Kaihara, I. H., *Conflict and Cooperation, Essays on the Maori Since Colonization*
    (Wellington, 1975).
Kennedy, Paul H., *The Samoan Tangle* (Dublin, 1974).
Kuykendall, R. S. *The Hawaiian Kingdom, 1778–1854* (Honolulu, 1947).
Kuykendall, R. S. and Day, A. Grove, *Hawaii: a History* (New York, 1967).
Lensen, George A., *Russia's Japan Expedition of 1852 to 1855* (Gainesville, 1955).
Mander, L. A., *Some Dependent Peoples of the South Pacific* (New York, 1954).
Maude, H. E., *Of Islands and Men* (London, 1968).
Moorehead, Alan, *The Fatal Impact* (London, 1956).
Morrell, W. P., *Britain in the Pacific Islands* (Cambridge, 1963).
Nicolson, I. F., and Hughes, Colin A., *Pacific Polities* (Sydney, 1972).
Oliver, Douglas L., *Ancient Tahitian Society* (Honolulu, 1974).
Parry, J. H., *Europe and a Wider World, 1415–1715* (London, 1966).
Potter, E., and Nimitz, C., *Sea Power* (Englewood Cliffs, 1961).
Previte-Orton, J. (ed.), *The Shorter Cambridge History of Mediaeval History*
    (Cambridge, 1962).
Reed, A. H., *The Story of New Zealand* (Wellington, 1945).
Roberts, Stephen H., *The History of French Colonial Policy, 1870–1925* (London,
    1925).
Ross, A., *New Zealand Aspirations in the Pacific in the Nineteenth Century*
    (Oxford, 1964).
——, *New Zealand's Record in the Pacific Islands in the Twentieth Century*
    (Wellington, 1969).
Rowley, C. D., *The Australians in German New Guinea, 1914–1921* (Melbourne,
    1958).
Sharp, A., *The Discovery of the Pacific Islands* (Oxford, 1960).
——, *Ancient Voyages in the Pacific* (Auckland, 1963).
Sinclair, Keith, *A History of New Zealand* (London, 1959).
——, *The Origins of the Maori Wars* (Wellington, 1961).
Smith, T. R., *The South Pacific Commission* (Wellington, 1972).
Stavrianos, L. S., *The Balkans Since 1453* (New York, 1958).
Sutch, William B., *Poverty and Progress in New Zealand* (Wellington, 1969).
Tate, Morze, *Diplomacy in the Pacific* (Washington, 1973).
Thomson, Sir Basil, *Diversions of a Prime Minister* (London, 1894).
Thompson, V., and Adloff R., *The French Pacific Islands* (Berkeley, 1971).
Wright, Harrison M., *New Zealand, 1769–1840* (Cambridge, 1959).
Yanihara, T., *Pacific Islands Under Japanese Mandate* (London, 1940).
Young, J. (ed.), *Australia's Pacific Frontier* (Melbourne, 1967).

DATE	FIJI	HAWAII	MARQUESAS	NEW ZEALAND
100–300				
300–900	Close links with Tonga		Polynesians arrive	
900–1000		Polynesians arrive		Polynesians arrive from Tahiti
1200				
1568				
1595			Alvaro de Mendaña arrives	
1600				
1603				
1615				
1642				Tasman sights South Island
1643				
1760	Bauan conquests begin			
1767				
1768				
1769				Cook and de Surville both arrive
1772				Dufresne in Bay of Islands; clash with Maoris

of Events

SAMOA	TAHITI	TONGA	MELANESIA	DATE
Polynesians arrive	Polynesians arrive	Polynesians arrive		100–300
		Close links with Fiji		300–900
		Tui Tonga instituted		900–1000
Tongan occupation begins		Occupation of Samoa begins; Trilithon built		1200
			Alvaro de Mendana reaches Solomons	1568
				1595
Tongan occupation ends		Tongans leave Samoa		1600
			Dutch follow New Guinea coast	1603
		Tui Kanokupolu created; Lemaire and Schouten arrive		1615
				1642
		Tasman arrives; Fale Fisi founded		1643
				1760
	Wallis annexes Tahiti			1767
	Bougainville annexes Tahiti; civil war			1768
	Cook arrives			1769
	Domingo de Boenechea arrives	Finau of Vava'u makes bid for power		1772

DATE	FIJI	HAWAII	MARQUESAS	NEW ZEALAND
1774				
1777				
1778		Cook arrives; Kalaniopiu at war with Kahekele of of Maui		
1779		Death of Cook		
1786		Kahekele defeats Kamehameha; sealers arrive		
1790				
1794		Kamehameha I cedes Hawaii to Britain		
1799				
1808	Beachcombers aid expansion of Bau			
1809				Crew of *Boyd* massacred
1810		Kamehameha I supreme		
1811				
1814				Marsden in Bay of Islands
1815		Scheffer arrives		
1819		Kamehameha I dies; de Freycinet arrives		
1821				Hongi Hika uses firearms
1824		Kamehameha II visits London; dies; Boki acknowledges George IV as Lord and Protector		
1826		USA claims 'most-favoured-nation' treatment		
1828				
1833				Busby arrives as British resident

SAMOA	TAHITI	TONGA	MELANESIA	DATE
	Tomas Gayangos annexes Tahiti			1774
	Cook reaffirms annexation by Wallis			1777
				1778
				1779
				1786
		Finau II rules in Vava'u		1790
				1794
		Civil war in Tonga		1799
				1808
				1809
				1810
	Pomare I baptized	Death of Finau II		1811
				1814
	Pomare I supreme			1815
				1819
				1821
				1824
	Laplace arrives			1826
				1828
		George Tupou I unites Tonga		1833

DATE	FIJI	HAWAII	MARQUESAS	NEW ZEALAND
1835				De Thierry proclaims himself Sovereign Chief
1837	Cakobau suppresses rebellion	France claims 'most-favoured-nation' treatment		
1838	Raid by D'Urville			
1840		Kamehameha III constitutional monarch		Hobson annexes New Zealand
1842			French annex Marquesas	
1843		Kamehameha III cedes Hawaii to Britain; cession revoked		
1845				
1849	Cakobau challenges Verata; fails			
1850	Cakobau challenges Macuata; fails			
1853	Ma'afu arrives			
1857	Cakobau cedes Fiji to Pritchard			
1858				Maori King movement
1860				Maori wars begin
1861				
1867	Cakobau crowned King of Bau Dominions			
1868				
1869	Tongan claims ceded to Ma'afu			
1874	Britain annexes Fiji			
1875				
1877				

SAMOA	TAHITI	TONGA	MELANESIA	DATE
				1835
				1837
				1838
				1840
	French depose Pomare IV; Proctectorate			1842
	French annex Tahiti			1843
Catholic missionaries arrive				1845
				1849
				1850
		George Tupou I offers aid to Cakobau	French annex New Caledonia	1853
				1857
				1858
				1860
		George Tupou I claims right to rule in Fiji		1861
				1867
Civil war in Samoa				1868
				1869
				1874
Malietoa Laupepa King of Samoa				1875
Appeals to Britain for protection				1877

DATE	FIJI	HAWAII	MARQUESAS	NEW ZEALAND
1878				
1879				
1883		Kalakaua and Kapiolani crowned		
1884				
1866		Kalakaua seeks Confederation with Samoa		
1890				
1891		Kalakaua dies; Republic proclaimed		
1895		Liliukalani abdicates		
1898				
1899				
1900				Maori Councils Act
1902				Seddon proposes Federation with Fiji
1904				
1914				
1917				
1919				
1923				
1927				
1928				Ratana Movement formed
1935				

SAMOA	TAHITI	TONGA	MELANESIA	DATE
			New South Wales and Queensland seek annex New Guinea	1878
			New South Wales and Queensland seek annex New Guinea	1879
			Intercolonial Conference seeks annex New Guinea	1883
			Germans annex New Britain, New Ireland and New Guinea	1884
				1886
		Basil Thompson becomes Prime Minister		1890
				1891
				1895
Laupepa dies; civil war				1898
Germany and USA partition Samoa				1899
				1900
				1902
			Anglo-French Condominium in New Hebrides	1904
New Zealand occupies Samoa			Australia occupies German Melanesia	1914
			Rebellion in New Caledonia	1917
Epidemic; 8,500 die				1919
Richardson becomes Administrator				1923
O Le Mau formed				1927
Allen becomes Administrator; shooting in Apia; Mau resistance				1928
New Zealand grants New Constitution				1935

DATE	FIJI	HAWAII	MARQUESAS	NEW ZEALAND
1936	New Constitution granted			
1939	New Zealand garrisons Fiji			
1940				
1944				Anzac Pact with Australia
1946				
1947				
1948				
1955				Government orders economic survey of Cook Islands
1957				
1959				
1962				
1964				
1965				Grants Independence to Cook Islands
1970	Full independence granted			
1971	Rata Maru calls for South Pacific Forum			South Pacific Forum meets in Wellington
1972				
1973				

SAMOA	TAHITI	TONGA	MELANESIA	DATE
				1936
				1939
	Gaullist coup in Tahiti		Gaullist coups in New Hebrides and New Caledonia	1940
Samoans protest New Zealand rule to Newall				1944
Fono of all Samoa called to discuss Constitution				1946
New Zealand introduces Samoa Amendment Act		Joins Pacific Health Service		1947
			Solomons revolt against British occupation	1948
				1955
Legislative Assembly for Western Samoa meets				1957
New Zealand offers full Independence				1959
Samoa becomes independent				1962
Joint South Pacific Commission				1964
	Te Ora Autonomous Party formed	King Tupou IV amends Treaty of Friendship with Britain		1965
		Tupou renounces Treaty		1970
			Constitution for Independent State of New Guinea approved by Australian Parliament	1971
			Michael T. Somare elected chief Minister of Papua–New Guinea	1972
			Papua–New Guinea becomes self-governing	1973

DATE	FIJI	HAWAII	MARQUESAS	NEW ZEALAND
1975				
1977				

SAMOA	TAHITI	TONGA	MELANESIA	DATE
			Papua–New Guinea becomes independent	1975
			Solomons scheduled to become independent	1977

Index